Praise for *Read Until You Understand*

Winner of the 2022 PROSE Award in Literature

A *Kirkus Reviews* 2021 Best Book About
Being Black in America

"A book like *Read Until You Understand* takes courage to produce. . . . [Farah Jasmine] Griffin's evangelizing of Black literature does what the best sermons do: It sends you back to Scripture—Baldwin, Coates, Morrison, David Walker and others."   —Monica Drake, *New York Times Book Review*

"[Griffin] is both masterful critic and master teacher."
                              —Walton Muyumba, *Boston Globe*

"What I like about this book so much is that it shows that reading is a vital part of engaged citizenship."
                              —Carlos Lozada, *PBS NewsHour*

"Griffin shares, in a blend of memoir and criticism, the fruits of her lifelong journey to fulfill that aspiration [to read until you understand]. . . . She also richly evokes her childhood in Philadelphia, long a hub for Black activism, where she belonged . . . to a family whose women, skilled seamstresses and gardeners, cultivated beauty."   —*The New Yorker*

"*Read Until You Understand* is brought to life through Griffin's account of the ways in which Black culture was an integral part of her being. . . . It is a book that acknowledges life's conflicts while still valuing hope and beauty."
                              —Douglas Field, *Times Literary Supplement*

"Griffin gives readers gifts akin to the gifts her father bestowed on her. She provides insightful interpretations of iconic African American writers, including Richard Wright, James Baldwin, and Toni Morrison, Griffin's friend and mentor. And she celebrates lesser-known writers, like Frances Ellen Watkins Harper."
—Glenn C. Altschuler, *Florida Courier*

"The perfect storm of imagination, research, compassion, and intellectual analysis. [*Read Until You Understand*] soars to a new level of wisdom, community love, and enlightenment for readers and critics alike."
—Robert Fleming, *African American Literature Book Club*

"Thank you Farah Jasmine Griffin for this sage gift, for packaging all these sage gifts for us."
—Ibram X. Kendi

"*Read Until You Understand* gives us Farah Jasmine Griffin in full and mighty sail. Keen cultural analysis, storytelling, and gorgeous lyricism combine in this book that makes a genre of its own. In recollection there is profound insight here; we have a portrait of a rich Black community in place and time, and of the teachers Griffin finds in neighborhood, family, books, and music. The sounds, words, and wisdom that Black folks make also make us, and no one expresses that with more beauty and power than Griffin. This book is a talking book, a teaching book, and a treasure."
—Elizabeth Alexander

"Farah Jasmine Griffin's vivid, passionate, and powerful tribute to the great gifts of Black culture offers a deep dive into such fundamental human themes as freedom, justice, rage, death, beauty, and love, as lived and celebrated through her own experience, music, and creative art, and that of countless others in the community she embraces, from the legacy of Black history to her own family, her wide explorations of literature and art, and her close friendships with many artists and writers." —Elaine Pagels

"Farah Jasmine Griffin is one of the few great intellectuals in our time! This wise and powerful memoir is a masterpiece. Griffin beautifully weaves her profound devotion to the life of the mind with her deep and abiding love of Black people and culture. Her magical words enchant and empower us like those of her towering heroes—Toni Morrison, Billie Holiday, James Baldwin, and Wilhelmena Griffin!"
                                                                    —Cornel West

"Griffin writes with learned poignance. . . . Perfect for literature lovers, this survey and its moving insights will stick with readers well after the last page is turned."
                                        —*Publishers Weekly*, starred review

"An impassioned inquiry into the literary roots of Black culture. . . . [I]nsightful, profound, and heartfelt."
                                            —*Kirkus Reviews*, starred review

READ

UNTIL

YOU

UNDERSTAND

⇒ | ⇐

READ

UNTIL

YOU

UNDERSTAND

The Profound Wisdom of Black Life and Literature

⇒ | ⇐

FARAH JASMINE GRIFFIN

W. W. NORTON & COMPANY
Independent Publishers Since 1923

Copyright © 2021 by Farah Jasmine Griffin

"Dear Lovely Death" from *The Collected Poems of Langston Hughes* by Langston Hughes, edited by Arnold Rampersad with David Roessel, associate editor, copyright © 1994 by the Estate of Langston Hughes. Used by permission of Alfred A. Knopf, an imprint of the Knopf Doubleday Publishing Group, a division of Penguin Random House LLC. All rights reserved. Reprinted by permission of Harold Ober Associates. Copyright 1994 by the Langston Hughes Estate.

Excerpt from "A More Perfect Union" © Barack Obama, 2017, *We Are the Change We Seek: The Speeches of Barack Obama*, ed. E. J. Dionne Jr. and Joy-Ann Reid, Bloomsbury Publishing Plc.

"Evening Primrose." Copyright © 2004 by Rita Dove, from *Collected Poems: 1974–2004* by Rita Dove. Used by permission of W. W. Norton & Company, Inc.

Lyrics from Gil Scott Heron's "Winter in America" used by permission of Rumal Rackley.

Excerpt(s) from *Sula* by Toni Morrison, copyright © 1973 by Toni Morrison. Used by permission of Alfred A. Knopf, an imprint of the Knopf Doubleday Publishing Group, a division of Penguin Random House LLC. All rights reserved. Excerpt(s) from *The Bluest Eye* by Toni Morrison, copyright © 1970, copyright renewed 1998 by Toni Morrison. Used by permission of Alfred A. Knopf, an imprint of the Knopf Doubleday Publishing Group, a division of Penguin Random House LLC. All rights reserved. Excerpt(s) from *Song of Solomon* by Toni Morrison, copyright © 1977 by Toni Morrison. Used by permission of Alfred A. Knopf, an imprint of the Knopf Doubleday Publishing Group, a division of Penguin Random House LLC. All rights reserved. Excerpt(s) from *Paradise* by Toni Morrison, copyright © 1997 by Toni Morrison. Used by permission of Alfred A. Knopf, an imprint of the Knopf Doubleday Publishing Group, a division of Penguin Random House LLC. All rights reserved.

For information about permission to reproduce selections from this book, write to Permissions, W. W. Norton & Company, Inc., 500 Fifth Avenue, New York, NY 10110

For information about special discounts for bulk purchases, please contact W. W. Norton Special Sales at specialsales@wwnorton.com or 800-233-4830

Manufacturing by Lake Book Manufacturing
Book design by Lisa Buckley
Production manager: Anna Oler

Library of Congress Cataloging-in-Publication Data

Names: Griffin, Farah Jasmine, author.
Title: Read until you understand : the profound wisdom of Black life and literature / Farah Jasmine Griffin.
Description: First edition. | New York, NY : W. W. Norton & Company, [2021] | Includes bibliographical references and index.
Identifiers: LCCN 2021011719 | ISBN 9780393651904 (hardcover) | ISBN 9780393651911 (epub)
Subjects: LCSH: American literature—African American authors—History and criticism. | African Americans—Intellectual life. | African Americans—Social conditions. | Griffin, Farah Jasmine—Books and reading.
Classification: LCC PS153.N5 G74 2021 | DDC 810.9/896073—dc23
LC record available at https://lccn.loc.gov/2021011719

ISBN 978-1-324-02204-6 pbk.

W. W. Norton & Company, Inc., 500 Fifth Avenue, New York, N.Y. 10110
www.wwnorton.com

W. W. Norton & Company Ltd., 15 Carlisle Street, London W1D 3BS

1 2 3 4 5 6 7 8 9 0

For T.M.

CONTENTS

INTRODUCTION

This book begins with a girl and ends with grace. Along the way, through a combination of memoir and readings of African American literature, it touches upon the question of mercy, the elusive quest for justice, the prevalence of beauty, even in the presence of death, and throughout, hope in the face of despair.

Both the autobiographical reflections and my readings of the literature speak to the ideals and failures of the U.S. experiment with democracy. My goal in writing this book is to draw upon a lifetime of reading and almost thirty years of teaching African American literature to explore how, in addition to addressing concerns about democracy, perhaps even more than these, the works also speak to ideas and values that have concerned humanity since the beginning of time. Within these pages, I seek to share a series of valuable lessons learned from those who have sought to better a nation that depends upon, and yet too often despises, them. In the process, they have changed the world.

I am guided by the following questions: What might an engagement with literature written by Black Americans teach us about the United States and its quest for democracy? What might it teach us about the fullest blossoming of our own humanity?

What I offer here is a series of meditations on the fundamental questions of humanity, reality, politics, and art. Each chapter addresses a specific body of work and the issues it raises. Although you do not have to have read the books I discuss in order to grasp the lessons I share, I hope my words will entice you to pick up these works and read them. To do so will only enrich your experience, understanding, and life.

The voices that denounced chattel slavery, that spoke to the promise of meaningful freedom, that voiced pleas for justice which made the constitution a living document, the promise of which one day could be made real, have much to teach us. But even more than this, these works speak to us beyond the narrow boundaries of race and nation. They explore timeless values that guide us, reminding us of our responsibility to ourselves and others.

All Americans, indeed all freedom-loving people, should have exposure to and an understanding of this body of work. It reminds us of paths taken that should be avoided and paths not taken that may have yielded different futures. It encourages us to learn the bitter truths of our history as well as the transcendent beauty and humanity of some of our responses to it. This strikes me as especially urgent, now more than ever, when so many Americans appear ignorant of our history and of the importance of the democracy they claim to revere.

In the questions that I raise throughout these pages, I have been deeply influenced by a lifelong intellectual, aesthetic, political, and spiritual engagement with the writings of the late Toni Morrison. Informed by her writing, I ask a series of questions of selected works by Black writers. The authors do not posit or forward a system of ethics, but they do seem to bear witness to one that emerges from the community about whom they write.

In the midst of a hostile society, a society that wants our labor or our death, we live in pursuit of justice, in pursuit of freedom, and longing for a bit of grace. How shall we live, how shall we treat each other, how shall we treat our compatriots, some of whom are guilty of crimes against us?

Each year a multiracial group of students take my class, and each semester they encounter ideas that challenge their understanding of themselves, their relationships to each other, and what they thought they knew about the nation's history. They are forced to rethink their notion of what the United States is and their place within it and within the world. It is my hope that readers of this book will have a similar experience. And, along the way, I hope that they, like my students and myself, will take pleasure in the brilliance and the beauty of the literature.

Through the meditations presented within these pages, I think we will learn that writing by African Americans holds many important lessons for all people interested in the survival of this fragile democracy and the planet on which it exists.

A NOTE ON STRUCTURE

Read Until You Understand is structured around specific concepts, themes, and ideals. These have been chosen from a myriad of possibilities because they most consistently emerge in literature written by Black American authors. They also have the potential to transcend the differences that divide us. All people feel despair, long for love, create beauty, and face death. I have not organized the chapters chronologically as I might do for a literary survey. Instead, the book is designed as a seminar where we readers, together, seek a deeper understanding of the works and the principles they explore. Works written in different periods are placed in conversation with each other to demonstrate both consistency and change over time. Each chapter provides an autobiographical meditation that may be informed by some mixture of history, philosophy, or politics. *Read Until You Understand* demonstrates how a people have lived with style, grace, brilliance, and beauty in the face of persistent crisis and catastrophe. This is one of the many underappreciated gifts of Black Americans to the nation they have helped to shape and build. In fact, because of them, it is one of this nation's greatest gifts to the world.

I began writing this book shortly after the 2016 presidential election. I finished it in the midst of a global pandemic and a glorious uprising that seeks to advance Black freedom. Throughout this time, the stories that I tell, the literature that I share, and the values it explores remain urgent and necessary.

READ

UNTIL

YOU

UNDERSTAND

⇒|⇐

Legacy, Love, Learning

My formal study of African American history and literature did not begin until college. My love of them began much earlier, with my father, who believed teaching was an act of love. Because I adored my father and cherished being with him, I experienced learning as love. A natural-born storyteller, he would make our weekly visits to the public library, bookstores, and many of Philadelphia's historic landmarks come alive. The history of the nation's founding was more than a rendering of facts. Through my father's eyes it became an epic tale of bold and courageous characters challenging stuffy old men in Europe. His tellings were cinematic in their sense of adventure. An old fedora became a tricornered hat like those worn by the eighteenth-century Philadelphians who changed the course of history. On days off from his job as a welder at the Sun Shipbuilding Company in Chester, Pennsylvania, after work and on the weekend, he took me to Philadelphia's Elfreth's Alley, "the nation's oldest residential street," to Independence Mall, and to the various sites that surround it. He purchased copies for me of the Declaration of Independence and the Bill of Rights, which were reproduced on parchment paper for tourists and history buffs. Before I started school, he had me memorize and recite the Preamble to the Constitution, the opening of the Declaration of Independence, the Gettysburg Address, and the Presidents of the United States—all the skills he had learned as a Philadelphia schoolboy during the Depression. He followed my recitations with questions. "What do you think that means? Let's look up that word and use it in a sentence." This was not a practice he reserved for me, nor did he do it out of recognition of my intellectual precocity. My cousins, my older sister Myra, and her children all received the same instruction.

My father's lessons did not derive from an uncritical patriotism. At times I think he exposed me to our nation's founding fathers and the ideals they espoused so I would understand the enormity of their transgression, the enormity of the betrayal.

Along with the founding fathers, he also introduced me to Toussaint Louverture, Nat Turner, Frederick Douglass, Harriet Tubman, the Black Panther Party, and Angela Davis. He held dear intellectual freedom fighters who risked their lives to combat not only the men and women who oppressed them, but also the system of oppression itself. We read and discussed the Panthers' Ten Point Program, which appeared on the back of the Party's newspaper, and he pointed out the similarities to the Declaration of Independence. *The Black Panther*, along with *Muhammad Speaks, Black World, The Philadelphia Tribune*, and a bevy of other Black publications, showed how divided, as a nation, our understanding of events and actions could be. For instance, although mainstream print and broadcast media portrayed Angela Davis as a dangerous Communist and a fugitive from the law, who was on the FBI's most wanted list, these

Black publications described "Sister Angela" as a brilliant philosopher, committed to the project of our freedom. These publications also showed that Black thinkers articulated a sense of
Black history and culture that stretched beyond the borders of
the United States. Thus, my father used them to introduce me
to figures such as Kwame Nkrumah, first prime minister and
president of independent Ghana, Jomo Kenyatta, prime minister
and president of the Republic of Kenya, Patrice Lumumba, first
democratically elected prime minister of Congo, and others, all
founding fathers of modern Black nations engaged in the intellectually rigorous process of nation building.

My father did not limit his pantheon of Black brilliance to
political thinkers. Miriam Makeba joined Abbey Lincoln and
Nina Simone as shining examples of gifted artists who used their
art to speak out against racism and the plight of Black women.
Their images graced the pages of the publications we read, radi-
ant Black women who did not seek to emulate white beauty
standards and whose intellectual legacies continue to challenge
democracy to live up to its radical promise of equality.

Our frequent visits to Philadelphia's historic sites were supplemented by our attending protests and rallies. Among these I
vividly remember the Black Panther Party's Revolutionary Constitutional Convention of 1970, which was hosted by the activist Church of the Advocate in North Philadelphia. (My mother
let me wear an Afro and made me a dashiki dress for the occasion!) I recall the excitement of the people who crowded the
street. I reveled in their expressions of affection and concern
for me: "Look at that little sister!" I also recall the heavily armed
police who stood with guns and riot gear, and the anticipation of the pending arrival of Huey P. Newton, the charismatic
chairman of the Black Panther Party. The proximity of the gun-

wielding officers to the entrance of the church is an image that lives with me still.

Interestingly, unlike many of his generation, my father was not a religious man. One of the earliest words I recall him teaching me was "agnostic." He had eschewed the church of his youth long before I was born. As a young man he aligned himself with the beboppers: hip intellectuals, skeptical of all orthodoxies and race-proud. He had a brief flirtation with the Nation of Islam, drawn to it more by its harsh critique of white supremacy than by any belief in its religious dogma. He eventually left because he thought it was hostile to independent, critical thinking. Nonetheless, he passed his love and admiration for Malcolm on to me. While he did revere democratic principles, he never talked about religious or spiritual concepts like mercy or grace.

One Friday night, my father came home complaining of a bad headache. Within an hour he suffered what we later learned was a severe cerebral hemorrhage. In the middle of the crisis, two Philadelphia police officers, who had been called to our home, debated taking him to the hospital because, as they insisted, he was "drunk." He was not. He was not a drinking man. The difficult truth is, my father was a hardworking man who struggled with heroin addiction and, through much effort, recently had overcome his habit. Eventually, the officers relented to my mother's pleas, put him on a stretcher, and placed the stretcher in the back of the paddy wagon. My mother and I sat on the rough wooden benches and she alternated trying to hold me and trying to hold my father's stretcher down with the weight of her small body. The stretcher had not been secured and would slide with every sharp turn of the vehicle. At one point it slid back and my father's head hit the door. "Oh, Muzzy! My head!" he cried. (Muzzy was one of his nicknames for my mother.) Those were the last words I recall hearing him say. When my mother and I heard news of Freddie Gray's 2015 death in Baltimore, we called each other, each of us quietly crying. Gray had been injured during an arrest, and the officers failed to secure the stretcher in the van while transporting him to the police station. Echoes of that night in March 1972 shook both of us. And, as we have done countless times in the years since, we sought comfort in each other.

On that night, when finally, we arrived at Philadelphia General Hospital, the doctors and nurses rushed the stretcher down the hall. I never saw my father again. Within a week of this traumatic incident, he was dead. He was forty-five years old; I was nine.

Emerson Maxwell Griffin did not grant me any meaningful conception of heaven, so I never assumed he was looking over me from the clouds above. Nor was I concerned about him burning for an eternity, as I only learned of that possibility years later from "saved" Christian classmates who sought to frighten me into salvation. I did instinctively feel his presence, and chose to believe his spirit guided me, especially in my reading.

A voracious lover of books and jazz music, my father was rarely without a paperback book in his back pocket. When he died, I inherited all of his books and albums, and the love of learning that he had bequeathed to me. An upstairs clothing closet held hundreds of books, as did the dining room china cabinet. Another set of drawers under the buffet held albums and 45 rpm records. And the cellar, where we had a coal-burning stove before transferring to gas heat, housed crates full of old magazines including *Ebony, Jet, Sepia, Tan, Negro Digest,* and *Black World,* scrapbooks holding newspaper clippings from the *Pittsburgh Courier* and the *Philadelphia Tribune,* and a number of black-and-white composition books filled with notes. (I carry a tremendous sense of loss and guilt about the notebooks: loss because I no longer have them, guilt because I carried them to college, placed them in a storage space over the summer, and never retrieved the box that held them along with my high school yearbook and a volume of Shakespeare.) Following my father's death, our little row house was a virtual archive, my mind's playground. In addition to the books, there were two of his paintings. One was a self-portrait, which hung in the hallway upstairs. The other was of a slave coffle, filled with Black bodies and Black overseers, a slave castle in the distance; this one graced a wall in our living room.

Under the careful guidance of my mother, I lost myself in the pages and sounds my father left behind. This was my inheritance; my legacy. Little did I know, it would also become my life's work. Driven by my desire to make sense of and give meaning and order to a life forever unavailable to me, I chased him in the ideas he bequeathed me. What did he read? What did he listen to? What did he think about James Baldwin and Mary Lou Williams? How did he learn to paint and why did he make lists of dynamic verbs? Did he ever believe in God?

In the absence of my father, African American literature served as a constant spiritual and intellectual companion. In the Queen Memorial Branch of the Philadelphia Public Library on Point Breeze Avenue, I had a second home. I was seduced by the power and allure of the language, by the ways words brought to life other times, places, and people, even as they made sense of my own present. As I began to read, and later to study, the novels, essays, and poems written by American Blacks, I learned that this body of literature bore witness to both the hypocrisy and the promise of the nation. It debated the nation's potential for redemption against the forever curse of its original sins of genocide and chattel slavery. Frederick Douglass's "What to the Slave Is the Fourth of July?," Langston Hughes's "I, Too," Richard Wright's *Native Son*, Gwendolyn Brooks's "Negro Hero," Ann Petry's *The Street*, Ralph Ellison's *Invisible Man*, and James Baldwin's *The Fire Next Time*, collectively, and beautifully, portrayed the difficult story of our nation.

Later, the works of Toni Morrison joined this canon. She painstakingly reveals the ways whiteness has been the greatest threat to the democracy we claim to hold so dear. The novelist Ayana Mathis encompasses what Morrison means to so many of us formed in her wake: Morrison more than any other figure is "both lighthouse and anchor." I regret that my father did not live to read Morrison's work. Long before I met her in person, through her writing, she, like my father, shaped the way I saw and thought about the world.

Every time I read one of Morrison's novels, I find passages that seem to imply, "Once upon a time there was a people." She records their speech, their poetry, and then mines both diction and syntax for larger philosophical and ethical implications. In all her works there is a sense of loss, not nostalgia, but loss of this peoplehood, this village, and the values it sustained to survive.

Before I had a critical understanding of this historical and ethical dimension of Morrison's work, I was in awe of the way in which she found so much meaning in the words, phrases, and practices that were part of my everyday life. For instance, consider her first novel, *The Bluest Eye* (1970). The story is sometimes narrated by nine-year-old Claudia MacTeer and relays the story of Pecola Breedlove, a foster child who comes to live with the MacTeer family, and who later gives birth to her father's child. Early in the novel, Claudia recalls:

Outdoors, we knew, was the real terror of life. The
threat of being outdoors surfaced frequently in those
days. Every possibility of excess was curtailed with it.
If somebody ate too much, he could end up outdoors.
If somebody used too much coal, he could end up outdoors. People could gamble themselves outdoors, drink
themselves outdoors. Sometimes mothers put their sons
outdoors, and when that happened, regardless of what
the son had done, all sympathy was with him. He was
outdoors, and his own flesh had done it. To be put outdoors by a landlord was one thing—unfortunate, but an
aspect of life over which you had no control, since you
could not control your income. But to be slack enough
to put oneself outdoors, or heartless enough to put one's
own kin outdoors—that was criminal.

"Outdoors, we knew, was the real terror of life." This sentence signals that there is more to the word than the dictionary definition.
The phrase "we knew" asserts a knowledge held by a particular
group: the two sisters Claudia and Frieda, Black residents of Morrison's hometown of Lorain, Ohio, Black people in America. The
sentence gestures the reader to be attentive to the meaning that
lies beneath. Outdoors is not only an inconvenience, it constitutes
terror, intense fear or dread, or that which causes it. There is the
suggestion of violence. Outdoors is a condition imposed from
without and from within. Those who are put outdoors require our
sympathy. Those who put someone outdoors are judged. It goes
against Christ's dictum in Matthew 25:35–40 that we are to provide food, clothing, and shelter to those from whom it has been
denied, even the least of these. To put someone outdoors is to lose
honor in the eyes of the Lord. It is to fail before the Final Judgment.

To put your kin outdoors is the ultimate sin. It is not illegal by the law of the state but by judgment of the community. Evictions are common and beyond one's control, therefore not a judgment on your character. But to impose this condition on oneself or upon one's kin is an act against humanity. Throughout my life my mother always told me, "We don't put people out, we take them in." Take them in we did, time and time again.

If the first paragraph defines outdoors, the second uncovers the philosophical implications of the term.

> There was a difference between being put *out* and being put out*doors*. If you were put out, you go somewhere else; if you are outdoors, there is no place to go. The distinction was subtle but final. Outdoors was the end of something, an irrevocable, physical fact, defining and complementing our metaphysical condition. Being a minority in both caste and class, we moved about anyway on the hem of life, struggling to consolidate our weaknesses and hang on, or to creep singly up into the major folds of the garment. Our peripheral existence, however, was something we had learned to deal with—probably because it was abstract. But the concreteness of being outdoors was another matter—like the difference between the concept of death and being, in fact, dead. Dead doesn't change, and outdoors is here to stay.

The girl, Claudia, the storyteller, the burgeoning artist, interprets meaning here. Note the words *irrevocable, final, concrete*. Each shares this sense of finality only with death. The terror of outdoors exacerbates and underscores the community's social condition. Here Morrison takes a common word from the Black vernacular and, in translating it, reveals the depth and dimension of that language. The throwaway phrase contains a people's worldview, a fear that could be universal, an ultimate dispossession, rootlessness, a tearing asunder for which there is no remedy. It causes a psychic scarring. To have been put outdoors is to have experienced a major trauma from which one never fully recovers. You may endure, but you have been put outdoors, and that is forever a condition of your existence. When Billie Holiday sings, in "Billie's Blues," "He put me outdoors," she is identifying an act of betrayal beyond the end of a romantic relationship. It is a physical act that instills a psychic wound. It is metaphysical and transcendent.

No one in *The Bluest Eye* is more "outdoors" than the child Pecola Breedlove. She is outdoors in relation to everything surrounding her. The blues sing about a condition in order to gain some control over it, to narrate it and therefore contain it within the blues woman's own narrative. The blues song is then given to the listener like a sacred text, a tool to help build endurance, to help find the sweetness and humor in the midst of terror. But Pecola has no blues song. She is not socialized into this alternate universe, except as its victim and scapegoat. Her father twice puts her outdoors, first by burning up their house, putting him "beyond the reaches of consideration." It is this trauma of dispossession that contributes to the stripping of the child's self, which makes her completely vulnerable to the others, undesired and unloved. However, throughout her literary career, including in this first work, Morrison portrays moments that are governed by what I refer to as an ethic of care. Her expressions of goodness are most often guided by an ethic of care.

Goodness, the Good, as implied in this passage, is the opposite of putting someone outdoors. Early in *The Bluest Eye*, Claudia recalls having had a cold. At first, she thinks her mother is angry at her for having gotten ill. She later realizes her mother is angry at the illness itself. Looking back, Claudia reconsiders and recalls that during childhood illnesses, "Love, thick and dark as Alaga syrup, eased up into that cracked window. I could smell it—taste it—sweet, musty, with an edge of wintergreen in its base—everywhere in that house."

Love here is neither abstract nor romantic. It is embodied in action, in forms of maternal care:

> It coated my chest, along with the salve, and when the
> flannel came undone in my sleep, the clear, sharp curves
> of air outlined its presence on my throat. And in the
> night, when my coughing was dry and tough, feet padded
> into the room, hands repinned the flannel, readjusted the
> quilt, and rested a moment on my forehead. So when I
> think of autumn, I think of somebody with hands who
> does not want me to die.

Here love is equated with care, and care is life-giving and life-affirming. The language is elevated and sensual. The metaphors are quotidian, yet rich. Alaga syrup is thick and syrupy sweet, a treat that turns biscuits and other breads into a dessert. To claim something good and loving as dark is notable in this novel, which reveals the destructive nature of white supremacy that claims darkness for all things evil and bad. Here love itself is thick and dark. The young girls who are recipients of this kind of care, especially during times of illness, freely give it to others in need. When the foster child Pecola came to live with Claudia's family, the MacTeers, "She came with nothing. No little paper bag with the other dress, or a nightgown, or two pair of whitish cotton bloomers. She just appeared with a white woman and sat down." The abandoned child doesn't even have a Black mother or aunt to accompany her. The MacTeers quietly take her in; feed her, give her shelter, a place to sleep, maternal and sisterly care. Claudia says, "Frieda and I stopped fighting each other and concentrated on our guest, trying hard to keep her from feeling outdoors." The two sisters agree, together, to take care of Pecola. They enact an ancient hospitality by treating their guest well, making her comfortable, giving her a sense of home, in this case in order to counter the trauma of being outdoors. They make her laugh and feed her graham crackers and milk. They ask nothing in return. The young girls grow in their effort to comfort and care for Pecola. They are nurtured in love and governed by an ethic of care. And they are transformed by the act of caring for one in need of it.

Unfortunately, the MacTeer home is the only place where Pecola receives such care. Outside of that space she falls victim to white supremacist notions of beauty and value, which are so internalized by her community that she becomes their victim first, and then ultimately the victim of the most heinous crime—incest at the hands of her father. There is no call for justice for Pecola, the crimes against her go unpunished, the care given her not enough to address the causes and extent of her trauma. *The Bluest Eye* makes no mention of the pursuit of justice for Pecola. And, by novel's end she is utterly defeated and destroyed. When the community goes against its own ethic of caring for those who are put outdoors, the most vulnerable are destroyed, betraying the community's own capacity for cruelty. In failing to save Pecola, it has lost yet another battle against white supremacy. The novel, in telling that story, becomes a tool, a weapon, in that ongoing war. *The Bluest Eye* offers a critique of Black people's exclusion from America, but more importantly, it asks, "How do we treat each other? Do we mirror and echo the values of the larger society or do we live by an alternative set of values?"

Although I was a dark-skinned girl, who often experienced teasing at the hands of my playmates, I did not identify with Pecola. My family spent a great deal of time countering the teasing and bullying, and unlike Pecola, as a very little girl, I lived in the age of "Black Is Beautiful": While Pecola and her peers admire Shirley Temple and Betty Grable, I was surrounded by images of dark brown beauties like the '70s actresses Brenda Sykes and Judy Pace, and model Beverly Johnson. More importantly, however, I felt much more akin to Claudia, the observant storyteller, disciplined by my mother but deeply cared for. Even as a girl, I knew I was especially fortunate that I would never experience "outdoors" or another condition often described as "like a throwed away child." Although sometimes my mother and aunts would say, "Look at your dress buttoned up wrong! You look like a throwed away child." The implication of course being that you have no one to care enough about you to groom you, love you, feed you. Like "outdoors," it was a condition of being without love, guidance, or protection. In my case it was a hyperbolic simile, not a true description of my reality.

I never feared being "outdoors." My father left not only his books and records, but also a house, which my mother had turned into a home. It was small, two stories, two bedrooms, and a backyard, just big enough for a clothesline and a little garden. The house was our security, our safety. Many people on our block were renters, vulnerable to the whims of landlords, but we owned our home. Ownership meant stability, longevity. Our neighborhood changed over the years, from a mix of Black and Italian to predominantly Black with a sprinkling of Vietnamese, Cambodian, and Laotian, from predominantly homeowners to renters, from two-parent households to single mothers and their children (and, in one instance, a single father of three, who reminded me of our version of the popular television series, *Family Affair*). Because I was surrounded by a loving and protective family, I was never a "throwed away child," although I encountered many young people who were. This knowledge made me especially aware of and grateful for the care given to me by my family, and to my mother and me by both our family and our neighbors following my father's death. I also had a home in pages and pages of books filled with another kind of legacy—one that stretched far back and seemed to project me into a distant future. My home, my family, the memory of my father—the lessons he taught me and the books he bequeathed me—provided the greatest inheritance, a sense of safety and security, a space and a context in which to be granted the freedom to read, to imagine, to develop a sense of self, to expect possibility and to see limitations as but an inconvenience, whenever possible, to overcome.

= 2 =

The Question of Mercy

In the nighttime.
Mercy.
In the darkness.
Mercy.
In the morning.
Mercy.
At my bedside.
Mercy.
On my knees now.
Mercy. Mercy. Mercy. Mercy.

Toni Morrison, *Song of Solomon*

That night in 1972, as my father lay in distress, it was certainly within the power of the white officers to grant him mercy. It was within their power to see his suffering and choose to alleviate it either by calling for an ambulance or immediately taking him to the hospital. It was within their power to grant my mother and me an act of mercy. If they could not, would not, assuage his suffering, could they not have eased ours? My mother—in spite of a lifetime of evidence to the contrary—

wanted to believe in their capacity for empathy. "Please," she said, "He is not intoxicated. He is sick. Please take us to the hospital." My petite mother attempted to lift her husband herself. Perhaps it was the vision of her doing so that led the younger policeman to finally suggest to his partner they transport him to Philadelphia General Hospital. Was he being merciful?

I remember one of their filthy shoes on my mother's white sheets, I heard the crack of the bed frame as a foot landed on the mattress and they began to lift him. Had they gone back downstairs to retrieve the stretcher? That detail I cannot remember. But I recall the odd mixture of anger and gratitude that engulfed me as they placed him in the police wagon, ill-equipped to relieve the suffering of a sick man. I recall the fear I felt as my mother and I climbed in back with the stretcher. Police were the source of trepidation and disdain in my community. Rarely were they called upon, their presence not often welcome, certainly not in our homes. The idea of voluntarily getting inside the police wagon filled me with confusion and fear, but also relief that perhaps they really would help us. Years later I lived with sadness that it was a police vehicle instead of an ambulance, where trained workers might have revived him, offered him comfort and treatment on the way to the hospital. Years later, I often wondered why God didn't seem to grant us mercy on that occasion, when, in fact, we had done no wrong. My father did not believe in a Just and Beneficent God. Here was evidence that he may have been right.

And yet . . .

If we did not experience mercy at the hands of the police— perhaps because we had not—the days and weeks that followed my father's death were awash with the warmth, generosity, indeed mercy, of my family and neighbors. At least, that is how I remember them. Though consumed by grief, my mother and I were the beneficiaries of a love and kindness so deep as to defy description. Our family and neighbors protected and provided for us. I experienced this as a thick blanket covering us and holding us close. We did not have a church community, because we were not church members—we weren't even Christians—though there were many self-proclaimed ·Christians among those who cared for us. There were Muslims and Jehovah's Witnesses, Freethinkers and Doubters as well. They gave us the necessary distance, while standing vigilant watch over us, ready to address our needs. Anonymous envelopes with small cash gifts were slipped through our mail slot. My mother suspected these may have come from one of Daddy's friends, perhaps my godfather, called by his last name, Somerville, a handsome streetwise man who knew she would never accept money if offered. The city had mistakenly torn down the fence of our yard, leaving the back of our row house exposed and easily accessible to predators. However, during the days of my father's hospitalization and the weeks that followed (until the fence was replaced), a big dog sat watch just outside the dining room window, arriving each night as darkness descended and leaving at the break of day. Had his owner instructed him to stay there and keep watch over the young widow and her child? We never knew.

The streets outside held danger, but somehow, we did not experience it. My cousins, uncles, and self-appointed godfathers were men whose reputations guaranteed that no intruder would dare enter our home. Elders carefully monitored our comings and goings—always quick with greetings and offerings of food and solace. Gestures of kindness greeted us in the form of extra tomatoes from a garden, a plant clipping, a pitcher of iced tea.

Inside our home, a quiet filled the empty hole left by my father's absence. And in that quiet I read and wrote, did homework and sometimes listened to my father's records, soothing instrumental jazz, mostly Miles, and the occasional vocals of Lady, Carmen, or Sarah. I started a diary and began a lifelong habit of letter writing. My aunts couldn't provide enough boxes of stationery or little books with keys. My mother shared her stamps for the letters that I sent to activists (the Panther Party headquarters in Oakland), artists, journalists, Black models (Naomi Sims and Beverly Johnson). Many of them, like Johnson, Ed Bradley, and Gregory Hines, wrote back. I wrote stories and poems about my father, about my parents' love story, about characters I invented. A compulsion to read and write addressed my loneliness and seemed to release something close to euphoria in my head. In writing I found, if not joy, then contentment. In reading I found information but also worlds that fed my imagination. A voracious, undisciplined reading both discomfited and brought a sense of well-being. I read Mario Puzo's *The Godfather* and Billie Holiday and William Dufty's *Lady Sings the Blues*, both books readily available because the movies that had been made from them were released at this time; *Tom Sawyer*, because my father had chosen *Huckleberry Finn* to read to me at bedtime; a navy blue hardback children's biography of Frederick Douglass; anthologies of poems; and profiles of historic figures like Hannibal, Makeda, Queen of Sheba, and Phillis Wheatley. I sent away for book club offers that reeled you in with a number of books for a penny but then saddled you with monthly purchases and steep shipping and handling fees. My favorites were novels and biographies, until my mother discontinued my membership. Eventually school reading at my new magnet school took over, including *Ethan Frome*, which I hated, but which introduced me to Edith Wharton, whom I would grow to love. Later as an A Better Chance scholarship student at an elite girls' school, The Baldwin School, I fell in love with works by

Andrew Marvell, Charlotte Brontë, T. S. Eliot, James Joyce, and Dostoyevsky. At Baldwin I was introduced to and fell in love with the canon, which was presented to me as a precious prize, and I, like Phillis Wheatley before me, consumed it with delight. I did not read Black authors in class at Baldwin, but the library had a copy of Jean Toomer's *Cane*, which I found mesmerizing, if confounding. Unlike Wheatley, on my own, in my small row house, I continued to read Black authors, who I now placed in conversation with the revered white ones I encountered in school. Wasn't James Baldwin's *Go Tell It on the Mountain* similar to *A Portrait of the Artist*? Weren't Morrison's literary gifts as extraordinary as any modernist? And she still managed to reference things familiar to me like Dixie Peach hair pomade and Alaga Syrup.

Those days, weeks, months, years following my father's death are a blur, but I remember the love, the books, the writing paper, and a mother with softly falling tears. We were vulnerable ones who were shielded and protected by a people, themselves in need of mercy, who granted it freely to us. And I was comforted and nourished by a cascade of words, those of others, and many that danced in my head.

Slowly, we incorporated our loss, no longer experienced as crisis, but now as a quiet emptiness at the core of our existence. We carried it with us as we re-entered the world—my mother to factory work, me to ever broadening educational opportunities that were always guided by "What would Daddy have wanted?"

Having been the beneficiaries of mercy, both God's and our people's, it was something we cherished, held dear, and extended to others. In mercy lay the possibility of redemption and renewal. We had little expectation that whites would grant it; in fact, we held tightly to the belief that it was best to avoid ever being in need of their mercy.

I don't recall anything about mercy in my early readings, but many years later, as I came to teach literature by African American writers, I noticed it appeared again and again. Writers such as Phillis Wheatley, Charles Chesnutt, and Toni Morrison leave us with more questions about it than answers.

Phillis Wheatley was an enslaved African prodigy, a girl poet. Hers is a litany of firsts: In 1773 she became the first Black person, the first enslaved person, and the third woman to publish a book of poems in the colonies. Her most famous work is also her most controversial one:

On Being Brought from Africa to America

'Twas mercy brought me from my *Pagan* land,
Taught my benighted soul to understand
That there's a God, that there's a *Saviour* too:
Once I redemption neither sought nor knew.
Some view our sable race with scornful eye,
"Their color is a diabolic die."
Remember, *Christians*, *Negros*, black as *Cain*,
May be refin'd, and join th' angelic train.

Celebrated, reviled, and eventually revisited, this poem has had many lives. Initially celebrated as evidence of Africans' capacity for intellectual pursuit, evidence that genius exists amongst the darker races, later it was reviled by Black thinkers because of its representation of Africa as unenlightened and pagan, and because it expressed a sense of gratitude for the slave trade. Wheatley seems to assert that neither human violence nor greed brought her from Africa to America. These were but the vehicles for an act of mercy granted by God. Enslavement is the price paid for salvation, for conversion, for Christianity. When the poem is revisited in the 1980s, we move, finally, from the opening lines to the closing ones. Christianity gives her the authority to challenge racism and claim equality. She speaks as an equal to those she addresses, and offers them a challenge. Here, she may be said to initiate a Black prophetic tradition in the Americas, speaking truth to power and issuing an admonition. However, in order to be granted a hearing, she must accept the absurd terms presented to her: Africa is pagan, slavery is an act of mercy. This seems to me a major dilemma of the Black artist and intellectual in the West; in order to be heard by those who oppress you, you must first accept the false premise that justifies your oppression. The enslaved understand that their masters assume slavery is justified. At best, the masters think they are acting mercifully; they do not believe themselves to be acting unjustly. They are in the position to grant mercy to their slaves, when, in fact, what the slaves deserve is justice.

Wheatley's title offers the poem as a meditation on her journey. She is brought from Africa to America. She does not travel of her own volition. She is transported, led, carried. "From Africa to America"—as with the poem's persona, the phrase moves through time and space, from one place to another, from one group of people to another, from one idea to another. What brings her? The poem says "mercy," but in fact it was a slave ship, a schooner, the *Phillis*.

A child of seven years old when she arrived in Boston in 1761, over a decade before the birth of the United States, her frail frame was barely covered by "a dirty carpet." She is like a thrown-away child. It is a wonder she survived the journey; at least ten of the original ninety-six captives did not. Someone—we don't know who—determined her age by her missing front teeth. The sickly child was not of great value to the slave trader. On the morning of her arrival, John and Susanna Wheatley, a prominent Christian couple, came to the Boston docks seeking a new house slave. According to Margaretta Matilda Odell, a woman who claimed to be Mrs. Wheatley's grandniece, the family wanted "a young negress," who would be trained "under [Mrs. Wheatley's] eye, that she might, by gentle usage, secure herself a faithful domestic in her old age." So moved by the child's features, frailty, and vulnerability, Mrs. Wheatley insisted upon purchasing the African girl. The child's new owners named her Phillis, after the slave ship that "brought" her from Africa to America. They named her for a site of her trauma. No one knew her actual age; no one knew her name. Imagining the moment of her arrival and her purchase, the poet June Jordan writes that "Until then Phillis had been somebody's child. Now she was about to become somebody's slave."

Scholars have determined that Wheatley came from the Senegambia region of West Africa. By what name had she been called in her homeland? What term of endearment might her mother have used to beckon her near, to soothe a minor scrape, reassure her after a scare, or to embrace her after disciplining her? Did the child recall words or phrases from her native tongue (perhaps Wolof)? Had she been a precocious and curious toddler, quick to walk and talk? What were the lyrics to the lullabies that enticed her to sleep? Was her mother, or father, or sister, or brother, among the captives who did not survive the journey? Perhaps they all survived but were separated from her. By what name had this girl-child been called by those who claimed her as kin?

We will never know. Perhaps, the trauma of her kidnapping, the trauma of the Middle Passage, ripped memories of her past from her. Perhaps she recalled it all in intimate detail, but chose to keep her recollections inside, close, where they could not be taken from her. Perhaps she returned, occasionally, to that interior landscape of her memory and her imagination.

In the Wheatley home, she was separated from the other enslaved people. She became a constant companion to her mistress. Odell tells us that her owners became aware of Wheatley's "uncommon intelligence" and that she "was frequently seen endeavoring to make letters upon the wall with a piece of chalk or charcoal." So intense was her desire to write that she was driven to do so on any surface and with any material made available to her. Within a few years she became fluent in English; she later learned Latin as well. The Bible, Greek mythology, Alexander Pope's poetry, and a translation of Homer were among her favorite works. The Wheatleys' eldest daughter, Mary, became her tutor, instructing her in astronomy, geography, Latin, and the Old and New Testaments. In writing about Clarence Thomas, by way of Robinson Crusoe's Friday, Toni Morrison seems to address Wheatley as well: "The problem of internalizing the master's tongue is the problem of the rescued. Unlike the problem of survivors who may be lucky, fated, etc., the rescued have the problem of debt." I think in Wheatley's case, she pays that debt in gratitude.

All during this time, she shared but one recollection of her life prior to her capture. She remembered her mother, who each morning faced the rising sun and poured a libation: her mother in a spiritual practice. This tells us Wheatley was inculcated with a sense of spirituality, of devotion, long before her introduction to Christianity. She was not a blank slate. What were the names of her Gods? Had she been taught to revere her ancestors? Might she have known of Islam before Christianity?

Perhaps her spiritual life made her open to the religion of her master and mistress. She was baptized on August 18, 1771, a decade after her arrival in Boston, a city struck by both religious and political fervor. In this place, young Phillis learned not only religious doctrine, but also the language of freedom and liberty, the language of a burgeoning revolutionary sensibility. Both attracted her. Both would be of central importance to her throughout her short life. (She died in 1784.)

The nonconformist Christianity of her environment informed the young convert's understanding of mercy. Hers was the New England of the Puritans; it was also a city that had been touched by the first Great Awakening, which converted many there, including many enslaved peoples. Like many Bostonians, the Wheatleys were Congregationalists who believed that all people had direct access to God's word through the Bible. Therefore, they encouraged literacy. They followed a Calvinist doctrine, which held that humanity was corrupt, that only a few, chosen by the Grace of God, not by deeds, would achieve a state of salvation. It was God's mercy that granted an undeserving humanity access to eternity. Wheatley's most astute biographer, Vincent Caretta, notes that enslaved converts were taught that theirs was a "fortunate fall" into slavery. According to Caretta, St. Augustine wrote of the fortunate fall, *felix culpa*: "For God judged it better to bring good out of evil than not to permit any evil to exist." Caretta explains how the fortunate fall was understood in relation to enslaved individuals—how young Phillis would have understood it: "The discomfort of the slave's present life was compensated by the chance given them of achieving salvation," of having an equal chance with their masters of being chosen by God. Without slavery, they would have never had the opportunity to convert and to worship the Lord, God, Jesus Christ. An act of mercy, one that introduces her to Christ, offers her conversion, and puts her on equal spiritual standing with whites: "Remember, *Christians*, *Negros*, black as *Cain*, / May be refin'd, and join th' angelic train." The fixed mark of Cain, her skin color, is juxtaposed with the mobility of the train. Color is fixed but status is not.

I have always been struck and haunted by the word *mercy* in Wheatley's poem. Over two hundred years after Wheatley encountered the concept in Boston, I heard it in that other historic colonial-era city, Philadelphia. "Lord Have Mercy" was both a plea and an assertion, an insistence. It was a request made of God by someone in need of kindness, consideration, a respite from the difficulties of life. It was sometimes shortened to "Have Mercy!" or simply "Mercy!" In this instance it was not entirely sacred. If someone was pitiful, or dressed in poor taste, or had delivered a poor performance, then the call for mercy was more like, "God please help this child/fool/untalented soul, because they are not going to get a break from their fellow humans." And, of course, there was Marvin Gaye imploring, "Whoa, ah, mercy, mercy me / Oh things ain't what they used to be, no, no." His was a most eloquent plea for God's consideration in the face of human-made ecological disaster.

The most common understandings of mercy have to do with God's compassion for humankind. But mercy is also the compassion human beings grant to another who is within their power to harm or punish. Finally, mercy is the dispensation of compassion and forgiveness toward someone who deserves punishment. In all of these instances, mercy is granted to someone who has not earned it. In Wheatley's poem, mercy brings her Christianity, and Christianity grants her the equality and authority upon which to challenge white Christians. This is the Calvinist notion of the "fortunate fall." However, if mercy is defined as being spared the punishment you deserve, who actually is in need of it: the African child, or those who capture and enslave her?

Certainly, throughout much of this nation's history, whites have held tremendous power over Black people's lives; in slavery that power was absolute. Under these circumstances one might say they held the capacity to grant mercy out of the capricious whims of their power and authority. But isn't the possession of that kind of power itself worthy of punishment? At the end of her novel, *A Mercy*, Toni Morrison writes: "To wrest dominion over another is a wrong thing."

In an extraordinary book of poems inspired by Wheatley's life and writing, the poet Honorée Fanonne Jeffers meditates on the word *mercy* in two poems: one set in West Africa and the other on the slave ship that transported Wheatley to Boston. "*Mercy, girl*" is an opening line, an African mother's prayer. "Lord, Lord have *mercy*" closes another poem describing the devastating condition of her transport from Africa to America.

This question of mercy, initiated by Wheatley's poem, drives much of my understanding of Black literature. For instance, the act of mercy with which Charles Chesnutt ends *The Marrow of Tradition* (1901) is an act granted not by God but by a Black mother of a dead child to her white sister, who has failed to acknowledge their kinship until she needs something. The Black mother's child is killed in a race riot. The white woman's child has been sickly from birth and is dying. Only the town's Black doctor, the Black woman's husband, can save him. Here, in the absence of justice for the Black woman, in the absence of recognition or reparation, she grants mercy to her undeserving sibling and implores her reluctant husband to save the white child's life. It is the only moment in the novel in which a Black character has the power to grant mercy. The novel has always left me wondering if these conditions when the oppressed grant mercy to their oppressors are the only ones by which an undeserving nation, founded in genocide and slavery, can be saved. Does it require the mercy of God to be granted in the forgiveness of the oppressed? Are the oppressed even in the position to offer mercy? James Baldwin thought so. In "My Dungeon Shook: Letter to My Nephew on the One Hundredth Anniversary of the Emancipation," he writes: "There is no reason for you to try to become like white people and there is no basis whatever for their impertinent assumption that they must accept you. The really terrible thing, old buddy, is that you must accept them. And I mean that very seriously. You must accept them and accept them with love." Is the willingness of Black Americans to forgive their tormentors actually an act of God's mercy toward whites?

In religious terms, each time the oppressed chooses to forgive the oppressor, each time, on those rare occasions, they find themselves having a modicum of power over them and offering mercy instead of vengeance, might be interpreted as an act of mercy in favor of the oppressor. Black history is replete with these instances. I believe the very fact that Black Americans formed no vigilante groups akin to the Ku Klux Klan is evidence of such an instance.

These questions about mercy and forgiveness arise again upon my reading and re-reading of Toni Morrison's *A Mercy*, published in 2008 but set in the colonial era. At the end of that text an enslaved mother recalls begging a white man, Jacob Vaark, to take her little girl, Florens. Having herself been the victim of gang rape and fearing her master, who'd taken notice of her little girl, will molest the child, she says, "There is no protection. To be female in this place is to be an open wound that cannot heal." She tells Florens that Vaark "see(s) you as a human child, not pieces of eight." When she asks that he take the child, he agrees. She determines, "It was not a miracle. Bestowed by God. It was a mercy. Offered by a human." For the mother, the white man offers a gift of mercy, but is the mercy an act granted to the slave child by the man Vaark, or one granted to the white man to whom she is given? Is the act of mercy his ability to see Florens as a child and not only a piece of property over whom he has power? Or is it God's mercy that the enslaved mother sees Vaark as a human being who might do right by her child and not as a monster who would cause her great harm? All she knows of white men would lead her to see them, to believe them, to be monstrous and evil. Yet, she sees this one as a human being capable of kindness.

The theologian Reinhold Niebuhr tells us, "If, for instance, the white man were to expiate his sins committed against the darker races, few white men would have the right to live. They live partly because they are strong enough to maintain themselves against their enemies and partly because their enemies have not taken vengeance upon them. They survive, in other words, both by the law of nature and the law of grace." Niebuhr here says that grace is what saves, but it would seem to be mercy, for the first part of the sentence asserts justice requires whites pay with their lives for their crimes against people of color. Grace is unmerited favor. No one deserves it. Mercy is not getting the punishment you deserve. In her first novel, *Grace*, Natashia Deón says it better than I do: "[J]ustice is getting what you deserve. And mercy is not getting the bad you deserve. Grace is getting a good thing, even when you don't deserve it."

It is not insignificant that in the three works of literature I discuss, the question of mercy revolves around Black children who are the most vulnerable: A child kidnapped and enslaved, a dead child whose life is sacrificed for the possibility of racial reconciliation, and a child given away by her mother. Children, dead or orphaned. Who can be more deserving of mercy than a child, and, perhaps, who has a greater capacity to embody God's offer of it?

If mercy is granted by humans who have the power to punish but choose not to act upon it, then Black people, and others who are near the bottom of the nation's color hierarchy, certainly benefit if and when white people or the state offer them mercy; but the greater benefit would be the dispensation of justice. If mercy is granted to those who deserve punishment for their deeds against others, then in many ways the United States, particularly its white citizens, have been among the greatest recipients of mercy. It would seem they are in need of it. African American literature raises the question of mercy in a variety of scenarios and certainly seems to value it as an eternal ideal to which we as individuals and as a nation should aspire. Black writers have prized the pursuit of freedom even more than the longing for mercy, because there is a sense of precarity involved in hoping for mercy from white people.

In 1772, one year after her baptism, Phillis Wheatley composed "To the Right Honorable William, Earl of Dartmouth." It is an expression of gratitude to William Legge, the 2nd Earl of Dartmouth, upon the occasion of his appointment as Secretary of State for the Colonies. Wheatley welcomed his appointment because she believed him to be sympathetic to the concerns of the colonists: "Hail, happy day, when, smiling like the morn, / Fair Freedom rose New-England to adorn:"

She sings the praises of freedom, using metaphors of slavery, to describe the condition of the colonies in relation to England. Until the third stanza the persona may very well be a white colonist. However, the narrator distinguishes herself when she says there:

> Should you, my lord, while you peruse my song,
> Wonder from whence my love of Freedom sprung,
> Whence flow these wishes for the common good,
> By feeling hearts alone best understood,
> I, young in life, by seeming cruel fate
> Was snatch'd from Afric's fancy'd happy seat:
> What pangs excruciating must molest,
> What sorrows labour in my parent's breast?
> Steel'd was that soul and by no misery mov'd
> That from a father seiz'd his babe belov'd:
> Such, such my case. And can I then but pray
> Others may never feel tyrannic sway?

Here, her authority to speak about freedom comes not from conversion to Christianity, but from her status as a slave. She says her love of freedom is born of her enslavement. Here, Africa is no longer a pagan land, but "Afric's fancy'd happy seat" from which she was snatched. The poem's persona goes on to imagine a sorrowful parent, a father, whose "babe belov'd" is snatched from him. Although the enslaved would call themselves the "motherless child," here Wheatley recalls the traumatic separation from a loving father. What a shift from "On Being Brought from Africa to America"! She stands on the authority of having been victimized by the traffic in human flesh, the transatlantic circulation of bodies. She uses that authority to bear witness to the colonists' desire for freedom. The enslaved poet has the moral authority, and not only desires her own freedom, but also that those who enslave her not experience the tyranny they have imposed on Black people. She advocates for those who continue to enslave her in the hopes that their freedom will lead to hers. Does her advocacy embody mercy? The nation that emerges in just a few years would not return the favor. Given the opportunity to end slavery as it proclaimed its own status as a free society, it chose instead to maintain the hateful institution for another century.

The nation, which has granted little mercy to Black people, has relied upon their willingness to offer an abundance of mercy and forgiveness. Over and over again. Some of Wheatley's literary progeny would reject her privileging of Christian mercy for an insistence upon justice and freedom and, occasionally, revolt.

Let us turn again to Toni Morrison. *A Mercy* is as much a meditation on freedom as it is on the act for which it is named. As with Wheatley, that novel's protagonist Florens is also literate, also enslaved, also precious and protected. And, as with Wheatley, "from the state of [her] teeth [she is] maybe seven or eight when [she is] brought" to New England. Her first-person narration is in fact written in a fervor on the walls of her owner's dream house, now a ruin. Recall here, the child Wheatley writing on the walls with charcoal. To write is to take control, to reclaim one's reality. The compulsion to write is a strong one. Might it also be an act of one's will to be free? At the novel's end, Florens is not in search of mercy. She instead claims her violent and vengeful self. For Florens, Christianity only renders people evil. The coming of organized Protestantism brings with it a new cruelty and violence. In fact, it is the "pagan" Native American Lina, and the disabled Daughter Jane (who, accused of being a demon because of her disability, proudly claims to be one), that treat her most humanely and with love, who free her internally and literally. Florens does not seek mercy. As with the later poems of

Wheatley, she instead contemplates freedom. And she does so after striking out in an act of violence which allows her to claim, not religious salvation, but a passionate and willful wild nature, for which she has no remorse.

Perhaps it is better to strike a blow for freedom than to rely on mercy.

⇒ 3 ⇐

Black Freedom and the Idea(l) of America

At some point, in first or second grade, administrators from my neighborhood school reached out to my parents expressing concern that I refused to stand for the "The Star-Spangled Banner" during school assembly. I attended the neighborhood elementary school, McDaniel, less than a block from my home. It was predominantly Black and sat diagonally across the street from St. Edmund, a Catholic school, which was predominantly Irish and Italian. I didn't sing the National Anthem or say the Pledge of Allegiance because, according to my father, our country refused to recognize us as full citizens or even as human beings. When my father died, my family decided not to request a flag for his coffin. He'd served in a segregated navy just after World War II and was honorably discharged, but he never spoke to me about his service. It appears to have been a traumatic experience for him.

My mother, ever the diplomat, instructed me to stand for both the anthem and the pledge, though I didn't have to sing the former or recite the latter. "Do like the little Jehovah's Witness boy does." The Jehovah's Witness she referred to was one of two or three remaining white students in the entire school. At one point I resumed reciting the Pledge of Allegiance because I like reciting things from memory and I especially liked the sound of the declarative ending: "With Liberty and Justice for All!" "The Star-Spangled Banner" never held that kind of appeal for me, since it's so militaristic and bombastic. Even today, I stand for it, but I do not sing.

"The Star-Spangled Banner" is my least favorite of the patriotic American songs. Another, "My Country, 'Tis of Thee," has been forever ruined for me by my father's rewriting of the lyrics: "My country, 'tis of thee, land of *no* liberty." In contrast, I've grown to love Woody Guthrie's "This Land Is Your Land" because of its expansive, inclusive sense of the nation. However, "America the Beautiful" is the one that I find most appealing, perhaps because of Ray Charles's soulful rendering of it, or because it portrays the country's wondrous natural beauty. I especially came to appreciate the magnificent landscape after a cross-country drive when I was a young adult. It is the one thing I love about this land without ambivalence.

During my brief time with my father, I learned of his disdain for what he saw as the country's hypocrisy. He taught me that the Vietnam War was a travesty, and shared his belief that Black people shouldn't fight for the country, especially not against other poor people of color. I can still recall reciting *my* opinions on the war to his buddies when I accompanied him to the barbershop. They showered me with praise: "That little sister sure can rap!" From my current vantage point, I would describe my father as a Black nationalist. His nationalism was informed by his youth as a bebopper and his stint in the Nation of Islam. (As I said, he loved Malcolm. He prided himself on having met with him during the latter's frequent visits to Philadelphia. He claimed to have "fished," or made an effort to recruit new members of the Nation, with Malcolm.) My father had Communist sympathies, but found the Communist Party's pursuit of racial integration of the working classes naive and unappealing. He lamented being "too old" to join the Panthers, though his admiration for them was immeasurable.

Nonetheless, Emerson Griffin possessed a deep admiration for the Founding Documents, and though critical, he held a kind of disdainful awe for U.S. military might. What I have learned of my father in the years following his death tells me that at some point he was a bit more hopeful about the country's possibility for racial reconciliation. In his 1958 Temple University yearbook he lists his membership in the NAACP, so at some point he believed in the reformist politics of that august organization. In fact, my three earliest memories of my father are (1) the sound of his melodic whistle as he turned the corner on his way home from work; (2) watching from our living room window as he built me a snowman; and (3) his returning home following a march he'd participated in. This latter memory stood out because it was one of the rare times I saw him in a suit (gray) and tie, and because of the round yellow button he wore on his lapel: "Back to the Wall!" He had been protesting the racial exclusion of Girard College, a boarding school for fatherless boys founded by Stephen Girard, who was a nineteenth-century banker and philanthropist. There are many things named for Girard in the city of my birth, including Girard Estates in South Philadelphia, within walking distance of our row house. A small exclusive enclave of well-kept homes, the Estates seemed to have operated under a restrictive covenant. In my childhood, no Black people lived there. Upon his death, his will established a boarding school for "poor, male, white orphans," which opened in 1848 in North Philadelphia. Girard College sat behind ten-foot walls in the midst of what became a Black working-class neighborhood in the mid-twentieth century. Although Raymond Pace Alexander, esteemed lawyer, activist, politician, and later judge, brought court cases to desegregate the school, he was unsuccessful. Under the leadership of the charismatic Cecil B. Moore, the Philadelphia branch of the NAACP launched a campaign of direct-action protests against Girard College. Starting in May 1965, protestors held daily marches and weekly rallies. On August 3, 1965, Martin Luther King Jr. joined Moore to address the rally. I think this was the event my father attended. I cannot imagine him wearing a suit to any of the other marches. Five years later, in 1968, the Supreme Court finally struck down the ban on Black students.

By word and example, my father taught me that protest and resistance were both personal and collective. We march, we stand up (or sit down) for what we believe, and we read. He insisted that reading and study were central to our struggle as a people and to my overall development as a human being. One morning, before I left for school (I was in third grade), my father gave me two paperback books. I remember being surprised that he was home from work and that he wore a dress shirt and slacks, rather than his work clothes. Inside each book there were handwritten notes.

On the title page of *Black Struggle: A History of the Negro in America* by Bryan Fulks he wrote:

Jazzie read this book
You may not understand it
At first. But read it and understand
    Daddy

Baby read it until you understand
Ask your teacher if you don't understand
She will like you for it.
If you just know this book by the time I get home. I will be
happy.
     Daddy

The second book was a small paperback with a red, white, and
blue cover, titled *The Little Red White and Blue Book: Revolu-*
tionary Quotations by Great Americans. He'd written notes, not
on the title page but within the book, and placed asterisks by or
parentheses around specific quotations:

Start here Jaz
There's lots of Frederick Douglass

He gave me these books because he thought he might be
arrested following a trial or a hearing for failure to file or pay
taxes. My mother filed the federal income tax and prepared tax
forms for family and neighbors (she had briefly studied book-
keeping). My parents paid the real-estate tax as well. I don't
know which tax he refused to pay, but I am sure he saw it as
yet another form of protest. This one carried potentially terrible
consequences for our family. I was nervous all day in school, but
when I returned home he was there, and there was no more talk
of serving time. I assume the case was dismissed or perhaps he
paid the required amount. I just recall feeling relieved. However,
this relief was short-lived, as within months he was dead. Then
the notes in the books became even more precious. His hand
had touched them, his distinct, careful handwriting contained
something of him. He had cared enough to write notes to me. He

wasn't coming back, but I was determined to know everything contained within his books.

These books held a version of history I did not learn in school. This was no "Star-Spangled Banner" history. *The Little Red White and Blue* book offered a "This Land Is Your Land" perspective. *Black Struggle* was closer to Gil Scott Heron's "Winter in America":

> From the Indians who welcomed the pilgrims
> And to the buffalo who once ruled the plains
> Like the vultures circling beneath the dark clouds
> Looking for the rain
> Looking for the rain . . .
> The Constitution, a noble piece of paper,
> Would free society. It struggled but then died in vain
> And now Democracy is ragtime on the corner
> Hoping for some rain
> And looks like it's hoping
> Hoping for some rain.

Heron's song appeared the year after my father's death; its mood expresses disappointment in the failed promise of the nation, a nation whose origins Heron situates in Native Peoples welcoming their enemy and a Constitution whose ideals have been smothered by our failure to live up to its noble goals. His is a song of a post–Civil Rights, post–Black Power era:

> And now it's winter
> Winter in America
> Yes and all of the healers have been killed
> Or sent away, yeah . . .

And ain't nobody fighting
Because nobody knows what to save
Save your soul, Lord knows
From Winter in America

The books, though published just a brief time before Heron's music first appeared, are of a related but different era. They were inspired by and seeking to fuel movements for revolutionary, social change. They were to be found on the tables and bookshelves of independent bookstores, like Robin's, the one we frequented in Center City, Philadelphia. Robin's, owned by the ever-friendly Larry Robin, who resembled Jerry Garcia of the Grateful Dead, was a gathering place where you not only purchased books, but also went to find out where the meetings and rallies were going to be held; where there was always lively political debate and dialogue. Along with these two books, my father also purchased and owned Mao's *Little Red Book*. All three were light in weight and inexpensive.

Published by Dell in 1969, *Black Struggle* was a book for young readers. *The Little Red White and Blue Book*, published by Grove, also in 1969, has been described as a work from the counterculture movement and compiled by Johnny Appleseed Rossen. In the sixties Grove published books that spoke to the anti-war, student, feminist, and Black Power movements. Among these were works by Franz Fanon, Che Guevara, and Malcolm X. The books are a testament to the political, cultural, and intellectual tenor of the times: heady, exciting, revolutionary and full of the sense that a better world awaited us if only we would build it. I am struck by the titles' invocation of the America they describe. The word *Negro* in the Fulks title was anachronistic even then. Given the number of factual errors within the work, the *Negro* in the title may have been an oversight. Perhaps the book was rushed out in anticipation of a newly identified audience of young Black readers like me. The cover had a sepia-tone drawing of an Afro-wearing Black man. On his body are portraits of Martin Luther King Jr., Sojourner Truth, Joe Louis, Malcolm X, and others. *The Little Red White and Blue Book* claims the colors of the American flag (the cover looks like the French flag, as there are no stars) and the phrase "Great Americans." It tells the history of the nation as a revolutionary history, a tradition in powerful prose and peopled with heroic figures who eloquently called for an expansion of rights for women, Blacks, Native Americans. These freedom fighters included Jefferson, Paine, Thoreau, King, and H. Rap Brown, among others.

Frederick Douglass appears in both books. My father owned copies of the 1845 *Narrative of the Life of Frederick Douglass* and the 1855 *My Bondage and My Freedom*. He revered both Malcolm and Douglass, as much for their auto-didacticism, which he shared, as for their eloquence and courage, to which he aspired. I now understand that the two of them, Frederick Douglass and Malcolm X, had very different conceptions of the nation that gave birth to them. For Douglass, the United States was a work in progress, capable of being perfected; for Malcolm, it was irredeemable. Perhaps my father started out like Douglass and ended up like Malcolm. Interestingly, I do not recall his ever talking about Du Bois, whom I would not discover until I was a teenager, although I'd heard his name throughout my childhood. As a high school student I began working, after school, for Federal District Court Judge A. Leon Higginbotham. In addition to answering phones and doing some light typing, I also began to catalogue the books in his dark wood-paneled chambers, where he had floor-to-ceiling bookshelves. I would quietly go through them taking notes, while he sat at his desk working. I was welcome to borrow any book that I liked. As with my father, Judge Higginbotham loved Frederick Douglass. It was in his bookshelves that I first recall coming across *Three Negro Classics*, which contained Du Bois's *The Souls of Black Folk*. It was also where I first discovered Harriet Jacobs's *Incidents in the Life of a Slave Girl*. When, eventually, I studied *The Souls of Black Folk* in college, it became one of the many books I longed to discuss with my father.

Douglass's heroism was a favorite childhood story, and since those first encounters with Douglass, I have read, studied, and taught his three autobiographies and his numerous speeches many times over. I am struck always by his powerful prose, and I remain enamored of his story of self-realization. Under the tutelage of my beloved college professors—the literary critic Werner Sollors, the historian Nathan Huggins, and, in graduate school, the philosopher Cornel West—I came to read Douglass closely and critically, growing to appreciate him as a writer and political theorist as well as an activist. Huggins was an insightful biographer of the great man.

Douglass's story is familiar to many: The slave who became a man, who freed himself, first psychologically and then physically. The slave boy taught to read by a kind mistress. The young man who refused to be beaten and who fought his master to a draw. The fugitive who became a radical abolitionist, a gifted orator who bore witness to the horrors of slavery. The race leader who advocated for his people with Lincoln. Generations have revered the truth-telling prophet who became a political insider and elder statesman. Drawn, photographed, and sculpted, Douglass's chiseled features and abundant hair make for one of the most iconic figures in our history.

Douglass was clear-eyed about the vicious nature, fundamental lies, and pathology of white supremacy. He was disheartened but not surprised by its persistence. And yet, he remained devoted to what he believed was the promise of American ideals as articulated in the Constitution and the Declaration of Independence. Perhaps this core belief allowed him to become, in later life, a functionary of the U.S. government, first as Marshal of the District of Columbia, Recorder of Deeds, and then later as the United States Minister and Consul General to Haiti, thus becoming part of an American imperialist project.

But that is what he would become. On July 5, 1852, at the invitation of the New York Ladies' Anti-Slavery Society of Rochester, Douglass delivered what is perhaps his most famous oration, "What to the Slave Is the Fourth of July?" Recited by schoolchildren and accomplished actors alike, posted on social media, alluded to by activists and politicians, segments of the speech are still used to rebuke a nation that continues to fall short when it comes to Black people. During the summer of 2020, a summer marked by protests against police brutality, systemic racism, and the emergence of a protest movement for Black Lives, Douglass's young descendants recited the speech. A recording of their recitation circulated widely, and his words were as powerful and relevant in the younger generation's America as they had been in his. In this speech, Douglass, at the height of his fire and militancy, at once congratulates white Americans on the celebration of their freedom from British tyranny, celebrates the Founding Fathers' courage and conviction, eviscerates the nation and its churches for hypocrisy and their tolerance of slavery, and concludes that he has hope that the United States may yet live up to the ideals articulated by the founders. His hope lies in the nation's youth and in its founding documents, especially the Constitution, which, by this time in his career, Douglass claimed as an anti-slavery document. He does this with a remarkable rhetorical strategy—the use of the word "your": July 4th "is the birthday of your National Independence, and of your political freedom." The signers of the Declaration of Independence are "your fathers." The United States is "your nation." From the very beginning, even as he sings praises for those who did imagine a new nation into being, he creates an uncomfortable distance. He refuses the pretense of claiming the history and legacy as his own. In the use of the word "your," he is making an indictment. For where there is a "your" there is no "our," and there is an implication that the distinction between "your" and "our" is one forged in injustice and hypocrisy. Next, he marks the space between whites and himself among Black Americans. "What have I, or those I represent, to do with your national independence? Are the great principles of political freedom and of natural justice, embodied in that Declaration of Independence, extended to us?"

This is "Your Country, 'Tis of Thee," not "My Country." Douglass asserts this distinction while insisting upon the integrity of the ideas and prose that gives them meaning. He asserts it so that he may appeal to his audience for the claims that he and his people would make upon the nation. Here Douglass builds upon a rhetorical tradition initiated by David Walker's *Appeal in Four Articles; Together with a Preamble, to the Coloured Citizens of the World, but in Particular, and Very Expressly, to Those of the United States of America* (1829).

Walker was a militant anti-slavery activist and writer. Douglass differs from Walker in that he addresses his oration to white Americans, while Walker addresses his to Black people, especially, but not exclusively, those in the United States. But like Douglass, Walker indicts the United States, especially its white

Christians, for their betrayal of the fundamental ideals they profess to uphold. Furthermore, while Douglass will end on the hope and promise offered by the United States Constitution, Walker actually models his manifesto on the form of the Constitution. Like that document, the *Appeal* has a Preamble and four Articles. If the form echoes that of the Constitution, the content is much closer to the Declaration of Independence in that Walker provides a historically grounded indictment of the wrongs and cruelties white Americans have enacted upon Black people, while also calling upon the slaves to engage in armed revolt in order to secure their freedom.

The two writers, Walker and Douglass, lay the foundation for a strategy that extends into the twentieth century, from Dr. King's "I Have a Dream" speech to the Black Panther Party's "Ten Point Program," structured as a hybrid of the Declaration of Independence and the Bill of Rights. Echoing the Declaration of Independence, the Ten Point Program ends with a verbatim quotation from that document:

> We hold these truths to be self-evident, that all men are created equal, that they are endowed by their Creator with certain inalienable rights, that among these are life, liberty, and the pursuit of happiness. That to secure these rights, governments are instituted among men, deriving their just powers from the consent of the governed, that, whenever any form of government becomes destructive of these ends, it is the right of the people to alter or abolish it, and to institute a new government, laying its foundation on such principles, and organizing its powers in such form, as to them shall seem most likely to effect their safety and happiness.

The Panthers thus demonstrate the hypocrisy of the national creed while insisting on Black freedom from racist tyranny, on the necessity of self-defense and self-determination, and situating the contemporary struggle for Black freedom squarely within the revolutionary origins of the United States. They mark Black people as the true and legitimate heirs of that unfinished revolution, capable of realizing its truly radical potential. Furthermore, they remind us that the Declaration of Independence gives Americans the rights to overthrow a government that does not represent them and to create a new one in its place. In their use of the founding document's language, they join and extend the discourse of Walker and Douglass into a collective radical Black prophetic voice.

Before turning to the Constitution, in the midsection of his July 4 speech, Douglass offers his searing indictment of the moment in which he speaks: "Fellow-citizens; above your national, tumultuous joy, I hear the mournful wail of millions!" He then addresses the question of his title: "What, to the American slave, is your 4th of July? I answer; a day that reveals to him, more than all other days in the year, the gross injustice and cruelty to which he is the constant victim." Should his Northern audience try to distance themselves from the cruelty of the southern slaveholder, Douglass reminds them of the Fugitive Slave Act of 1850, whereby any Black person suspected of being a runaway slave could be arrested and sent into slavery. The accused could not request a jury trial and could not testify. Anyone who was suspected of aiding them, providing food or shelter, was subject to imprisonment and a fine. Douglass asserts that through the Act, "slavery has been nationalized." In a brilliant move, Douglass writes that the power of the Fugitive Slave Act "is co-extensive with the Star Spangled Banner, and American Christianity. Where these go, may also go the merciless slave-hunter." This hunter of Black men, women, and children is as American as "The Star-Spangled Banner" and its Christian Church. The church undergoes blistering criticism for its silence, at best, and at worst, its "actually taking sides with the oppressors."

If the churches and the courts betray the values of their civic and religious doctrines, Douglass nonetheless finds hope in the existence of the Constitution. In turning to it, the speech becomes part of Douglass's broader declaration of independence from his fellow abolitionist and mentor, William Lloyd Garrison. Garrisonians held that the Constitution was a pro-slavery document. Douglass came to believe it could be used to dismantle the institution. Of the Constitution, he writes: "In that instrument I hold there is neither warrant, license, nor sanction of [slavery]; but interpreted, as it ought to be interpreted, the Constitution is a GLORIOUS LIBERTY DOCUMENT." He says that those who framed the document purposely chose not to include the words *slavery, slaveholding*, or *slave* in it. While this is true, Douglass ignores the document's allusions to the institution of slavery. Article I, Section 2, Clause 3, commonly known as the three-fifths compromise, allowed the slave states to count a portion of their enslaved population toward apportioning seats in the House of Representatives. Thus, compromises with the slavocracy are built into the document. This is but one of many instances where compromises are made on the backs of Black people to give even greater power to their oppressors. (The Fugitive Slave Act is the result of one such compromise; so is the end of Reconstruction in 1877. Even the much-heralded New Deal legislation of the twentieth century is marred by concessions to Southern segregationists).

Article I, Section 9, Clause 1 of the Constitution, instead of ending the slave trade, prohibits Congress from banning it until 1808. Article V ensures that no amendments would repeal or nullify Article I before 1808. Article IV, Section 2 prohibits free states from sheltering and protecting fugitive slaves. None of these mention the word *slavery*, but they certainly recognize and support the institution. If they did not, there would have been no need for the Thirteenth Amendment, which finally does mention the word: "Neither slavery nor involuntary servitude, except as a punishment for crime whereof the party shall have been duly convicted, shall exist within the United States." The amendment at once abolishes slavery and re-establishes it under conditions of imprisonment.

A writer who was closely attentive to language, Douglass uses the absence of the word *slavery* to build a strategic, political argument that the document is indeed a powerful tool in the fight against human bondage. He writes: "Now, take the constitution according to its plain reading, and I defy the presentation of a single pro-slavery clause in it. On the other hand, it will be found to contain principles and purposes, entirely hostile to the existence of slavery." In truth, it contains both.

Douglass ends his oration on a high note of hope: "Notwithstanding the dark picture I have this day presented, of the state of the nation, I do not despair of this country. . . . I, therefore, leave off where I began, with hope." He bases this hope upon "encouragement from the Declaration of Independence, the great principles it contains, and the genius of American Institutions," and the powerful and influential abolitionist movement, which shaped him and which he is helping to further build.

There is much for us to learn here. The enslaved were not citizens, so Douglass has to indict the nation for allowing such acts of injustice and inhumanity to happen on this land, where liberty is deemed a sacred right. Imagine extending this critique to our moment: consider the immigrants seeking asylum at the nation's southern border. They do not find refuge, they are mistreated and abused, babies are snatched from their parents, children are forced to live in inhumane conditions. To view the United States through Douglass's lens is to issue an indictment of the country that would tolerate such practices. It is an indictment of our religious institutions that remain silent about them or, worse yet, that support and encourage them. Just as those who aided the fugitive slaves were subject to arrest and fines, so too are those who would assist the migrant at the border.

In our time, conservative politicians attempt to claim Douglass as a member of the Republican Party. First of all, the Republican Party that Douglass joined is a far cry from the Republican Party of today. Secondly, although Douglass did articulate a profound belief in America's capacity to live up to its ideals, he was an unrelenting critic of white supremacy. This certainly cannot be said of the Republican Party (at least since Ronald Reagan), which has aided and abetted avowed white supremacists, and which welcomed them into its fold.

Those who claim to take Douglass and his legacy seriously are required to follow the lead of his prophetic voice, speaking truth to power; or the lead of the listeners, overwhelmingly white, who gathered to hear him speak, organizing against the injustices he calls out. Douglass and his allies insisted that the nation take a different route and move in the direction of freedom and the shared rights of all humanity.

The forces that he identified are never fully defeated. Throughout the history of the United States, there is always a fight between those who would seek to oppress others for profit and greed and those who insist that the nation is better than that. History is not a straightforward process; at times it moves toward greater freedom, at other times it is jerked away by backlash.

A final question inferred from Douglass: Does movement building require hope? Of late, many of our progressive social movements seem to call this into question. The very notion of hope is under scrutiny and not faring well. Pessimism and Despair are the rule of the day and even seem to be lauded as points of departure for those who would build a better world. Those American institutions that Douglass so celebrated have certainly proven not to be worthy of an investment of our hope, which ought instead to be transferred to justice-seeking and freedom-loving people, engaged in and transformed by the project of building a better way.

In 1859, just before John Brown's raid on Harpers Ferry, Douglass published an editorial titled "The Ballot and the Bullet." It strikes a blow against his former Garrisonian comrades who asserted that abolitionists should use only the "sword of the spirit," forgoing both the voting booth and violence in their pursuit of slavery's abolition. In contrast, Douglass wrote:

> If speech alone could have abolished slavery, the work
> would have been done long ago. What we want is an anti-
> slavery government, in harmony with our anti-slavery
> speech, one which will give effect to our words, and
> translate them into acts. For this, the ballot is needed,
> and if this will not be heard and heeded, then the bullet.
> We have had cant enough, and are sick of it. When anti-
> slavery laws are wanted, antislavery men should vote for
> them; and when a slave is to be snatched from the hand
> of a kidnapper, physical force is needed, and he who gives

it proves himself a more useful anti-slavery man than he who refuses to give it and contents himself by talking of a "sword of the spirit."

Here Douglass calls for both the use of the ballot *and* the bullet in pursuit of Black freedom. Over a century later, at Cleveland Ohio's Cory Methodist Church, on April 5, 1964, one month after breaking with Elijah Muhammad, his mentor and father figure, Malcolm X delivered a speech that would become known as "The Ballot or the Bullet." In his Black nationalism, Malcolm is more the political heir of David Walker, Henry Highland Garnet, and Black nationalist and Pan-Africanist Marcus Garvey, than of Frederick Douglass. Similarly, in his global perspective and Pan-Africanism, Malcolm is more an inheritor to Du Bois than to Douglass. Nonetheless, Douglass is one of his political and rhetorical ancestors as well.

Elijah Muhammad had clear-cut answers to the Black man's problems. White people were capable of such inhumane cruelty against people of color, especially Black people, because they were devils. Islam, or his version of it, was the Black man's true religion. Black people in the United States would do well to turn within, to build families and businesses and serve the Black nation Elijah Muhammad was building. He discouraged his followers from participating in the political process. As with many young, urban Black men, Malcolm had been exposed to the Nation of Islam's teaching and discipline in prison. He emerged as the Nation's most charismatic disciple and loyal follower. Because of Malcolm, Muhammad's message spread nationally and gained wide admiration among many working-class and working-poor Black Americans, who did not necessarily flock to join the Nation, but who nonetheless appreciated Malcolm's message.

I do not know when my father discovered or joined the Nation. Looking at a scrapbook and notebooks he left behind, I think it may have been sometime in 1958–59. The scrapbook is filled with clippings of articles and columns from the Black newspaper *The Pittsburgh Courier*. There are a few from another newspaper, the *Islamic News*, which may have been the precursor to *Muhammad Speaks*. *The Courier* articles are by figures such as independent scholar J. A. Rogers and sociologist Horace Cayton, with a few by Elijah Muhammad. There are stories about various leaders of the African independence movements, about the Dixiecrats, a few about King, and some about Malcolm. By the time of my birth, my father was no longer in the Nation, but its continued influence was evident. We didn't eat pork. A framed crescent and star graced the wall above the mantle. On the back of one of the very rare pictures of me as an infant is written, in my mother's graceful penmanship, "Farah Jasmine Griffin. All Praises Due to Allah." In my childhood there was little mention of Elijah Muhammad, who was referred to as "The Messenger," but Malcolm's name resonated with great affection and reverence in our home.

My father left the Nation before Malcolm did. When Malcolm announced his own departure from the organization following revelations of a scandal involving Elijah Muhammad and young women who had given birth to children fathered by him, my father expressed concerned for Malcolm's safety. Following his departure, Malcolm continued to believe that neither the Democrats nor the Republicans had the best interests of Black people in mind. He pointed out the willingness of the Democratic Party to house the racist segregationist Dixiecrats as evidence of their betrayal of Black voters. Nonetheless he insisted: "That's why, in 1964, it's time now for you and me to become more politically mature and realize what the ballot is for; what we're supposed to get when we cast a ballot; and that if we don't cast a ballot, it's going to end up in a situation where we're going to have to cast a bullet. It's either a ballot or a bullet." While Douglass insisted that both the ballot and the bullet were necessary, Malcolm suggests that the ballot might help to prevent a situation where the bullet would be necessary. While the South actively disenfranchised Black voters through violence, intimidation, and laws,

> In the North, they do it a different way. They have a system that's known as gerrymandering, whatever that means. It means when Negroes become too heavily concentrated in a certain area, and begin to gain too much political power, the white man comes along and changes the district lines. You may say, "Why do you keep saying white man?" Because it's the white man who does it. I haven't ever seen any Negro changing any lines.

In "The Ballot or the Bullet," Malcolm calls for an expansion of the vision of the Civil Rights movement to include demands for human rights and to seek allies outside of the United States: "When you expand the civil-rights struggle to the level of human rights, you can take the case of the black man in this country before the nations in the UN." Here as elsewhere throughout his short public career, Malcolm refuses to romanticize the American past or have his listeners profess faith in its future. "Uncle Sam's hands are dripping with the blood of the Black man in this country. . . . Let the world know how bloody his hands are. Let the world know the hypocrisy that's practiced over here." For this reason, Black Americans cannot rely on appeals to the nation, "the criminal who's responsible." But using the example of the power of African nations in the United Nations to utilize their votes to keep the United States "in check," Malcolm argues for the importance of the ballot. Yet, he also notes, "in areas where the government has proven itself either unwilling or unable to defend the lives and property of Negroes, it's time for Negroes to defend themselves." Here, he echoes earlier thinkers such as journalist and anti-lynching activist Ida B. Wells, who called for Black self-defense in a period of unrestrained lynching.

Malcolm makes no pretense of claiming the United States for Black Americans. For him, Blacks are Africans, not Americans. In other versions of this speech, Malcolm uses America's national symbols as an opportunity to create some of his most effective wordplay: "Our forefathers weren't the Pilgrims. We didn't land on Plymouth Rock. The rock was landed on us." In opposition to Douglass, who insists that the Constitution is an anti-slavery document that does not endorse slavery, Malcolm tells his audience:

> We were brought here against our will; we were not
> brought here to be made citizens. We were not brought
> here to enjoy the constitutional gifts that they speak
> so beautifully about today. Because we weren't brought
> here to be made citizens—today, now that we've become
> awakened to some degree, and we begin to ask for those
> things which they say are supposedly for all Americans,
> they look upon us with a hostility and unfriendliness.

By this time Malcolm is not only advocating for the vote, he is also promising to register voters "not as Democrats or Republicans, but registered as independents."

At the end of his life, after decades of struggle, Douglass may have come to have a less optimistic belief in the possibility of the United States for its Black citizens. With the rise of lynching, disenfranchisement, and Jim Crow, he grew more and more skeptical about the nation's commitment to Black freedom. "I cannot shut my eyes to the ugly facts before me," he said. For him the Republican Party was the "party of money rather than a party of morals, a party of things rather than a party of humanity and justice." For Malcolm X, neither party represented the interest of Black people, but he envisioned the ballot, the electoral process, as an important tool and strategy in the ongoing struggle for Black freedom.

I don't imagine either Douglass, with his hope in America having been consistently challenged, or Malcolm, who never acquired hope in the nation's possibilities, could have imagined the rise of Barack Obama. For that matter, neither would my father have imagined the possibility of Barack Obama's political career. I know he would have been ambivalent about anyone who wanted to be president of the United States, though I expect he would have been as proud of Obama the candidate as my mother was, if less enamored than she.

The foundations laid by Douglass and Malcolm (as well as Martin Luther King Jr.) provided the ground from which Obama ascended. As a young man, Obama became fully aware of the tradition represented by Douglass and Malcolm, and he engaged with their ideas as he sought to shape his own identity and worldview. All three men were readers and thinkers, and each penned powerful and influential autobiographies: *Narrative of the Life of Frederick Douglass*, *The Autobiography of Malcolm X*, and *Dreams from My Father* are all true works of

American literature. All three were orators of great power, charisma, and dynamism.

As a young senator from Illinois, Barack Obama excited the electorate in ways not seen in generations. It wasn't his race only, though that surely played a part. The nation had a brilliant, progressive Black candidate in Jesse Jackson in 1984. This time was different: after the Iowa primaries, there was viability for his candidacy. Perhaps this time white Americans, and not just a small group of them, would vote for the Black liberal candidate. The days of the campaign were exciting, and at times breathtaking. Barack Obama was handsome, intelligent, cosmopolitan. He was a reader, a thinker, and a beautiful writer. He appealed to Black Americans for all of these reasons and more. For many Black people, his respectability was a plus: He was married to Michelle, a lovely, equally accomplished Black woman, and he was the father of two precious little Black girls, Malia and Sasha. (That he had chosen to marry a Black woman and raise Black children was significant to many Black voters.) He was scandal-free. He would not embarrass us. He appealed to white Americans for similar reasons of intellect and charisma, but also because he didn't appear to be angry (this was most important), couldn't be linked to previous activist struggles, though he seemed to be the culmination of them, and not insignificantly, genuinely appeared to like white people. He even held forth the promise of loving them. After all, he loved his white mother and grandparents. He seemed neither aggrieved nor bitter.

Barack Hussein Obama first aroused the nation's interest with a spellbinding speech at the 2004 Democratic National Convention in Boston with talk of a United States of America: a nation that could transcend political, regional, racial, and ethnic divides. With soaring rhetoric and an oratorical style deeply influenced by the African American homiletic tradition, he presented a vision of the nation as it wanted to see itself, progressing steadily toward a united, post-racial future. With his youth and his mixed-race identity, he seemed to represent a truly American future.

In a street-capitalist's act of marketing genius, during the 2008 presidential campaign Black vendors hawked tee shirts and posters with photographs of Obama superimposed alongside those of Martin and Malcolm. Some of their buyers were aware that though Douglass and Malcolm helped to make him possible, Obama was not a prophetic voice of the Black freedom struggle, nor would that struggle culminate in his election. (In fact, the election would erupt into a horrific backlash.) King and Malcolm were unrelenting critics of American racial politics and of America's imperialist wars and its rampant greed. While he was critical, Obama did not seek to dismantle these structures, but instead to correct them in the nation he sought to lead. He espoused a hope in America that Malcolm never had, and that King possessed even while knowing that it was an act of faith in things unseen. But Obama learned from them, and from Douglass, Du Bois, and Baldwin. (He'd learned from and been mesmerized by Morrison as well.)

In his eloquent autobiography *Dreams from My Father*, Obama writes:

Malcolm X's . . . repeated acts of self-creation spoke to me; the blunt poetry of his words, his unadorned insistence on respect, promised a new and uncompromising order, martial in its discipline, forged through sheer force of will. . . . And yet, even as I imagined myself following Malcolm's call, one line in the book stayed

with me. He spoke of . . . the wish that the white blood
that ran through him, there by an act of violence, might
somehow be expunged. . . . [T]raveling down the road to
self-respect my own white blood would never recede into
mere abstraction.

Throughout *Dreams from My Father* Malcolm informs Obama's
understanding of Black nationalism: "Ever since the first time
I'd picked up Malcolm X's autobiography, I had tried to untan-
gle the twin strands of Black nationalism, arguing that nationalism's affirming message—of solidarity and self-reliance,
discipline and communal responsibility—need not depend on
hatred of whites any more than it depended on white munifi-
cence." Here Obama is trying to carve out an ideology of Black
self-sufficiency divorced from disdain of or accusations against
whites. It is a form of conservative Black nationalism that might
better be associated with Booker T. Washington, and it forms
a long and sustaining thread in Black American life. This is the
origin of a perspective Obama would share time and again in his
speeches to Black audiences, though often it came off as chastis-
ing them for looking for "excuses" in their identifying white racism as the major obstacle to Black progress. Obama is inspired
by Malcolm's act of self-creation, by his discipline, even his militancy and his ability to grow beyond a racist theology. However,
Malcolm could never embrace the white part of himself. In fact,
he described it as that "white rapist's blood." Obama's white relatives were not, or not only, slave-owning whites. Having been
raised by his hardworking, devoted white mother and her parents, he believed in the capacity of white people to embrace,
indeed, to love him. Unlike Malcolm, Obama writes, "I was left

to wonder what else I would be severing if and when I left my mother and my grandparents at some uncharted border."

At the time of his first campaign it was not clear that Obama fully understood the unrelenting capacity of white supremacist ideology to stoke deep, profound, and irrational hatred and fear. For many, his election would be that occurrence, which James Baldwin had described in 1963 in the essay "My Dungeon Shook": It constituted a "danger, in the minds of most white Americans . . . the loss of their identity. Try to imagine how you would feel if you woke up one morning to find the sun shining and all the stars aflame . . . the Black man has functioned in the white man's world as a fixed star, as an immovable pillar: and as he moves out of his place, heaven and earth are shaken to their foundations."

Many white liberals loved Obama. Most African Americans did as well. Progressives of all races were divided. Some saw him as a charismatic, dangerous representative of neoliberalism, lending to it the symbolic legitimacy of the Black freedom struggle. Others saw him as an important step toward the goal of a multiracial democracy. But we were all excited. And many of us, myself included, worked to get him elected. We sent money, canvassed, worked phone banks, attended forums, and endlessly debated ideas, policies, and platforms. We wrote columns, editorials, and blogs. It was the first time many people who had never been politically involved participated in the political process. The campaign represented an expansion of American political democracy.

In the midst of all the excitement, as the campaign gained momentum and headed toward the Denver convention, snippets of recordings from Obama's pastor, the Reverend Jeremiah Wright, surfaced. Taken out of context, whittled down to incendiary comments, the remarks were made to seem anti-American. As is often the case for Black candidates, there were demands that Obama disown his pastor. At first Obama distanced himself, and then when circumstances suggested that his candidacy might be threatened, he delivered a much-awaited speech on race, which satisfied those who insisted on complete disavowal and permanent severance of his ties to Reverend Wright. Here I am careful to use the word *disavow* rather than *disown*. In the speech, Obama *never* disowns Wright. In fact, he says, "I can no more disown him than I can disown the Black community. I can no more disown him than I can my white grandmother." To disavow is to repudiate, to disclaim, to refuse to accept. To disown is to deny the validity or authority of, to refuse to acknowledge as one's own. One disavows an idea; one disowns a person.

Demands to disavow and disown put Black candidates in impossible positions: disavow a figure admired by large swaths of Black America or risk losing support of large groups of whites. (Obama's successor, the 45th president of the United States, not only did not disavow white supremacists; his failure to do so did not threaten his candidacy. He fully embraced them once in office, including welcoming them into his administration and espousing white supremacist rhetoric himself.) In Obama's case, the disavowal wasn't simply of an incendiary and polarizing figure. Wright had brought Obama to Christ, served as a spiritual mentor, officiated at his wedding and baptized his daughters. Furthermore, he inspired the young leader and, through his sermons, offered him the seeds that he would develop into his own oratorical masterpieces (the phrase "audacity of hope" comes from a Jeremiah Wright sermon). The disavowal marked a breach. As Douglass broke with Garrison and articulated the ideological dimensions of that break through "What to the Slave Is the Fourth of July?," and Malcolm broke from Elijah Muhammad and articulated the ideological dimensions of that break through "The Ballot or the Bullet," so too did Obama break with Wright, articulating the ideological dimensions of that break through "The More Perfect Union" speech delivered on March 18, 2008, in Philadelphia.

At the time of the controversy, Jeremiah Wright was a widely respected and admired African American pastor, an electrifying preacher, a man of ideas and action who built one of the nation's most admired churches. He sat firmly in the Black prophetic tradition, delivering Black jeremiads in the style of David Walker and Frederick Douglass, speaking truth to American Power and offering a way forward toward not just a more perfect union, but a more just world. His theology was shaped by Black liberation theology, described by its founder, James Cone, as "a theology that sees God as concerned with the poor and the weak." At its core Black liberation theology seeks to make the gospel story relevant to the struggles of Black people and to encourage a sense of self-affirmation in Black followers of Christ.

During the campaign I had the honor of meeting and corresponding with Reverend Wright. Obama's description of Wright in the "More Perfect Union" speech matches the Reverend Wright I met and came to admire:

The man I met more than twenty years ago is a man . . . who spoke to me about our obligations to love one another; to care for the sick and lift up the poor. He is a man who served his country as a U.S. Marine; who has studied and lectured at some of the finest universities and seminaries in the country, and who for over thirty years led a church that serves the community by doing God's work here on Earth—by housing the homeless, ministering to the needy, providing day care services and scholarships and prison ministries, and reaching out to those suffering from HIV/AIDS.

Upon our first meeting, Reverend Wright and I bonded over our Philadelphia origins, especially after we realized that my Aunt Eunice later purchased the Germantown home in which he'd been born. I found him to be erudite, humorous, and generous. In his brilliance, militance, and charisma, he reminded me of my father. The congregation he built at Trinity United Church of Christ was guided by an ethic of care for all of its members and the surrounding community. I developed a great fondness for him, and I still smart whenever anyone portrays him as a caricature. But I understand this country, and I knew Obama would be forced to disavow Wright if he wanted to appease the majority of whites who might vote for him, even as I hoped he would not. In his description of Wright, Obama went on to say, "Not once in my conversations with him have I heard him talk about any ethnic group in derogatory terms, or treat whites with whom he interacted with anything but courtesy and respect."

The speech Barack Obama gave on March 18, 2008, will go down in history as one of his most important. Obama begins by quoting the opening of the United States Constitution: "We the people, in order to form a more perfect union." As such he situates himself and the remarks he will make directly in the political tradition that gave birth to the nation he was seeking to lead. He follows that sentence with a rhetorical allusion to another canonical speech. The words "Two hundred and twenty-one years ago" echo Lincoln's "Four score and seven years ago," which opens the Gettysburg Address. Both the Preamble of the Constitution and the Gettysburg Address call a united nation into being through language. The Gettysburg Address does so at a moment of great division and national unraveling. Obama does so at a different kind of juncture, at a moment that might undermine his efforts to become president, in order to once again weave together this nation, through words and person, into a kind of unified, if momentary, project. "Two hundred and twenty-one years ago, in a hall that still stands across the street, a group of men gathered and, with these simple words, launched America's improbable experiment in democracy." He quite literally stands in the history he evokes. Noting his geographical proximity to the birthplace of the document he cites, Obama, the constitutional scholar, invokes the moment in which a group of white men created our fragile democracy. In Obama's words, the Constitution is "unfinished." Here is a lighter version of Martin Luther King Jr.'s metaphor of the unpaid check from "I Have a Dream." Unlike Douglass, Obama does not ignore the Constitution's failings. He confronts head-on the fact that the Constitution "was stained by this nation's original sin of slavery, a question that divided the colonies and brought the convention to a stalemate until the founders chose to allow the slave trade to continue . . . and to leave any final resolution to future generations."

This compromise, this failure to finish, is embedded in the nation at the start. Even in the Declaration of Independence, Jefferson was forced to excise his harsh condemnation of the institution of slavery. South Carolina and Georgia demanded these passages be taken out, since they were determined slavery would continue. Thus, compromise on the backs of Black people is embedded in our very founding. Black freedom was sacrificed then and would be sacrificed again and again and again. Obama acknowledges this fundamental fact. If he differs from Douglass in this way, he does share with the great man a sense of the document's fundamental truth: "Of course, the answer to the slavery question was already embedded within our Constitution—a Constitution that had at its very core the ideal of equal citizenship under the law: a Constitution that promised its people liberty, and justice, and a union that could be and should be perfected over time."

After briefly reflecting upon his own autobiography, he turns to Reverend Wright. He asserts that Wright's remarks "expressed a profoundly distorted view of this country—a view that sees white racism as endemic, and that elevates what is wrong with America above all that we know is right with America." Another fault of his view, according to Obama, is that Wright sees the Middle East conflicts rooted in the "actions of stalwart allies like Israel, instead of emanating from the perverse and hateful ideologies of radical Islam." (Here Obama makes no mention of the plight of the Palestinian people.) For Obama, Wright's remarks are racially divisive.

The man who would become the first Black president of the United States of America, the brilliant and careful writer, then creates rhetorical equivalences, between his love of Wright and his love of his grandmother, and between Wright's racial "divisiveness" and his grandmother's racially tinged fear of young Black men. His grandmother loves him, helped raise him, and nonetheless confessed her fear of Black men who passed by her on the street, and "who on more than one occasion has uttered racial or ethnic stereotypes that made me cringe." He then says that both Wright and his white grandmother are a part of him. It is a brilliant move on his part. They are of the past, products of the time that produced them: the one angry and bitter, the other fearful and stereotyping. He assumes the younger generation of Americans to whom he speaks will understand this. The speech implies that younger Blacks surely have old bitter relatives; while younger whites have racist parents, aunts, uncles, and grandparents. We love them, but we are not them, he implores.

But these are not equivalents. Older Black people (my parents included) who have endured and experienced white racism have earned every bit of their anger and so-called bitterness. Most of them harbor little of that bitterness, for they understand it would have destroyed them. Yet what whites fear is often a figment of their imaginations, fed and exploited by opportunistic politicians and sensationalist media. Their fears may be real, but they are often not based on a lived experience of Black violence. Obama here offered a "both sides" argument. The electorate, eager to move forward and get on with the business of building that more perfect union, welcomed it. And it was this kind of equivalence that allowed the majority of Americans to hear the truths that he was offering. Only after equating Black anger and white resentment could he then talk about slavery, Jim Crow, and other forms of "legalized discrimination." It is a history that explains current gaps in wealth, income, and education.

But according to Obama these gaps are also the result of Black parents who don't spend enough time with their children. According to him, Black anger keeps us from facing our own complicity in our problems—a consistent theme for him, especially in his speeches to Black Americans. Although many hardworking, socially conservative Black Americans probably agree with him, it should be noted that the vast majority of Black people to whom he spoke are not guilty of the practices he ascribes to them. As with my parents and Obama's in-laws, Fraser and Marian Robinson, they are hardworking, striving people who love, support, care for, and spend time with their children, build and sustain churches, civic groups, and other organizations. They move forward in spite of ongoing racism, and do not seek excuses for themselves because of it. While others see his tendency to offer these critiques as moments of political expediency at best or capitulation to whites at worst, I do not. I think Barack Obama has too much integrity to be doing either. I think he genuinely believes there is a lack of Black parental involvement, which is clear from his earliest writings, long before he became a presidential candidate.

An irony of the calls to disown or disavow Jeremiah Wright because of his views on race is that Wright's sermons were not primarily about race. The media had taken snippets from two sermons, "The Day of Jerusalem's Fall," delivered on September 16, 2001, and "Confusing God and Government," which was delivered on April 13, 2003. Though separated by two years, the two sermons both offer a critique of the United States' place in the world. "The Day of Jerusalem's Fall" insists that the rush to war is the wrong response to the tragedy of 9/11. It challenges Americans' claims of innocence (why do they hate us?). In this way Wright echoes James Baldwin, who writes in *The Fire Next Time*: "It is not permissible that the authors of devastation should also be innocent. It is the innocence which constitutes the crime." "Confusing God and Government" warns of the government misleading citizens in order to rush them to war. It is a call to America to reckon with the ways it has acted unjustly at home and abroad, and a call for Americans to refuse the conflation of blind allegiance to government with allegiance to God.

Obama's critics (both from the Clinton campaign and from Republicans) and the conservative media made Wright's anti-imperialist, anti-war critique into a domestic rant about race only. They used the issue of race in an attempt to derail the cam-

paign of the first viable Black presidential candidate, forcing him
to address a topic he had largely avoided until then.

At the close of his speech, Obama implores us that we must
believe that society can change, that we can work together to
perfect the union and to build a future that is better for all of our
children. Obama's race speech will go down in history as one of
the most significant in our national history. Unlike the speeches
of Douglass, it does not bear witness to whites about the suffering of Black people. Unlike the speeches of Malcolm, it is not
addressed to Black people about ways to organize and move forward in our struggle for freedom. It is addressed to the nation. It
is more closely aligned with the James Baldwin of *The Fire Next
Time*. However, unlike Baldwin, who assumed a relatively small
group of conscious Blacks and whites would forge change against
all odds, Obama insists this is the work of the new America, of
all of us—or at least the majority of us, or the majority necessary to ensure his election and thus stake the future in the project he represents. As with the speech he delivered at the 2004
Democratic Convention, it proposes a beautiful vision of American possibility. It invokes the liberal philosopher Richard Rorty's
reformist Left, which Rorty described as "all those Americans
who, between 1900 and 1964, struggled within the framework of
constitutional democracy to protect the weak from the strong."

Toward the end of *Dreams from My Father*, Obama writes:

> *We hold these truths to be self-evident.* In those words, I
> hear the spirit of Douglass and Delany, . . . Jefferson and
> Lincoln; the struggles of Martin and Malcolm and unher-
> alded marchers . . . I hear all of these voices . . . asking the
> very same questions that have come to shape my life. . . .
> What is our community, and how might that community

be reconciled with our freedom? How far do our obligations reach? How do we transform mere power into justice, mere sentiment into love?

These are the words, the questions, that drove the young man
who momentarily transformed us into a nation of believers, a
nation that was willing to give hope a chance. It paints a vision of
a nation we aspired to be. It raises the timeless questions, questions that ennoble us and lift us even in the asking of them. And
yet, the reaction to this vision so angered and so frightened a
swath of America, the backlash against it and Obama so harsh
and so swift, that it stunned even those of us who never shared
his optimism. Yet, we wanted to hold out . . . we did hold out
hope that the change he described might one day be possible.

Many of us understood the words of Toni Morrison, who in
an interview with *The Guardian*, recalled feeling "truly American" for the first time when she attended Obama's 2008 inaugu-
ration. She said, "I felt very powerfully patriotic . . . I felt like a
kid. The marines and the flag, which I never look at—all of a sud-
den it looked . . . nice. Worthy. It only lasted a couple of hours.
But I was amazed, that music that I really don't like—God Bless
America is a dumb song; I mean it's not beautiful. But I really felt
that, for that little moment."

Black Americans' understanding of America is too realistic,
too cautious, too conscious of the lessons of history to possess an
unbridled patriotism. We know that at best, our country is a work
in progress and that the battle to perfect it is an uphill climb.

Nowhere was this more evident in the electorate's response to
the two terms of an Obama presidency. The racial resentments
of large numbers of white voters had been simmering since his
first presidential campaign. One could witness elements of it in

the crowds that flocked to see and hear Sarah Palin, the running mate of Republican nominee John McCain. The not-so-subtle anger and racism of many of her supporters stood in full sight with the emergence of the Tea Party. This is the energy that helped to bring an explicitly vile racist into the presidency in 2016. Significantly, also under Obama, the nation witnessed a number of high-profile vigilante and police murders of Black people, which gave birth to the Black Lives Matter movement. I daresay that fear and anger over that movement and over the Obama administration's critical engagement with it also contributed to the political ascension of a white supremacist—an authoritarian whose administration presented a challenge to the very notion of democracy—to the heights of presidential power. The struggle for Black freedom continues. The struggle over the idea(l) of America is ongoing as well.

4

The Quest for Justice

Well, if one really wishes to know how justice is administered in
a country, one does not question the policemen, the lawyers, the
judges, or the protected members of the middle class. One goes
to the unprotected—those, precisely, who need the law's protection most!—and listens to their testimony. Ask any Mexican, any
Puerto Rican, any black man, any poor person—ask the wretched
how they fare in the halls of justice, and then you will know, not
whether or not the country is just, but whether or not it has any
love for justice, or any concept of it.

James Baldwin, *No Name in the Street*

Justice is what love sounds like when it speaks in public.

Michael Eric Dyson

I t was a cookout. Was it in someone's backyard, or at The
Lakes? It was probably The Lakes because the yards of those
South Philadelphia row houses weren't big enough for fam-
ily gatherings. The houses in Southwest Philadelphia, where my
cousins moved with their wives, also did not have backyards. The
South Philadelphia park was officially named for Franklin Delano

Roosevelt. All the working-class people, Black and Italian, who went there for respite, picnics, and family gatherings called it "The Lakes," for the manmade bodies of water that dot the green land-scape. We were often there on Memorial Day, July 4th, Labor Day. I don't remember the holiday, but I remember my family and the smell of the grill, the hotdogs, chicken, hamburgers. There had to have been potato salad and macaroni-tuna salad, Pepsi, Frank's Sodas in all their neon hues, and cans of beer. Surely there were playing children and laughing adults. These summer cookouts were like bigger versions of Saturdays at Mama's, Thanksgivings at Aunt Eunice's, and Christmas at Aunt Eartha's. Times when we gathered, where children reveled in the laughter and joy of the adults and adults showered us with affection and affirmation. Someone, one of the men—probably one of my cousins, Leon or Irvin—had gotten up early to scout out the perfect spot for the gathering. The women had been marinating the meats and mak-ing the various salads for days.

We were all related, biological and play kin. Adults who were not parents or grandparents were called Aunt and Uncle, and everyone else was a cousin. It was at one of these summer gath-erings that I recall first seeing the scars, dark brown, raised, and thick, that poured down Uncle Pitt's back. It must have been hot. Apparently, he had removed his shirt. He sat on a folding chair, eating. Was it a plate of potato salad and ribs? Surely, to the delight of us children, there were also crabs, bushels of them, cooked in beer and Old Bay Seasoning, poured out on a picnic table cov-ered in newspaper. Uncle Pitt was laughing. He laughed a lot, and occasionally he danced, grabbing my mother's hand and twirling with her in what seemed to me an old-fashioned partner dance. Here was a glimpse of them from earlier days, youthful and full of joy. Uncle Pitt had been my Aunt Eartha's teenage love, the father of her two boys and a close friend of my father's. He and Aunt Eartha were no longer together, not officially anyway, but he was family and always welcome. Having been raised as a proper Black child, I neither stared nor pointed, but I was transfixed by the scars and kept the image at the forefront of my mind until I could ask my mother about them. "Mommy, what is that on Uncle Pitt's back? Is he hurt?" She responded, "Shush . . . no, he is fine. I will tell you later. But he is fine. See how happy he is?"

Later she told me that sometimes when people had been imprisoned, scientists and doctors conducted experiments on them in exchange for things like cigarettes. Uncle Pitt had been "experimented on." Those scars were called "keloids." She said this as a matter of fact, if with a tinge of sadness. She said it in that same tone she used whenever she had to reveal something harsh. It was as if the tone would soften the blow of the knowledge she revealed. I knew he had been incarcerated. Aunt Eartha wrote letters to him and letters to her oldest son, who was in the military. I never knew why Uncle Pitt was imprisoned; I did not know where. On our side of the family, each generation had at least one young man who had "done time." Each generation had at least one who went to the military. My maternal grandfather served in the military. My father and Uncle Pitt had both done stints in prison and in the military. Daddy was in the Navy and later did four months for drug possession, before I was born. Uncle Pitt had been in the Army and later did time, for I don't know what. Of my male cousins, one had done a little time as a teenager, for gang fighting with a BB gun; his brother had gone to Vietnam. Another cousin, who was more like my brother, went into the Marines. Of my two nephews, one served time for manslaughter before he turned twenty and the other went into the Air Force right out of high school. All of them, whether on the right side or wrong side of the law, had encounters with the police, who stopped and questioned, sometimes harassed, at least in once instance brutally beat them. It was a regular part of our lives, a hated but almost expected occurrence. At any given time, we knew someone in the joint. At any given time, we were helping to fund someone's bail, or going to court to offer support, paying lawyers and bail bondsmen, receiving and writing letters to our loved ones there. That was the plight of our men. None of them spoke to the women or children about their time in prison. I hope they spoke to each other. Once they had been there, they did everything they could to avoid returning and to keep younger men from going.

Uncle Pitt's scars initiated me into another kind of understanding and concern: that something I could not have imagined might happen to the men who went "away." Later I saw the famous photograph of Gilbert, the formerly enslaved man whose back looks like a roadmap of scars. His were the result of brutal beatings with a whip. My uncle was one of hundreds of Philadelphia area prisoners who "volunteered" to take part in various medical experiments. In his meticulously researched *Acres of Skin*, Allen M. Hornblum documents decades of medical experiments at Pennsylvania's Holmesburg Prison.

As a girl, I knew that men I knew and loved sometimes ended up in prison. I knew that some of them might have done something to land them there, but incarceration didn't have to be an indication of guilt. There were many innocents behind bars. Interestingly, though we all knew someone who had done or was doing time, we also knew that many of our neighbors who had been victims of crime rarely even bothered to call the police.

If I was haunted by the sight of Uncle Pitt's scars, other incidents haunted my peers and me more: the frequent occurrences of sexual assault, including gang rape. When such instances transpired, families rarely called the police. They feared girls would be further victimized by them. This was not an unfounded fear. There was the story of a young woman who after having been raped was subjected to "an examination" at the police precinct. It was later learned that the "exam" was actually another assault, not conducted by a medical professional, but by an officer. On March 9, 1974, *The Philadelphia Tribune* reported that the white officer, Detective Robert Bailey of the South Detective Division, had been dismissed "following a high-level investigation by police officials acting on a complaint from a WOAR (Women Organized Against Rape) volunteer" who assisted the fourteen-year-old victim at the Philadelphia General Hospital. However, the detective was "acquitted of indecent assault . . . in Family Court." The judge, Vito Canuso, ruled in Bailey's favor "after his attorney attacked the girl's credibility. The child told the court that the 'man in the trench coat' [who 'examined' her at the police station] had gray hair, Bailey's hair is blond." This in spite of a police sergeant's testimony that Bailey was wearing a trench coat and was carrying a stethoscope on the night of the incident, just as the girl indicated. The story made the front page of the Black newspaper and resonated throughout our community. Because of many incidents like this, even if the victim reached the point of going to court, families feared the way she would be treated by prosecutors and defense attorneys, and were almost certain her assailant would not be convicted.

Nonetheless, although the failure to report such sexual crimes was presented as an effort to protect the victim, my mother and I also understood it as a failure to fully value the lives of Black girls. Like many of the girls I knew, I, too, feared sexual assault. I believed one of the only things standing between me and such victimization was the protection and reputation of the men in my family. If I had been assaulted, I assume but I am not sure my family would have called the police; they too doubted the ability or willingness of the police to deliver justice. However, this I knew, deep in my bones: if my assailant were known to my family, if I or someone else identified him, he would have been maimed or murdered. In her first memoir, *I Know Why the Caged Bird Sings*, Maya Angelou reveals that in all likelihood, her uncles murdered the man who molested her when she was a girl. Although separated by time and location, I recognized that moment as one that could have been mirrored in my own life. In the world in which I was raised, prisons rarely offered rehabilitation and courts did not serve justice. Whites didn't do time for harming Blacks; Blacks were unjustly imprisoned. Justice as we understood it was Divine—God would take care of it; or it was retributive, meted out by gangs, friends, and family members. "They better hope the cops get to them first" was a common refrain whenever anyone had committed an act of violence against children or the elderly.

What is the nature and possibility of justice for the crimes of racism, slavery, segregation, and mass incarceration that Black people have experienced in the United States? What does justice look like for centuries of systemic abuse and violence enacted by a society built upon withholding justice from Black people? Black writers contemplate these questions over and over. From Richard Wright's *Native Son* (1940), to Ernest Gaines's *A Lesson before Dying* (1993), to Tayari Jones's *An American Marriage* (2018), Black literature is full of courtroom scenes where Black defendants, even those guilty of crimes, are treated unjustly. In these novels, the ultimate crime is to have been born Black in America.

Wright's Bigger Thomas is guilty of killing and dismembering the white heiress Mary Dalton, of raping and murdering his Black girlfriend Bessie Mears, and of evading capture, choosing to become a fugitive rather than turn himself in. He *is* guilty of a number of horrific crimes, and yet and still, the novel successfully puts the American judicial system on trial, for the horrific racism of the press and the prosecution reveal just how unfair, unjust, inhumane, and racist the courts are. Bigger's arrest and conviction are used as an excuse for upholding white supremacy as a means of containing Black people. He is tried for the rape and murder of Mary Dalton, even though he did not rape her. He is not tried for the rape and murder of Bessie Mears, because Black women only matter to the extent that they can serve the interest of whites. In this case, Bessie's body is a proxy for Mary's. Wheeled out and displayed like a specimen, her corpse is not allowed even a modicum of decency, and there is no quest for justice for the crimes committed against her.

Wright devotes the entire third book of the novel, "Fate," to Bigger's incarceration and trial. There is no question of his guilt. Wright makes him white America's worst nightmare: he has suffocated, beheaded, and burned a young, wealthy white woman. The Black community is ambivalent about him because he has bullied those he knows, and this horrific crime has brought the wrath of law enforcement and armed vigilantes upon them. Yet, Wright demonstrates the way that Bigger, his family, and Black people as a whole are victims of American capitalism and liberalism long before Bigger's crime. (Here, I use *liberalism* to mean the political philosophy that emerged during the Enlightenment and that supports individual rights, free-market economies, and other such rights associated with Western democracies. It is a philosophy espoused by both liberals and conservatives in the United States.) Wright demonstrates the ways the judicial system, the government, the police, the banks, and the press—all of those in possession of power and authority in a liberal society— work to dominate and exploit the Black poor such that some form of imprisonment and state-sanctioned death are inevitable and constitute a kind of Fate. Wright thus indicts the United States for crimes against its Black native sons (and, to a lesser degree, daughters as well).

In the absence of justice, the crime, indictment, and trial provide Bigger a chance to develop an interior sense of himself, to claim ownership and responsibility for what he has done without any hope of gaining a fair hearing. By novel's end he has a moment of self-realization and is able to experience his first truly human interaction with a white person, Jan, the Communist boyfriend of the woman he has murdered. Jan is not the average American white man; he is a radical, a Communist, and a Jew, and therefore a despised other. When he visits Bigger in prison, he tells him:

> I can't take upon myself the blame for what one hundred million people have done. . . . I'm here because I'm trying to live up to this thing as I see it. . . . Let me be on your side, Bigger. . . . I can fight this thing with you, just like you've started it. I can come from all of those white people and stand here with you.

It is Jan who locates Bigger's defense lawyer Max. On the eve of his execution, as he asks Max to deliver a series of messages for him, he says: "Mr. Max! . . . Tell . . . Tell Mister . . . Tell Jan hello . . ." Saying and then removing the "Mister" before Jan's name is a simple gesture, but one that connotes the achievement of something extraordinary: the opportunity to know a white man as a peer, an equal, with the potential of becoming a friend. Jan has had to let go of his whiteness and act mercifully toward him in order for Bigger to see him as a human to whom he wants to relate. No one is punished for the crimes committed against

Bigger, his family, and all the poor Black people they represent. There is only the opportunity for Bigger to acquire a sense of self-knowledge, and the opportunity for a moment of interpersonal recognition between him and Jan.

The novel warns white America: the bogeyman you've created, the figment of your racist imagination, has become your very own Frankenstein's monster. By novel's end Bigger constitutes an even greater threat than does the reckless murderer of the book's early chapters. He is now a self-aware man clear about the forces that have aligned against him his whole life, and willing to accept responsibility for having acted out against them. In the closing pages of the novel, Bigger asserts: "What I killed for, I am!"

While Wright devotes the entire third book of *Native Son* to Bigger's trial, almost fifty years later Ernest Gaines devotes very little time to the trial in the opening pages of *A Lesson before Dying*. His character Jefferson, charged with murdering a white store owner, is tried, convicted, and sentenced to death before the novel begins. Although Jefferson was with the young men who robbed the store, he is not the murderer. On the very first page, the narrator of the novel, the schoolteacher Grant, asserts, "I was not there, yet I was there. No, I did not go to the trial, I did not hear the verdict, because I knew all the time what it would be." Jefferson's godmother, Miss Emma, "knew, as we all knew, what the outcome would be. A white man had been killed during a robbery, and though two of the robbers had been killed on the spot, one had been captured, and he, too, would have to die. Though he told them no, he had nothing to do with it."

The rest of the novel is devoted to Jefferson's small rural Louisiana community and the consequences of his conviction for his family and neighbors, as well as the transformation both Jefferson and Grant undergo with the assistance of the children and elders of that community. Gaines's novel posits that in the absence of justice, Black people have only each other and the responsibility of acknowledging and nurturing a sense of humanity among themselves. If they are unable to successfully resist the forces arrayed against them, the people at least meet those challenges with dignity and self-respect.

Jefferson's godmother wants him to meet his death knowing he is a man and not the "hog" his defense attorney claims him to be. "I don't want them to kill no hog . . . I want a man to go to that chair on his own two feet," she tells Grant when she enlists him to meet with Jefferson on a regular basis and to tutor and mentor him.

At Grant's encouragement, the barely literate Jefferson begins to keep a diary, and one of the novel's final chapters presents its contents. These are among the most beautiful, moving, and, I daresay, eloquent pages in all of African American literature. Although in my classes we approach our reading of them as clear-headed, critical thinkers, these pages, which I have my students read aloud so as to hear the poetry, never fail to bring tears to our eyes. And I remind my students that this is the power of literature: to use language to remind us of another's humanity by touching our own. In the course of the diary, we witness Jefferson's unfolding, we witness his struggle to put his thoughts and feelings on paper, and we witness his deeply human connection with poor, ordinary, Black folk who offer him love and grace:

> lord have merce sweet jesus mr wigin where all them
> peple come from when you ax me if some chiren can
> com up here an speak to me i didn kno you was meanin
> all them chiren in yo clas an jus sitin ther on the flo all
> quite in they clean close lookin at me an I coud see som

was scard o me but mos was brave and spoke an my little cosin estel even com up and kiss me on the jaw an I
coudn hol it back no mo

then after the chiren here com the ole folks an look like
ever-body from the quarter was here mis juila an jo an mis
haret an ant agnes an mr noman an mis sara an mis lilia
an mr harry an mis lena an god kno who all an mr ofal an
mis felia wit her beeds an jus prayin an all the peple sayin
how good I look an lord have merce sweet jesus

In reading Jefferson's words aloud, students hear the deep humanity in what they may have dismissed as illiterate scribbling. Instead,
here is a man striving toward literacy, toward self-expression,
toward community. The entire community came out to envelop
Jefferson in love. They have made the jail house a sacred and holy
place. They have said to him, "We see you and we love you." The
word "merce" appears at the beginning and end of Jefferson's diary
entry. "Lord have merce." He has experienced mercy in action: the
action of love and care granted him by his people.

At the end of the diary, on the eve and morning of his execution, Jefferson's language becomes sparse, the sentences break
into lines, his prose turns into verse.

day breakin

sun comin up

the bird in the tree soun like a blu bird

sky blu blu mr wigin

good by mr wigin tell them im strong tell them im a man good
by mr wigin im gon ax paul if he can bring you this
sincely jefferson

The last words of a dying man are meant to feed and nurture his people: "tell them im strong tell them im a man." He has
received love and care, and he can now return it. His concern
is for the people who will be strengthened by his strength as he
faces death without fear.

Paul is one of the white prison guards. In both *Native Son* and
A Lesson before Dying, the authors provide a singular white character whose humanity is enriched by recognizing the humanity of the condemned Black person and the racial injustices of
our society. When Paul delivers the diary to Grant in the Black
quarters, he reports: "He was the strongest man in that crowded
room, Grant Wiggins.... He was, he was. I'm not saying this to
make you feel good. I'm not saying this to ease your pain....
When Vincent asked him if he had any last words, he looked
at the preacher and said, 'Tell Nannan I walked.' And straight
he walked, Grant Wiggins. Straight he walked. I'm a witness.
Straight he walked."

Paul is transformed by bearing witness for Jefferson. By
bearing witness, he is gifted with the opportunity to deepen his
own humanity. This is a necessary step toward building a more
just world.

Justice is denied both Bigger and Jefferson, but Bigger is
granted mercy and Jefferson is granted grace, which leads to
their transformation. Bigger does nothing to earn Jan's forgiveness, yet Jan freely gives it. As a result, Bigger comes to know a
white man whom he neither fears nor hates. When they visit and
write him, the Black community becomes a vehicle of grace for

Jefferson. Seeing himself through their loving eyes allows him to meet his death with dignity.

In all of her novels, Toni Morrison contemplates justice, but she doesn't devote any narrative space to the courtroom. Through-out *Song of Solomon* (1977), she explores the meaning of and quest for justice. She is especially interested in the nature of jus-tice and its relationship to vengeance and history, retribution and repair. Significantly, most of the discussions about justice take place between the novel's men, often in all-male spaces. The first and most explicit discussion occurs in the barbershop. The narrator tells us:

> A young Negro boy had been found stomped to death in Sunflower County, Mississippi. There were no questions about who stomped him—his murderers had boasted freely—and there were no questions about the motive. The boy had whistled at some white woman, refused to deny he had slept with others and was a Northerner visit-ing the South. His name was Till.

The statement does a great deal of work. It declares the matter-of-factness of the murder. It is spoken like it might be a com-mon occurrence. There is no mystery to be solved. The culprits are known. They feel neither remorse nor guilt. In fact, they are boastful. They do not fear arrest, trial, or conviction. The passage ends with the brief sentence, "His name was Till." This situates the narrative temporally. The dialogue that follows occurs in the shadow of Emmett Till's murder in August 1955. Till is the Black fourteen-year-old from Chicago who, while visiting family in Mis-sissippi, is falsely accused of molesting a white woman whose husband and brother-in-law then brutally beat and murder him. Till's death offers a rich opportunity for the men gathered in the barbershop. The conversation that ensues illustrates the diversity of opinion and ideology in the Black community. The more conservative speaker almost blames the teenager for provoking his own death. His open defiance of the rules and norms governing contact between Black men and white women constitutes a refusal to stay within the confines that the Jim Crow South sets for Black people. Another man counters by noting that Till was murdered for daring to act like a man. The end of the conversation leaves us with questions: Is it possible to be a Black man in the United States? What constitutes masculinity? Is survival an act of cowardice?

No matter their politics, each man in the barbershop knows that his Black skin constitutes guilt in the eyes of whites and that they are all vulnerable to any white vigilante without recourse to justice. The very arbitrariness of white power is what makes it so frightening. At any given time, in any given place, they too might share Till's fate. Guitar, a militant young Black man, member of a vigilante group that seeks eye-for-an-eye justice, articulates an argument based in the historical truth of justice denied, and this is what makes it both compelling and frightening. He says:

We poor people, Milkman. I work at an auto plant. The rest of us barely eke out a living. Where's the money, the state, the country to finance our justice? You say Jews try their catches in a court. Do we have a court? Is there one courthouse in one city in the country where a jury would convict them? There are places right now where a Negro still can't testify against a white man. Where the judge, the jury, the court, are legally bound to ignore anything a Negro has to say. What that means is that a Black man is a victim of a crime only when a white man says he is. Only then.

In an era when the murderers of Trayvon Martin, Alton Sterling, Mike Brown, Walter Scott, Korryn Gaines, Sandra Bland, Rekia Boyd, Tamir Rice, Philando Castile, and too many more Black Americans walk free, readers will feel the ongoing truth of Guitar's assertion. Morrison demonstrates the persistence of injustice through time and place, past and present, North and South. The only justice her male characters can imagine is vengeance. Most advocate survival over revenge; in so doing they forgo seeking justice.

Morrison offers another possibility in the figure of an elderly woman named Circe, a midwife and servant who lives in the ruins of a plantation mansion once owned by a white family, the Butlers. Circe is the subversive agent who undermines everything her white employers lived and died for. She is over 100 years old, and her face is a map of wrinkles. After the murder of Milkman's paternal grandfather Macon Dead Sr., Circe rescues, hides, and *takes care* of his two children, Milkman's father Macon Dead Jr. and aunt Pilate. She takes from the Butler's wealth, made by slavery and then by stealing the land of freedmen, to *care* for the orphaned children of one of their victims. She feeds them, provides them shelter and love, hides them from harm, and sends them on their way. She is *kind but not coddling.* She "told them to stay with her until they could all figure out what to do, someplace for them to go." Their problem becomes her problem. She "would bring them food, water to wash in, and she would empty their slop jar." She enacts an ethic of care that helps ensure their well-being and their ability to become self-sufficient.

Circe guides the novelist's protagonist Milkman to seek his

family's history and consequently his own identity. Circe is healer, nurturer, protector. She is skilled in the use medicinal herbs and other natural remedies. Milkman thinks, "Healer, deliverer, in another world she would have been the head nurse at Mercy [the novel's segregated hospital]." Morrison's Circe, like Homer's, serves as Milkman's escort, and guide to the spirits of the dead . . . in that she fills in the story of Macon Sr. and his Native American wife, Sing, and then sends Milkman further South, where he will encounter his ancestors. She is a healer, but she is also a justice seeker. She helps to bring a long-term sense of justice into being. It is not justice for those who were the immediate recipients of harm, nor does it punish those who have caused the harm. But it helps to create a more just society for the progeny of both.

Morrison's Circe is a keeper of the past. With their large columned mansion, the Butlers laid claim to a classical past, but Morrison assures us it is the enslaved whose roots are more ancient than Eden and whose progeny reach into the present (though perhaps not into the future).

In naming Circe for the *Odyssey*'s bewitching seductress, Morrison calls attention to the relationship between that text and her own, and in so doing, she questions the Homeric Quest, with all of its plunder, traffic in women, slavery, and its seeking a return to re-establish the order of the patriarchy. As Circe explains: "They [the Butlers] loved this place. Loved it. . . . Stole for it, lied for it, killed for it. But I'm the one left. Me and the dogs. . . . Everything in this world they lived for will crumble and rot." What doesn't rot on its own, she will allow the dogs to destroy. "Ha! And I want to see it all go, make sure it does go, and that nobody fixes it up."

Western democracies like the United States claim a cultural, philosophical, and political lineage that links them to the ancient

Greeks and Romans. Through Circe, Morrison reminds us that those ancient civilizations were also slave societies. (In fact, American slaveowners often jokingly named their slaves after figures from Greek and Roman mythology and history.) In Morrison's hands the progeny of the enslaved and their quest for justice outlast the material wealth that their labor helped to create. The grand plantation, an ode to temples of the past, is now, like those of the ancient world, a ruin.

There will be no romantic plantation tours at the Butler place. Circe does not act out of a love of whiteness, nor out of loyalty. Neither does she act out of revenge. She lives with a patient sense of justice, a kind of divine retribution, and for the return of the Black son. She gains pleasure not by killing the Butlers, but by watching what they loved rot, by watching their monument to history and greed decay from within and bearing witness to its ruin.

Through Circe, Morrison juxtaposes the *Odyssey*'s version of the Quest narrative with a quest that will yield a suppressed history, that will narrate the lives of those who have been victims of the West, and that will thoroughly question the patriarchy by insisting on a reconstructed masculinity at quest's end.

In *Song of Solomon*, Morrison explores the potential of retributive justice, which she rejects in favor of a long-term divine justice toward which the universe bends. She also introduces the ethic of care and suggests its relationship to the pursuit of justice. She will not fully develop this idea until the late novels.

In *Home* (2012) Morrison turns most fully to an exploration of the relationship between an ethic of care and its potential for achieving a kind of *restorative* or, better still, *transformative* justice. I should say here that Morrison does not represent restorative justice as a process, but instead suggests that this might be a guiding principle of a society governed by an ethic of care. There is nothing that can make up for the crimes against her victimized characters. At best, they can learn how to live, how to survive, how to be healed, not cured, and how to go on and "do some good in the world." In her model, the offender is not reconciled with the victim, but the victim is cared for and embraced by the community. And witnessing this, the victim's brother, who in another instance has been an offender, must come to terms with the trauma he has caused and, rather than continue to be paralyzed by it, he must do something ethically productive, indeed good. As a result, at novel's end a victim and a victimizer are transformed.

Set in the 1950s United States, during the height of McCarthyism, *Home* is the story of a Korean War veteran, Frank Money. Living in the Pacific Northwest and suffering from a form of post-traumatic stress, Frank receives word that his younger sister Cee is in harm's way in Georgia, and he sets out on a cross-country trek to rescue her. Cee has been working as a domestic servant in the home of a white doctor, Beauregard Scott, and his wife. Unbeknownst to Cee, Scott is a eugenicist who "occasionally performed abortions on society ladies," and who, like the so-called father of gynecology, J. Marion Sims, set out to improve the speculum and in the process has mutilated a number of poor Black women. Cee quickly becomes victim to Scott's experimentation, and her suffering is so extreme that the house's other domestic reaches out to Frank, and aids him when he comes to rescue his sister.

Frank carries his sister in his arms until they are able to hire a hack to take them to the small Georgia town of their childhood, Lotus. There he hands her over to Miss Ethel and a band of local women, who set out to heal her. Morrison writes, "Once they knew she had been working for a doctor, the eye rolling and tooth sucking was enough to make clear their scorn." At no point does anyone call the police, nor do the women issue a complaint to a medical board. These are not options that will do Cee any good, since they won't render justice to her.

First, they tend to her bodily wounds. Miss Ethel, the older woman, "parted [Cee's] legs" and whispers, "Have mercy. . . . She's on fire." The women take turns providing her medicinal herbs and potions. The "final stage of Cee's healing" includes being "sun-smacked, which meant spending at least one hour a day with her legs spread open to the blazing sun. Each woman agreed that that embrace would rid her of any remaining womb sickness." They believe access to the sun's healing powers provides "a permanent cure. The kind beyond human power."

The ten days exposed to the sun is a ritual, a transition, an absorption of energy to combat evil and harm. At the end of two months in their care, "Cee was different. Two months surrounded by country women who loved mean had changed her. The women handled sickness as though it were an affront, an illegal invading braggart who needed whipping. They didn't waste their time or the patient's with sympathy and they met the tears of the suffering with resigned contempt." Like the care-giver mother in *The Bluest Eye*, so too do these women confront illness as an enemy they must vanquish. Their care is without sentiment or even sympathy, and it certainly holds no pity. As Cee heals from their potions and food, they "change tactics." They bring her embroidery and crocheting to do and finally when she's ready they invite her into their quilting circle. They incorporate her and teach her. "Laziness was more than intolerable to them; it was inhuman. Whether you were in the field, the house, your own backyard, you had to be busy." Finally, when she is healed to their liking, Miss Ethel tells her:

Look to yourself. You free. Nothing and nobody is obliged to save you but you. Seed your own land. You young and a woman and there's serious limitation in both, but you a person too. Don't let . . . some trifling boyfriend and certainly no devil doctor decide who you are. That's slavery. Somewhere inside you is that free person I'm talking about. Locate her and let her do some good in the world.

Freedom lies not in her social condition but in her self-perception. She must understand herself to be a self-reliant, self-possessed grown woman before she can fully enter, as an equal, the community of women who cared for and healed her. She must have a sense of herself beyond her victimization so as never again to give herself over to those who would further victimize her. Freedom here is a mental state, one that she must claim for herself. Standing in this truth, she will then be positioned to fulfill her purpose, which is "to do some good in the world."

In the posthumously published "Goodness," Morrison identifies the women's work to heal Cee as an "instance of innate group compassion." She asserts, "It was important to me to give that compassion voice," and in so doing to mark it as significant, worthy of our attention: to highlight this act of goodness. The women's ethic of care gives Cee herself, transformed, wounded but standing strong. Like many of her contemporaries, Black and poor women in the South, she has been sterilized by a doctor without her knowledge and consent. She carries the burden of that loss within her, and yet she leaves the women stronger, economically self-sufficient (she sells her quilts to visiting tourists), and no longer in need of her brother's rescuing. Frank notices:

This Cee was not the girl who trembled at the slightest touch of the real and vicious world. Nor was she the not-even-fifteen-year-old who would run off with the first boy who asked her. And she was not the household help who believed whatever happened to her while drugged was a good idea, because a white coat said so. Frank didn't know what took place during those weeks at Miss Ethel's house surrounded by those women with seen-it-all eyes. . . . They delivered unto him a Cee who would never again need his hand over her eyes or his arms to stop her murmuring bones.

In *Home*, there can be no justice for what Dr. Scott has taken from Cee, especially as it is unlikely that what he did to her even counted as a crime. In her recent work *Intimate Justice: The Black Female Body and the Body Politic*, political theorist Shatema Threadcraft reminds us that Black women who suffered forced sterilization at the hands of the state are largely responsible for the shift in feminist language from a right to abortion to "reproductive rights." So pervasive was this practice that it became commonplace and was nicknamed a Mississippi appendectomy. And it was legal. When one of the victims, Elaine Riddick, finally sought justice forty-three years later, Threadcraft wonders "What, in this instance, does justice require?" The project of intimate justice, she writes, "is still incomplete."

There is no movement demanding justice for Cee, just a community of women, who heal her wounds, teach her how to incorporate her physical and emotional scars into the woman she has become, and send her off to do some good in the world. They integrate her into their community, hold not just the doctor but the whole medical establishment accountable, and vow to do all they can to keep themselves and those for whom they care out of any entanglements with doctors, hospitals, and the like. They model a kind of behavior and ethical practice that lays the foundation for her transformation. They do not invite her victimizer into the restorative justice process or into their community, because he is pure evil. And yet, their community can and does offer healing to those who have victimized others. As we learn, part of Frank's mental trauma is a result of his own horrific action during his time in Korea. He is broken from the guilt he bears. Returning to Lotus to rescue his sister, an act of brotherly love and goodness, restores him as well. Before returning home, he sees the world in black and white, but once there, once he has delivered his sister, he notices "It was so bright, brighter than he remembered." He notes "marigolds, nasturtiums, dahlias. Crimson, purple, pink, and China blue. Had these trees always been this deep, deep green?" *Clarity* and an appreciation for the world's beauty return to him after he cares for his sister. After he risks himself to save her. After he acts out of love for her.

Restorative justice advocate Dr. Fania Davis, building upon Dr. King's philosophy, says, "Justice is love correcting that which stands against love." She asks, "How do we heal from structural and interpersonal trauma?" Healing is necessary to stop the cycle of harm—healing individuals as well as communities. Morrison has suggested that the very act of putting stories of suffering on display is necessary for the acquisition of justice. Restorative justice seeks to offer repair, to put things as they should be. Many progressive thinkers and activists have argued for restorative justice to replace the punitive paradigm, which governs so much of American society.

Others are beginning to turn from restoration to transformation. Activist and scholar Zaheer Ali writes:

If things are restored back to the way they used to be, the same arrangements of power, the same relationships, the same mindsets, etc., is that really justice? But if we think about *transformative justice* as a means by which to create a space that allows people to exercise agency to make new (and better) decisions in their lives—maybe that is closer to justice.

As a form, the novel can raise questions about the possibilities and goals of justice. It allows us to imagine what a society governed by an ethic of care, a society devoted to restoring and repairing those who have been harmed, giving them the space for transformation, might look like. It is not easy, it does not offer the possibility of a cure, but it encourages healing. The scar is still there. It becomes a part of the new person, who is scarred but not broken. As such she can go on living a productive life devoted to goodness and breaking a cycle of harm. In a joint interview with her sister Fania, activist and philosopher Angela Davis says: "I think that restorative justice is a really important dimension of the process of living the way we want to live in the future. Embodying it. We have to imagine the kind of society we want to inhabit. We can't simply assume that somehow, magically, we're going to create a new society in which there will be new human beings. No, we have to begin that process of creating the society we want to inhabit right now." This, I think, is, in part, the work of the novel, especially in Morrison's hands. Her late fiction imagines worlds that were, and in so doing, provides a template for what might be. In the case of *Home* (and to some extent *God Help the Child*), it is a template for a just society guided by the principles of love and care. Interestingly in Morrison's case, achieving justice is secondary to the acquisition of self-knowledge. She

asserts that "a satisfactory or good ending for me is when the protagonist learns something vital and morally insightful that she
or he did not know at the beginning." I wonder if the acquisition
of self-knowledge, having gained moral insight, might not be the
end result of a process of restorative justice.

By novel's end, both Frank and Cee stand like the tree with
which Morrison closes the novel, a sweet bay with olive-green
leaves, split down the middle. The final page contains a poem, in
the voice of Frank:

> I stood there a long while, staring at that tree.
> It looked so strong
> So beautiful.
> Hurt right down the middle
> But alive and well.
> Cee touched my shoulder
> Lightly.
> Frank?
> Yes?
> Come on, brother. Let's go home.

This image, of the tree, scarred but not broken, sustains me. I
hold on to the possibilities of communal love and care in the
ongoing struggle for justice. I hold on to it even in the midst of
ongoing trauma, in large part because I have been the beneficiary of transformative love and care. It is this love and care for
those denied justice that motivates us to continue to seek it. Our
movements hold the victims of injustice dear, say their names,
weep for them and struggle to hold those who caused them harm
responsible, struggle to transform the society that allowed for
their victimization. The theologian Serene Jones writes, "Mercy

grants freedom from the bondage of harms. Justice is the struggle to make sure those harms stop."

The struggle for justice in ongoing. In the meantime, we work to heal, to love, to transform ourselves and the world we live into a more just place.

Even now, in this moment, I am still haunted by her precious baby girl voice. Long before I saw her, I had already fallen in love with her: "It's OK, Mommy. I'm right here with you," she says soothingly to her mother from the back seat of a car. They had both just witnessed a police officer, Jeronimo Yanez, shoot and kill her stepfather, Philando Castile. She was four years old and we later learned her name—Dae'Anna Reynolds. But at first, it was her voice—that voice of a little girl, taking on the responsibility of caring for a distraught parent. I immediately understood the impulse. She evoked in me a tenderness, a desire to shield her eyes from a sight she will never forget. And even then, before witnesses, before protests and indictments, I knew there could never be anything like justice for this little girl. How would she be made whole?

Her mother, Diamond Reynolds, had filmed the entire encounter and broadcast it via Facebook Live on July 16, 2016. We watch as she calmly tries to negotiate with the officer, as she watches in disbelief while the policeman panics and shoots her boyfriend, a man who offers no threat, having informed the officer that he is licensed to carry a weapon and that it is in the car. Like many of us, I thought maybe this time, maybe because it is unambiguous and we all can see it, maybe this time, the officer will be found guilty. The killing of Philando Castile joins a long list of names from Trayvon Martin in 2012, through to Eric Garner, Tamir Rice, Walter Scott, Freddie Gray, Sandra Bland, Korryn Gaines, and on and on. And although we knew it was unlikely his killer would be convicted, we still waited, hoping for a miracle, that some jury will find the loss of this Black life enough of a travesty to warrant punishment. I kept returning to the presence of the girl. Surely, we as a country want her to experience some sense of justice, some sense that there is a price to be paid for wrecking her life. Surely . . .

And yet, as hurt and angry as we always are when the killers walk away, each time, we are still disappointed because we want to be wrong about this place we call home.

It is the innocence of the child, Dae'Anna, that makes the pain, anger, and disappointment especially unbearable. When I finally find photos of her, she is beautiful. Her hair is meticulously groomed and braided, her dress and shoes selected with care. She is anything but a thrown-away child. There she sat, in the back of the police cruiser: "It's OK, Mommy. I'm right here with you." The officer who murdered her father figure, Jeronimo Yanez, was acquitted of all charges.

Justice. Dae'Anna Reynolds will never receive justice for the trauma inflicted upon her. Yet, we, scarred and broken though we are, work for a world where no child witnesses the murder of a parent, guilty of no crime, at the hands of the police. There is no justice, not yet, but we strive for it anyway. Because we must. And if, in the process, we love and care for each other, we are transformed. Is it any wonder that the movement born of the need to seek justice for victims of police violence, the Black Lives Matter movement, would take as its inspiration the insistence of '70s revolutionary Assata Shakur:

It is our duty to fight for our freedom.
It is our duty to win.
We must love each other and support each other.
We have nothing to lose but our chains.

5

Rage and Resistance

We cannot shrink from our rage; it is the fire that lights the kiln.

Eddie Glaude, *Begin Again*

Hatred is the fury of those who do not share our goals, and its object is death and destruction. Anger is a grief of distortions between peers, and its object is change. . . . For anger between peers births change, not destruction, and the discomfort and sense of loss it often causes is not fatal, but a sign of growth.

Audre Lorde, "The Uses of Anger"

A t some point before he died my father wrote a poem and shared it with me. In fact, he led me to believe I helped him write it by saying I had selected the rhyming words. I don't remember if this is true; I do know I committed it to memory and can recite it even now:

Behold the man that sits and nods
And laughs at those who wait on God
For supernatural intervention

To right atrocities too cruel to mention.
It must have been a drag to be
A Christian's slave in history.
How glad I am my generation
Did dare as churchmen reparation.
But for me would be more fun
To do like Panthers say is done.
To face the tyrant with a gun,
And die brown, but bravely
In the sun.

Is this an autobiographical poem, stating in succinct verse my father's relationship to drugs, religion, and resistance? On first reading, it appears to be the voice of a drug user, an unbeliever, who holds praying Christians up for ridicule, and stands firm in his own militancy. There is affirmation and pride in his generation of activists like Martin Luther King Jr., but he most identifies with the revolutionary impulse of a younger generation embodied by the Black Panthers. However, upon closer reading, the persona of the poem seems to set himself apart from both the nodding man and the Christians. "Behold the man" places him at a distance. Look at this man who nods and looks with disdain and condescension at those "who wait on God." In this reading, the poem is critical of him. Both the nodding man and the Christians are passive. Each is in a state of waiting, the nodding man even more so than the Christian. The churchmen are at least actively engaged in seeking justice. The Panthers are even more so. By saying "But, for me," the persona sets himself apart from the nodding man, the waiting Christians, the justice-seeking churchmen, and the Panthers as well. The persona chooses armed self-defense and the death that it surely will bring. And yet the poem does not strike a mournful note. It ends with his courage at having faced and fought an enemy and with the dawn of a new day.

I rarely saw my father angry, but I do remember the few occasions when he was. He would become still and quiet, and a large vein would pop out on the right side of his forehead. I used to watch it, with fear and fascination, wondering if it would explode. I wonder if some such instance, something that caused the vein to pop, led him to write this poem. Or was it instead a picture of armed Black Panthers that sparked the sense of longing to join their ranks?

Years later when I read Claude McKay's sonnet "If We Must Die," I wondered if my father knew it. Did its last lines inspire his own literary effort?

> If we must die, let it not be like hogs
> Hunted and penned in an inglorious spot,
> While round us bark the mad and hungry dogs,
> Making their mock at our accursèd lot.
> If we must die, O let us nobly die,
> So that our precious blood may not be shed
> In vain; then even the monsters we defy
> Shall be constrained to honor us though dead!
> O kinsmen! we must meet the common foe!
> Though far outnumbered let us show us brave,
> And for their thousand blows deal one death-blow!
> What though before us lies the open grave?
> Like men we'll face the murderous, cowardly pack,
> Pressed to the wall, dying, but fighting back!

Born in Jamaica in 1889 and migrating to the United States in 1912, Claude McKay was a radical poet, novelist, and journalist, who became one of the most respected writers of the New Negro Movement. "If We Must Die," published in the July 1919 issue of the *Liberator*, was written in response to the Red Summer of 1919 during which hundreds of Black people were murdered at the hands of vigilante mobs and in race riots throughout the country, including Philadelphia in May and July of that year. Red Summer was not the first time that white mobs, threatened by the growing presence and economic competition of Black people in urban centers, resorted to vigilante violence. However, it was one of the first times that large numbers of Blacks, especially returning veterans, defended their communities. The genteel nature of the poem's sonnet form belies the militancy of its subject and imagery. Although I don't recall my father ever mentioning it, I like to think that he had encountered and been inspired by it.

The years that I had my father were marked not only by racist violence but by heightened Black political activity. They were movement years. Young people were at the forefront of both the Civil Rights and Black Power movements. He and I closely followed the Panthers' activities in Philly and in Oakland. We read about them in the newspaper, sought stories about them on the nightly news, and purchased and read the Panther paper. This dynamic group of young people between my father's generation and mine filled us with pride and hope. They seemed to be New Black people: bold and unafraid. It was only later that I learned they stood in a long lineage of resistance. Even the combination of political militancy, eloquence, and aesthetic style had roots in earlier eras. Throughout time, Black resistance movements have produced writings explaining and stating their case and bearing witness to the suffering of Black people. The books of the sixties and seventies found their way into my father's library, and following his death I read them. My father owned *The Autobiography of Malcolm X* (1965), Eldridge Cleaver's *Soul on Ice* (1968), and George Jackson's *Soledad Brother: The Prison Letters of George Jackson* (1970). We had Toni Cade's *The Black Woman* (1970), which I'd asked him to buy for me, primarily for the pretty Afroed brown lady on the cover, and poetry by Nikki Giovanni, Audre Lorde, and others. With my allowance, I later purchased Angela Davis's *If They Come in the Morning* (1972) and *Angela Davis: An Autobiography* (1974).

Interestingly, it wasn't until much later as an undergraduate at Harvard, while taking an Introduction to African American Literature course taught by Werner Sollors, that I learned of the long legacy of resistance in Black literature. A respected scholar of African American literature, Werner was originally from Germany, where he wrote a doctoral dissertation on Amiri Baraka and received his PhD from the Free University of Berlin. When I took his class, he'd just come to Harvard from Columbia University, where he'd also taught American and African American Literature.

Of the works we read, I was especially blown away by David Walker's *Appeal to the Coloured Citizens of the World* (1829) and Henry Highland Garnet's "An Address to the Slaves of the United States of America." The rhetoric that I'd associated with Malcolm X flowed throughout these documents: appeals to Black history, assertions of Black humanity, calls to armed self-defense and proclamations of Black masculinity. The lineage of Black resistance literature legitimizes, gives voice to, and seeks to organize Black rage.

In a document modeled on the United States Constitution, with a preamble and four articles, Walker's *Appeal* is a historical analysis of the condition of Black people, slave and free, a radical call for resistance—even revolt—against the institution of slavery and the hypocrisy of many white Christians. Walker was a free Black resident of Boston and the owner of a secondhand clothing business. When he published his *Appeal* in 1829, he'd already become an activist who assisted runaway slaves and generously offered financial and other assistance to his fellow Black Bostonians. Walker distributed his 76-page *Appeal* through a network of sailors, ministers, and other mobile Blacks, even sewing copies into the lining of garments. The *Appeal* was found as far south as North Carolina and Louisiana.

Within the pages of the *Appeal* Walker notes that since the Greeks and Romans "The Whites have always been an unjust, jealous, unmerciful, avaricious and blood thirsty set of beings always seeking after power and authority," but as Christians, they are especially cruel: "For while they were heathens, they were bad enough . . . they were not so audacious as to go and take vessel loads of men, women, and children, in cold blood, and through devilishness, throw them into the sea, and murder them in all kinds of ways."

Although Walker expresses gratitude to whites who have taken up the cause of Blacks and who have argued for their intellectual and spiritual equality, he insists that it is the responsibility of Blacks to refute White Supremacist assaults on their intellectual capacity and on their morality, and to resist acts of violence committed against them.

When copies of Walker's pamphlet were found in North Carolina, Governor John Owen sent a copy to the state legislature, which enacted further measures to inhibit both slaves and free Blacks, including penalties for anyone who taught slaves to read or write or who circulated publications believed to be seditious. These measures also prevented any Black entering the state from having contact with Black residents.

Walker is one of the first Black writers to call upon Blacks to defend themselves against white violence. He writes, "believe this, there is no more harm for you to kill a man who is trying to kill you, than it is for you to take a drink of water when thirsty." This call to arms in writing would be taken up over twenty years later by abolitionist and minister Henry Highland Garnet. Born into slavery in Maryland in 1815, at age ten Garnet escaped with his mother and siblings, with the assistance of a group of Quakers, to New York. Educated in that city's African Free School, he eventually moved to Troy, New York, where he became pastor of the Liberty Street Presbyterian Church and founded an abolitionist newspaper. Upon returning to New York City, he joined the American Anti-Slavery Society and became a well-known speaker on the abolitionist circuit.

Garnet delivered "An Address to the Slaves of the United States of America" before the National Convention of Colored Citizens in Buffalo, New York, on August 16, 1843, and later published it along with Walker's *Appeal* in 1848, thus aligning his statement with that of the earlier figure. The address is from the perspective of activist free Blacks who have organized against slavery. From this vantage point, Garnet writes to the enslaved:

Brethren and Fellow Citizens:—Your brethren of the North, East, and West have been accustomed to meet together in National Conventions, to sympathize with each other, and to weep over your unhappy condition. In these meetings we have addressed all classes of the free, but we have never, until this time, sent a word of consolation and advice to you. . . . While you have been oppressed, we have also been partakers with you; nor can we be free while you are enslaved. We, therefore, write to you as being bound with you. Many of you are bound to us, not only by the ties of a common humanity, but we are connected by the more tender relations of parents, wives, husbands, children, brothers, and sisters, and friends. As such we most affectionately address you.

For Garnet, it is the Christian duty of the enslaved to resist slavery, for the institution of slavery prohibits them from obeying and loving God, from keeping the Sabbath day holy, and from raising their children to worship God. Echoing the language of the American Revolution, Garnet writes: "If you must bleed, let it all come at once, rather die freemen, than live to be slaves." Garnet ends his appeal, "Let your motto be *resistance! resistance*! No oppressed people has ever secured their liberty without resistance."

Garnet was among a number of prominent Black abolitionists to attend the 1843 National Convention, which also included Frederick Douglass, Charles L. Remond, and William Wells Brown. Though Douglass, at that time a believer in non-violent "moral suasion," denounced Garnet's call, the address almost became the official resolution of the Convention, falling short by one vote. Within a decade, Douglass too would join in the call for armed resistance to slavery.

As a student, Walker and Garnet were not the only nineteenth-century activists who piqued my interest. Even before taking Werner's class, I found my way to a lecture on free northern Black women in the nineteenth century given by the educational historian Linda Perkins. During my undergraduate years Harvard had only one Black woman professor, the esteemed musicologist Eileen Southern, but the Bunting Institute for Research on Women and the W. E. B. Du Bois Institute yearly welcomed postdoctoral fellows, many of them African American women who were just beginning to create a body of historical and literary scholarship on Black women. As a curious undergraduate I attended a number of lectures and Professor Huggins and Professor Sollors made sure to introduce me to extraordinary scholars and writers who came through the two institutes, including Black feminist literary critics Valerie Smith (who became president of Swarthmore College) and Deborah McDowell (an early director of the Carter G. Woodson Institute at the University of Virginia). That day during my freshman year when I attended the lecture by Professor Perkins, I realized that although I'd learned a great deal about historic Philadelphia, I'd never come across any mention of the Black women who lived and worked there. I may have first heard of Frances Harper during her lecture.

As I began to seek more information, I found various references to Frances E. W. Harper—here she appeared as a poet, there as a novelist, and elsewhere as an abolitionist. I wondered, "Was this the same woman?" More so than Walker, Garnet, or Delany, my search for Harper would be one of the most intellectually transformative experiences of my undergraduate career. I credit her (along with my professors) with setting me on the path to becoming a scholar. As a History and Literature major, I made Harper the subject of my Junior Essay and my Senior Honors Thesis. At the time there were few secondary sources on her, so these projects provided me the opportunity to do primary research, taking me to archives like those at the Philadelphia Library Company and the Schomburg Center for Research in Black Culture. Little did I know in March of 1985, when I turned in my thesis, that a number of Black women scholars had been researching and writing about Harper. Cultural historian Hazel Carby published a groundbreaking article "'On the Threshold of

Woman's Era': Lynching, Empire, and Sexuality in Black Feminist Theory," in August 1985, which discussed Harper. Harper was also the subject of her book *Reconstructing Womanhood: The Emergence of the Afro-American Woman Novelist*, published in 1987. (A few years later, Carby became a most influential member of my dissertation committee, though by then, after having published my first article on Harper, I'd left the nineteenth century behind.) The ever supportive and intellectually generous Frances Foster collected and published two volumes of Harper's writing, *A Brighter Coming Day: A Frances Ellen Watkins Harper Reader* (1990), along with three of Harper's unpublished novels, *Minnie's Sacrifice, Sowing and Reaping, Trial and Triumph* (1994). Scholars continue to discover new works by Harper and to fill in the gaps in her biography.

None of these works were available to me in college. I fell in love with primary research while exploring Harper's life and legacy, and I came to admire her as a model of a feminist-minded activist-artist devoted to Black freedom. Finally, I especially found great joy in discovering the city of my birth anew through Frances Ellen Watkins Harper.

Through Harper, I discovered a history of Philadelphia that had been previously unknown to me. Though my father and I spent many hours walking among the city's well-known historic sites, he never talked about its great abolitionist history. And, although I'd often walked through the neighborhoods where Harper and countless other nineteenth-century Black activists had lived, I did so without knowing anything about her or her contemporaries. I don't recall historic markers indicating the vibrant past of the streets east of Broad Street between Bainbridge and Pine (the area overlaps with the Seventh Ward of W. E. B. Du Bois's *Philadelphia Negro*). I did know the area was home to large numbers of Black people immediately follow-ing the First Great Migration beginning in 1916, and that South Street had boasted a number of stores and clubs frequented by my grandparents' and even my parents' generation. But following Harper unearthed a whole new understanding of the layers of history that make up that portion of South Philadelphia.

Now when I returned home from Cambridge and walked the streets near Penn's Landing, which runs along the Delaware River waterfront, I did so with a newfound excitement. I imag-ined Black women in long, high-necked dresses, their thick hair neatly groomed in buns and twists.

As early as 1787 Richard Allen and Absalom Jones founded the Free African Society, a mutual aid society that also held religious services for the city's free Black population. In 1794 Allen founded Mother Bethel African Methodist Episcopal Church, while Jones founded the African Episcopal Church of St. Thomas, the first Episcopal Church for Black people. These institutions also opened a number of schools to educate the city's Black children. Philadelphia's Black population established civic and literary organizations, and, together with a historic Quaker community, they also created a vibrant abolitionist presence as well, helping to make Philadelphia one of Black America's cul-tural and political capitals. During the first half of the nine-teenth century, the city was home to one of the most significant and politicized free Black communities in the nation. Historian Margaret Washington writes, "Philadelphia, the eastern Under-ground Railroad headquarters, was the most important radical abolitionist hub in the mid-Atlantic region." Philadelphia was a place of transit and transition. It sat on the southeast corner of a state bordered by the slave states Delaware and Maryland. Many escaped slaves found their way to the city, where they were aided by agents of the Underground Railroad. Some settled there, but still more traveled further North, to cities like Buffalo, New York, and New Bedford, Massachusetts, and to Canada. In 1834 mixed-race abolitionist Robert Purvis and his father-in-law, the African American businessman James Forten, organized the Vigilant Association of Philadelphia. The association, made up of African American men and women and their white allies, charged itself with aiding fugitives. The Pennsylvania Anti-Slavery Society assisted the committee, which operated out of Purvis's home at Ninth and Lombard Streets.

Black and white abolitionists, including Purvis, James and Lucretia Mott, and John C. Bowers, founded the Pennsylvania Anti-Slavery Society in 1838. By the time the 1850 Fugitive Slave Act passed, the PAS and the Vigilant Committee were well prepared to resist its extension of slavery into the free state of Pennsylvania. Passed by Congress in September 1850, as part of the Compromise of 1850, the law required runaway slaves residing in free states be returned to their masters. It inspired many otherwise complacent Northern citizens to join the anti-slavery cause or to at least support it.

One of the committee's best-known incidents involved the enslaved woman Jane Johnson and her two children. In July 1855 Johnson and her children accompanied her owner, John H. Wheeler, U.S. Ambassador to Nicaragua, to Philadelphia, where she encountered a group of free Blacks and shared with them her desire to escape. They sent word to the PAS. As Wheeler boarded a ferry with Johnson, Passmore Williamson, a white Quaker and secretary of the Pennsylvania Anti-Slavery Society, and William Still, a Black member of its Vigilance Committee and writer, activist, and Underground Railroad conductor, and five Black dockworkers also boarded the ferry in search of Johnson. Williamson approached her and informed her that under Pennsylvania law she was free. Two of the dockworkers, John Ballard and William Curtis, restrained Wheeler while Still removed Johnson and her children from the ferry and rushed them to an awaiting carriage.

Wheeler petitioned the courts to have Johnson returned, and the court charged Passmore Williamson with abducting her. Still and the others were charged with rioting and assault. Williamson served three months in Moyamensing Prison, but he used his imprisonment to call attention to the abolitionist cause. Prominent visitors like Frederick Douglass and Harriet Tubman brought even greater attention to the case. Eventually, Williamson was released. Still and the dockworkers were tried for assault. Johnson, accompanied by a group of women abolitionists including Lucretia Mott, returned to Philadelphia from New York, testified that Still and Williamson had not abducted her and that she had gone with them of her own free will. Still was found not guilty, while two of the dockworkers who restrained Wheeler were convicted of assault. The incident only helped to solidify the reputation of Philadelphia as a hotbed of abolitionist activity and further established the militancy of its free Black community. Even before the well-publicized Johnson incident, Philadelphia's community of activists attracted Frances Harper to the city. They welcomed her when she relocated to the City of Brotherly Love after having lived in Maryland, Ohio, and south-central Pennsylvania. Philadelphians like Still embraced her upon her arrival. Inspired by their devotion and their courage, Harper vowed to join them in their resistance against slavery.

Born in Baltimore, Maryland, on September 24, 1825, to free parents, Frances Ellen Watkins was orphaned by age three. Upon the death of her parents, her uncle, William Watkins, became her guardian. One of Black Baltimore's leading figures, Watkins was a radical abolitionist and the founder and director of Watkins Academy, a school for Black children. Young Frances attended his school, where she and her classmates studied History, Math, English, Philosophy, Latin, Music, and Rhetoric. She especially excelled at writing. For reasons unknown to scholars, when she was thirteen years old, her uncle put her out to service with a white Quaker bookseller. She worked as a domestic and seamstress for his family, and he allowed her free access to his library. While still living in Baltimore, Harper published her first volume of poetry, *Forest Leaves*, in 1846. Long lost to scholars, one copy of the collection was eventually found at the Maryland Historical Society; subsequently it has been reprinted.

In 1850, Harper relocated to Ohio, where she became the first woman faculty member of the AME Church's Union Seminary (the seminary would later become Wilberforce University). There she taught sewing, embroidery, and domestic science. But she could no longer go back home. Maryland had long passed laws restricting its free Black population. In response to the 1831 Nat Turner revolt, which took place in nearby Virginia, Maryland enacted laws in 1831 and 1839 prohibiting free Blacks from entering or re-entering the state on threat of enslavement. Thus although the state's largest city, Baltimore, was home to a large and robust free Black community, they lived in a state of precarity, always vulnerable to enslavement. Consequently, Harper became an exile from her home. Instead of returning to Maryland, she found work as a teacher of young Black children at another AME-run school, the Smallwood School in York, Pennsylvania. While at Smallwood she experienced a crisis of vocation, which was exacerbated by yet another case involving a free Black man who was tricked and sold into slavery.

In 1852 Harper wrote to her friend William Still about her growing depression and restlessness: "What would you do if you were in my place? Would you give up and go back and work at your trade [dressmaking]? There are no people that need all the benefits resulting from a well-directed education more than we do. The condition of our people, the wants of our children, and the welfare of our race demand the aid of every helping hand, the God-speed of every Christian heart." Here was a young woman who wanted to use her gifts and talents in the service of her people, a people in great need of education. She had chosen a vocation deemed fitting for her sex: teaching children and a trade, sewing, that could bring in steady income. Yet, she wanted to do more. Lacking a big enough arena to act upon her passion for justice, she had fallen into despair and was requesting the guidance of a trusted friend and mentor.

Two years later the Ned Davis case became the impetus for Harper to finally commit her life to the anti-slavery cause. Davis's case was made possible by Maryland's Black Codes and the 1850 Fugitive Slave Act. In September 1851, Edward Davis, a 37-year-old free Black laborer from Philadelphia, traveled from Pennsylvania to Maryland at the urging of two white men, who later betrayed him. In Baltimore, he worked for one day on a schooner, fishing and unloading the catch. He then obtained work at a grocery store. While working he was arrested because he had violated the law prohibiting free Blacks from entering the state. Davis could not afford to pay the $20 fine required of him by the law. Because he did not pay the fine, as required by law, on November 10, 1851, he was sold into slavery to pay "all other costs incurred by his violation of the 1839 act of Assembly," and eventually sent to a Georgia plantation. Davis escaped from Georgia on the *Keystone State*, a steamship that regularly ran between Savannah and Philadelphia. When the ship arrived in Delaware, Davis was discovered and returned to Georgia under the auspices of the Fugitive Slave Act. He later died there having been "work[ed] . . . to death" by his owner.

The case caused an uproar in Philadelphia's Black and abolitionist communities. Harper was enraged and credits the Davis case with radicalizing her. She wrote to Still: "Upon that grave I pledged myself to the anti-Slavery cause. . . . God himself has written upon both my heart and brain a commission to use time, talent and energy in the cause of freedom." More than a century later, poet Audre Lorde may have been speaking of her foremother Harper when she wrote, "Anger . . . births change, not destruction, and the discomfort and sense of loss it causes is not fatal, but a sign of growth." Harper's growth would include her radicalization, which became the basis of her career as a lifelong activist-artist.

In Philadelphia Harper lived with Still and his wife Letitia (who was also a seamstress). The Still home was a station on the Underground Railroad where Harper heard firsthand the stories of fugitive slaves. Although free-born, like Henry Highland Garnet, she recognized that the existence of slavery threatened the freedom of all Blacks regardless of their legal status. Northern free Blacks, including those in Philadelphia, experienced racial discrimination on streetcars and lived under the constant threat of violence by whites. Many had been disenfranchised. Harper insisted "a blow has been struck at my freedom, in every hunted and down-trodden slave in the South."

Frances Ellen Watkins Harper became one of the most important, highly regarded, and widely recognized abolitionists, orators, and writers of her time. Blacks and whites purchased her books and enthusiastically attended her lectures and speeches.

She shared stages with Henry Highland Garnet, William Nell, and other well-known activists. While on the road she often recited her poetry as part of her lectures, and she wrote detailed letters back to Still, who would publish them in his book *The Underground Rail Road*, a collection of letters and other primary documents.

One of her most famous poems, "Bury Me in a Free Land," started out as a few lines in a letter to Still. In 1858 Harper wrote to him:

> I might be so glad if it was only so that I could go home among my own kindred and people, but slavery comes up like a dark shadow between me and the home of my childhood. Well, perhaps it is my lot to die from home and be buried among strangers; and yet I do not regret that I espouse this cause; perhaps I have been of some service to the cause of human rights. . . . I have lived in the midst of oppression and wrong, and I am saddened by every captured fugitive in the North.

She includes a brief poem in the letter:

> Make me a grave where'er you will
> In a lowly plain, or a lofty hill,
> Make it among earth's humblest graves
> But not in a land where men are slaves.

Like other letters, this one was written by Harper to Still from the road, from the anti-slavery circuit—a woman alone, who has devoted her life to the anti-slavery cause. Here is the voice of exile. She contemplates her own death and burial far from home. The short poem grew into an eight-stanza 32-line ballad, "Bury Me in a Free Land," published in *The Anti-Slavery Bugle* in November 1858. To the four lines sent in her letter to Still, Harper added stanzas where the speaker describes her potential grave:

> I could not rest if around my grave
> I heard the steps of a trembling slave;
> His shadow above my silent tomb
> Would make it a place of fearful gloom.
>
> I could not rest if I heard the tread
> Of a coffle gang to shambles led,
> And the mother's shriek of wild despair
> Rise like a curse on the trembling air.
>
> I could not sleep if I saw the lash
> Drinking her blood at each fearful gash,
> And I saw her babes torn from her breast
> Like trembling doves from their parent nest.
> I'd shudder and start if I heard the bay
> Of bloodhounds seizing their human prey,
> And I heard the captive plead in vain.
> As they bound afresh his galling chain.
>
> If I saw young girls from their mother's arms
> Bartered and sold for their youthful charms,
> My eye would flash with a mournful flame,
> My death-paled cheek grow red with shame.

The poem's persona imagines her corpse as sentient, and tortured by the sights and sounds of slavery. That the grave is the central image here is significant. Recall, Harper dedicated her life to the cause of anti-slavery upon the Georgia "grave" of Ned Davis, who was buried far from his home in Philadelphia. The rhyming couplet ending in "grave" and "slave" is repeated three times in the course of the poem. Bringing the two words together suggests that slavery is a kind of grave. (In this way she precedes twentieth- and twenty-first-century theorists of Black Studies for whom, building upon the assertion of sociologist Orlando Patterson, slavery constitutes social death.) In Harper's poem, the grave is a tomb of unrest. The refrain "I could not rest," repeated at the opening of the second and third stanzas, begs the question of what happens to a soul that does not find rest in death. Does it, like the ghosts of Toni Morrison's novel *Beloved* (1987), continue to haunt the nation?

The sights and sounds throughout the rest of the poem constitute the imagery of slavery; coffles, auction blocks, slave mothers whose children are ripped from their breast, bloodhounds and the lash—all are familiar to Harper's readers and listeners. These are images that emphasize that slavery is a brutal trade in human flesh, characterized by forms of violence including sexual abuse.

"I could not rest" is not only the refrain of the speaker from the grave; it may also be understood as "I cannot rest," as spoken by the poet herself: "I cannot be complacent in this life as long as slavery exists." In this way it anticipates the Sweet Honey in the Rock lyric from "Ella's Song" (dedicated to the twentieth-century activist, organizer, and strategist Ella Baker): "We who believe in freedom cannot rest until it comes."

In the clarity of language repetition and rhyme scheme, the poem has all the elements of a ballad, which poet and Harper biographer Melba Joyce Boyd identifies as one of Harper's preferred forms. Boyd writes, "The ballad form embraces the natural lyrical patterns of nineteenth-century mass culture, and with its flexible meter, it coincides well with the elocutionary format." Harper often recited "Bury Me in a Free Land" during her lectures.

Harper affiliated herself with the most radical abolitionists, even befriending John Brown. After the Harpers Ferry raid she wrote to him while he awaited trial and ultimate execution:

> Dear Friend: Although the hands of Slavery throw barrier
> between you and me, and it may not be my privilege to
> see you in your prison-house, Virginia has no bolts or bars
> through which I dread to send you my sympathy. In the
> name of the young girl sold from the warm clasp of a moth-
> er's arms to the clutches of a libertine or a profligate,—in
> the name of the slave mother, her heart rocked to and fro
> by the agony of her mournful separations,—I thank you,
> that you have been brave enough to reach out your hands
> to the crushed and blighted of my race. You have rocked
> the bloody Bastille; and I hope that from your sad fate great
> good may arise to the cause of freedom.

She closes the letter with an offer to assist his "fellow-prisoners": "If any of them, like you, have a wife or children that I can help, let them send me word." And she signs the letter, "Yours in the cause of freedom, F.E.W." Brown is friend and comrade. Her letter expresses her gratitude for his act of insurrection against the slavocracy. Her gratitude is that of an individual, but also in the name of Black people, especially those most victimized by slavery. She thanks him on behalf of enslaved women, subjected to sexual violence and the brothel that is the plantation, and of the slave mother whose child belongs not to her.

In addition to writing to John Brown, Frances Harper also penned a letter to his wife Mary:

> In an hour like this the common words of sympathy may seem like idle words, and yet I want to say something to you, the noble wife of the hero of the nineteenth century.... I thank you for the brave words you have spoken. A republic that produces such a wife and mother may hope for better days.... If there is one thing on earth I can do for you or yours, let me be apprised. I am at your service.

Shortly after writing this letter Harper traveled back to Philadelphia to be with Brown's wife and daughter, who were staying at the Still home during his trial. Harper wrote a number of letters to those men who accompanied Brown and were now awaiting execution. She included "Bury Me in a Free Land" in her letters. One man, Aaron A. Stevens, wrote back, thanking her for the poem and explaining that the "verses . . . go to the inmost parts of my soul." According to her biographer Boyd, the poem "was found in his trunk among his most precious possessions" after his execution.

Harper's poem had many lives and served many purposes. It is a statement of her ethics and values, it helped to rally the crowds to whom she spoke and organized in the anti-slavery cause, and it brought comfort and inspiration to those who gave their lives in the cause of Black freedom.

Following the Civil War Harper traveled to the Reconstruction South, where she taught and learned from the freed men and women who would greatly influence her poetry and novels. This is especially the case with her dialect poems, spoken in the voice of Aunt Chloe, a former slave, and her best known novel, *Iola Leroy, or Shadows Uplifted* (1892), the story an educated, mixed-race woman who has been wrongfully enslaved in North Carolina.

Although Harper spent much of her life on the road, in 1870 she purchased a house in South Philadelphia at 1006 Bainbridge Street—a little over a mile from my childhood home. From that base she continued to write and to work for the causes that remained of utmost importance to her, including temperance, women's suffrage, and the ongoing struggle for Black freedom. In 1976, the year of the United States Bicentennial, Frances Harper's South Philadelphia home was listed as a National Historical Landmark.

Almost twenty years after this designation, in 1993, I returned to Philadelphia after completing graduate school to start a job at the University of Pennsylvania, where I would teach African American literature. That August, while walking through Rittenhouse Square I spotted the familiar face of a woman sitting on a bench reading *Cancer Journals*, a journal and literary record of Audre Lorde's battle with breast cancer. The reading woman looked up at me and smiled. I immediately recognized the writer Toni Cade Bambara, whose anthology *The Black Woman* had been so important to me as a girl, and whose fiction I greatly admired. I introduced myself and we talked briefly about writing and about what I planned to teach. She told me that she thought the body of literature designated Slave Narratives had been misnamed. "They are Freedom Narratives," she asserted, and I could not disagree. As an activist, writer, and teacher, it seemed appropriate that Bambara would have made Philadelphia her home. Leaving her that day, I thought of her as an heir to Frances Harper.

Bambara was a New York–born activist, author, and film-maker who lived and worked in Philadelphia during the final years of her life. She is widely recognized as one of the most talented of the Black writers to emerge out of the Black Arts Movement of the sixties. In all of her work, she sought to empower her readers to claim and act upon their strength as individuals and as communities. Her essays, short stories, and novels established her as a major American literary artist. In addition to writing, she was a dedicated teacher, having taught at City University of New York, Rutgers University, Duke University, Spelman College, and numerous nontraditional settings. Of teaching, she said, "My main thrust in the classroom has always been to encourage and equip people to respect their rage and their power."

Moving to Philadelphia from Atlanta in 1985, Bambara quickly found a community of like-minded activists and artists, including the beloved poet Sonia Sanchez and Louis Massiah, filmmaker and founder of the Scribe Video Center. In fact, film and video became another medium for her cultural activism. At Scribe, she worked on documentary films, most notably *The Bombing of Osage Avenue*, about the 1985 bombing of the radical group MOVE, and *W. E. B. Du Bois: A Biography in Four Voices*. She also helped to organize and mentor a group of younger Black women documentary filmmakers who called themselves the Image Weavers.

I have always been drawn to Bambara's short stories because they succeed in her goal of "making revolution irresistible" by providing narratives that are full of humor and humanity, and characters with whom we want to spend time and who seem like people we know. The charismatic movement leaders are not the focus of attention; instead she gives us the people who walk the community, who know the elders as well as the youth. She reminds us that the church mothers tend to be among the best organizers because they know to feed people; and the civic society ladies and Garveyite women, the Elks and the Masons, are all a part of a community network that supports and sustains a community's resistance efforts. These backbones of the community are the people who occupy center stage. In Bambara's fiction, the true revolutionary may never deliver a speech or hold a gun. In fact, the most effective revolutionary may be a girl who just wants to see her people free. Her characters are revolutionaries who are also "neighbors, lovers, and family members who plant gardens, hang out on the block, light candles and sing." The stories in *The Sea Birds Are Still Alive* were written following Bambara's trips to Cuba (1973) and Vietnam (1975), and they share her observations of those countries along with lessons learned from her activism in the 1960s. All of her characters are committed to resistance and to building new futures. This is what makes her work unique. It does not only focus on the destruction of systems of injustice but consistently asks, what world are we trying to build, and does our movement mirror the values and institutions we want to bring into being?

As Bambara did, her characters find links with and inspiration in other women revolutionaries. In "The Apprentice," the organizer Naomi "views . . . everybody as potentially good, as a possible hastener of the moment, an usherer in of the new day. Examines everybody in terms of their input to making revolution an irresistible certainty." Naomi sees the potential humanity in all figures, and believes revolution to be a way not only of expressing rage but also of experiencing joy. She embodies Alice Walker's assertion, "Resistance is the secret of Joy!" She has traveled to countries where ordinary folk had waged revolution, where they'd toppled corrupt regimes and "built schools and hospitals for themselves." She has visited Cuba and spent time with an activist who functioned in revolutionary institutions for mental health, taught, raised children, and "partied Naomi to death in all night outdoor dance halls." She has met organizers in the Georgia Sea Islands who "fought land barons, organized collective farms and partied hard."

The collection's title story, "The Seabirds Are Still Alive," is among my favorite of Bambara's writing. It is beautifully crafted, its form echoing its meaning. Through the eyes of the story's protagonist, a little girl, Bambara introduces readers to a number of figures on a boat. As the little girl physically circles the boat, feeding the seabirds, we learn the stories of each person and we meditate with them on the meaning of home. By the end of the story we learn that the child has been the victim of a brutal interrogation during which she revealed nothing about the resistance. Upon her departure from the site of interrogation, a guard gives her a package of food, which she expects to be poison. Upon learning that it is not, she thinks of the guard, that he had done something good, and that revolution will free him to live according to his "natural self" who knows "right from wrong." Because of this, because she has heeded the wisdom of her elders, she is now being sent for further revolutionary training.

Bambara's writing shows us the other side of rage: rage felt and expressed in disciplined emotions, organized and directed toward fighting injustice, imagining new possibilities, and building new worlds.

In the spring of 2020, during a global pandemic that disproportionately affected Black and Brown peoples, the nation witnessed the cold-blooded murder of Ahmaud Arbery, shot in the back by a white vigilante father and son near Brunswick, Georgia, and George Floyd, suffocated by a callous policeman, Officer Derek

Chauvin, in Minneapolis. In between these two, both of which had been recorded on video, police in Louisville, Kentucky, fatally shot twenty-six-year-old Breonna Taylor in her own home.

Following Floyd's murder, thousands of protestors took to the street, first in Minneapolis, then throughout the nation, and finally throughout the world. It became one of the largest protest movements in history. Along with fast-spreading images of protestors clashing with police on city streets, of political leaders and members of police brass kneeling with protestors, and broadcasts of press conferences with city officials, there also emerged a genre of video, showing politically astute, articulate, intelligent, and charismatic speakers. These circulated on social media, and a few went viral. Two young women in particular put language to the rage and frustration of those in the streets and on the front lines, and of many of us watching from quarantine. Tamika Mallory and Kimberly Jones put forth a new generation's idea of America and its relationship to Black freedom. Each of them as youth had been trained through stalwart Civil Rights organizations: Mallory's parents were co-founders of the National Action Network, and she came up through the organization as a youth organizer; Jones credits her economic analysis to her training as a young person in Jesse Jackson's PUSH. Each of these women's speeches are examples of what Black feminist Brittney Cooper identifies as the "eloquent rage" of Black women for whom rage should be a "legitimate political emotion." Similarly, writing about Nina Simone, critic Salamishah Tillet writes that "Black rage" is "a reasonable and righteous response to white violence."

While the media and sympathetic political leaders made a distinction between "peaceful protestors" and violent "looters," both Mallory and Jones refuse to demonize the "looters," but suggest that looting is also a legitimate action in the face of the systemic racism that has looted Black people of generational wealth since the days of slavery. In her press conference on Friday, May 29, 2020, now known as "The State of Emergency Speech," Mallory says, "I don't give a damn if they burn down Target. Because Target should be on the streets with us calling for the Justice that our people deserve." If you want to address the rage, she argues, "charge the cops" who are killing Black people. She closes:

> Do what you say this country is supposed to be about: the land of the free for all. It has not been free for Black people and we are tired. Don't talk to us about looters. Y'all are the looters. America has looted Black people. America looted the Native Americans when they first came here. So looting is what you do. We learned it from you. We learned violence from you. We learned violence from you. . . . So if you want us to do better, then damn it you do better!

In 2020, after eight years of the nation's first Black presidency and more than three years into the most explicitly racist presidency since Woodrow Wilson, Mallory puts forth a vision of America and its refusal of Black freedom that has much more in common with Malcolm (or David Walker, for that matter) than it does with the promise and hope of Obama's nation as a work in progress.

Kimberly Jones's remarks are even more impassioned than Mallory's. Recorded on Sunday, May 31, 2020, and released by filmmaker David Jones, "How Can We Win" provides a historically grounded economic analysis of America's exploitive relationship with Black Americans. She starts by acknowledging three types of people who have taken to the streets: the protestors who are invested in the movement for social change; the agitators and anarchists who just want to "f' things up"; and the looters who are rushing through broken windows to take consumer goods. Rather than turn her attention to the "peaceful protestors," she focuses on the looters to explore questions of the racial wealth gap. She provides an economic history of the enslaved who worked to enrich their oppressors, of the free communities of Tulsa and Rosewood that tried to build Black wealth but were bombed and "slaughtered" in response. Her voice raised, her language eloquent and profane, she returns to the looters in a dynamic and powerful closing. Quoting her does not do her remarks justice, because her performance of them contributes as much to their power as does the language:

> You broke the social contract when you killed us in the
> streets and didn't give a fuck. You broke the contract
> when for 400 years, we played your game and built your
> wealth. You broke the contract when we built our wealth
> again on our own by our own bootstraps in Tulsa and
> you dropped bombs on us, when we built it in Rosewood
> and you came in and you slaughtered us. You broke the
> contract. So fuck your Target. Fuck your Hall of Fame.
> Far as I'm concerned, they could burn this bitch to the
> ground and it still wouldn't be enough. And they are
> lucky that what Black people are looking for is equality
> and not revenge.

The rhetorical use of the second person "you" echoes Frederick Douglass's "What to the Slave Is the Fourth of July?" It is a searing indictment of the nation, formed in the exploitation of Black labor and the denial of Black humanity and freedom. The language is profane because the situation is profane, obscene even. Jones's comments are not quite in the tradition of the jeremiad because it doesn't end with a vision of how America might be saved, though it gestures toward it. You are lucky, she says, that Black people want equality and are not seeking revenge. The unspoken words on the other side of this warning are that America should grant equality, otherwise it will experience the vengeful wrath of Black people. This is a moment of reckoning. Should the nation fail to address it, there will be "fire next time."

Before the rage, we are weary, we are hurt, we are fed up. In the same way that depression makes you tired. The "I just don't know how much more I can take" kind of tired. Before the spark, before the straw, before the camel's back breaks, some of us become numb. Sometimes the rage has already been there, seething, turned within. Some of us internalize it in the form of self-destructive behaviors; others of us project it onto our neighbors, classmates, spouses, partners, sons and daughters. Just beneath the bullying, the domestic violence, the corporeal punishment, one can find the pent-up rage. What changes, what shifts when the rage is turned outward toward the police, toward the stores? This rage can also give birth to movements, and those movements in turn give birth to words, which in turn further nurture movements. Our writers and our organizers make poetry of the rage. They have been working, building, creating, envisioning, showing us how to live like the future we are hoping to build is already here.

6

Death

The anticipation of death and dying figured into the experiences of Black folk so persistently, given how much more omnipresent death was for them than for other Americans, that lamentation and mortification both found their way into public and private representations of African America to an astonishing degree.

Karla Holloway, *Passed On: African American Mourning Stories*

Black creativity emerges from long lines of innovative responses to the death and violence that plague our communities.

Elizabeth Alexander, *The Trayvon Generation*

We die soon.   Gwendolyn Brooks, "We Real Cool"

He was there on Friday night, and then he was not. He'd come home from work, told us he wanted to catch the man who sold crab cakes because they were so good and he wanted me to taste them. Friday nights were usually our seafood nights. He went out. A short while later a friend brought my father home, saying he'd told him he wasn't feeling well: "Take me home to Muzzy," he said. Because he'd suffered a massive stroke two years before, my mother looked at him, "Em . . . let's go to the emergency room." He agreed, but only if he could go upstairs, wash up, change from his work clothes. My mother begged him not to, but he insisted.

We followed him up the dark, narrow staircase, to their bedroom. He sat on the side of the bed, my mother urging him not to bother changing. He cried, "Where are my shoes?" "Emerson, they are on your feet," she said softly, her voice full of concern. He fell back, arms flinging above his head. My mother turned to me, "Jazzie, run across the street and ask Mrs. Jewel to call an ambulance." We didn't have a phone. We went nightly to the phone booth so my mother could call her mother and her two sisters. I ran down the street to my best friend Sandra's house. Her mother, a kind, Savannah-born woman, opened the door. "Mrs. Jewel, my daddy's sick, my mother said, would you call an ambulance please? Please?" "Yes, baby, of course."

I ran back across the street.

I don't know how long it took, but I remember two white policemen. Did I let them in? Did my mother let them in? I remember feeling awkward, feeling like it was a betrayal. White men were never in our home. White policemen were the enemy. No one would voluntarily let them in the house, let alone upstairs into the most private space of our lives. I remember them standing over the bed, just looking. I remember my mother pleading. I remember their reluctance. I remember the smirk on the older, fatter one's face as he said, emphatically, "He's drunk." I remember my mother saying, "No, he is not intoxicated." I remember thinking, "My father doesn't drink . . . beer sometimes, but that's in the summer and it isn't summer, it's spring break." I don't remember coming downstairs, but I do remember my mother helping me climb into the back of the paddy wagon. I remember the horrible ride. I remember the hospital and the doctors rushing him down the hall. And the next thing I remember, I am at my grandmother's, in her big, four-poster bed, listening to the rumble of the freight train as it rattles by on the rickety bridge just yards away from her home. I remember thinking, "Everything will be alright."

It was not. A week later, my mother and my sister pull me aside to tell me that my father died. I am numb. Why are they telling me this? I remember thinking, "They look so much alike. They are so pretty, but they are wrong." It is Friday.

The days that follow are a blur of activity. My aunts and my father's best friends take over. My mother seems to be in shock. I am fed. One uncle-godfather gives me a big bag of my favorite candy, Hershey's Chocolate Kisses. I sit on the front step and slowly unwrap each morsel, letting it melt in my mouth. I eat the whole bag. I feel comforted, loved, and sick. No one notices. I think I am invisible, sitting above it all, watching them. Why is everyone so upset? My father isn't gone. My father would never leave me without telling me he was going.

Even through the funeral, I have that strange experience of being disconnected from my body and all that is happening. It is as if I am sitting outside of myself, watching a movie or a play with muffled sound. All of the adults who bend down to talk to me at the funeral speak like the characters in a *Speed Racer* cartoon or the *Godzilla* movie: their mouths move at a different pace than the words that come out of them. There is music, all jazz: Gene Ammons's "Didn't We" seems to set the theme for the service, for my parents' story, for our lives. And there are flowers, mostly white, tall stately gladiolas and big, full chrysanthemums, with their spindly petals. I still think of the white versions of these two as funeral flowers.

The funeral is an event. First of all, it isn't in a church like most of the funerals in our world. It is at a local funeral parlor, Emery's. There are no preachers. My Aunt Eunice reads the obituary, which she wrote: his birth, his education, his creativity, and his love for Mena, Muzzy. I don't remember hearing my name. There are so many people, most of them men. My aunts think this is worth noting: "That's the kind of man Em was. He didn't have a bunch of women. He had brothers." I wear white-on-white chiffon: an Easter outfit my mother made from fabric purchased by my Aunt Eartha. That year Easter fell on the Sunday following my father's dying. Earlier that month my mother, my aunt, and I had shopped for the fabric on Fabric Row in South Philadelphia. I am surprised now that I didn't wear yellow to the funeral, as my father loved me in that color and many of my special occasion clothes were in various shades of the hue. But little Black girls wore white to funerals, so I did as well. I wore the dress to the viewing; and the matching coat, I wore as a dress to the funeral service and burial the next day.

My "uncles" stand post at the casket. Dressed in denim jackets and jeans, they stand, legs slightly parted, hands clasped in front of them. There is one white man at the funeral. When he steps forward and bends down to greet my mother, my uncles surround him. He was a co-worker of Daddy's at Sun Ship Company. Later I hear my mother tell her sisters that she'd heard of him: allegedly, he was a Klansman, but somehow, he and my father spent hours talking about race and formed a strange acquaintanceship. Afterwards at the house there are more people than I have ever seen. The door is open and neighbors come in with plates of food. There is chatter. There is laughter. The same thing the next day after we return from the cemetery. My mother is upstairs in her bedroom. A few visitors are escorted upstairs to greet her. Downstairs one of my "uncles" has set up a screen and slide projector. There are photos of my father at a younger age, handsome, dressed in a suit, and tap dancing. I've never seen these. I never knew him like this. There are photos of my mother dressed in a black strapless dress with a full crinoline skirt. I recognize the dress because I played dress-up in it and its matching bolero jacket.

At first, there is a lot of activity. And then there is not. The neighbors leave. My father's friends continue to drop by the house. My aunts take over. This one takes me shopping. That one teaches me how to bake. My grandmother, the love of my life, makes sure I get to school and eat dinner. My cousin, Little Irvin, who is my age and like my brother, is extra kind and protective. My grandmother's brothers, Uncles Joe, Ernest, and George, visit often; in their strong, tender presence I get a glimpse of the girl my mother had been.

My mother is sad; prone to fits of tears. When she picks up a coffee cup, her hand shakes. When she naps, I stand over her to make sure she is breathing.

Yet and still, I don't believe my father is dead. He visits me every night. I don't see him. But I feel the side of my bed go down as he sits on it, like he has done hundreds of times before. I smell him. I feel him. And, often, after falling asleep, I meet him in my dreams.

My father's people do not reach old age. His mother, aunt, and uncles all died before turning sixty. Aunt Essie, Uncle Joe, and Uncle Peter were alcoholics, which certainly contributed to their poor health. However, my paternal grandmother, Sammie Lou, was a clean-living, God-fearing church lady. Even she suffered a fatal heart attack at 57. Daddy's closest friends, those with whom he came of age, with whom he served in the military, those who were pall bearers at his funeral, Uncle Sammy, Uncle Joe, and Uncle Brother, also died in middle age. Among them there was one violent death, possibly a hit: he was found in his car, a bullet wound in the back of his head. The others died from complications of hypertension or diabetes—the diseases that plague poor people, especially the Black poor. Writing about impoverished whites, the journalist Nicholas Kristof lists substance abuse, accidents, and diabetes among what he calls "deaths of despair." I always thought my people died from being Black in America, its own kind of despair.

These deaths did not end with earlier generations. Between 2005 and 2013, my sister and three of her four children followed the pattern. Myra succumbed to lung cancer in 2007. She was sixty-five. One niece, my sister's youngest daughter, doe-eyed Karen, pre-deceased her by two years, having suffered a brain aneurysm at age forty-five. Myra's eldest son and daughter, the preternaturally beautiful Kenneth, and Phyllis, whose features, coloring, and hair I share, died within six months of each other, of prostate and lung cancer respectively. All of their days were cut short by what I believe to have been a toxic environment: the Tasker Homes Housing Project, which was located near an oil refinery, scarce of opportunity and plentiful in drugs and alcohol. My sister's youngest child, my nephew Warren, like me protected and ambitious, endures. He and I have lived to bury them—a macabre ritual that binds us. We are the survivors with all the gratitude and guilt that accompanies our status.

As a girl, I was familiar with the loss of loved ones. I convinced myself that I was on intimate terms with death and the dying. My presence could comfort but not save them. I could sense death, smell it, feel it, when the adults around me could not. This familiarity provided me with an illusion of control. I would never again be surprised. It would not unmoor me. And yet, I lived in constant fear that it would take my mother. Thankfully, the women in her family live longer, at least reaching their seventies. My mother knew her own great-grandmother, who had been enslaved and shared with my mother her memories of Emancipation. Similarly, I was fortunate to know my maternal great-grandmother, Mama Lula, who died months after my father.

In addition to my familiarity with death, I also had the sense that the dead were not actually gone. After my father died, I sometimes saw wisps of smoke like that from a genie's bottle, which I attributed to his presence. I come from a culture that makes room for the dead in our daily lives. No one found these visitations odd. They expected them. As long as I found them comforting, my family expressed no concern. My father did not believe in ghosts, but we believed in his.

The omnipresence of death in our lives might be the reason we were so open to the possibility of visitations from the dead. Might it have been yet another mechanism to help us have some sense of control over the otherwise senseless occurrence of frequent death? Was this some remnant of a spiritual tradition passed down to us from African cosmologies, some understanding of the presence of ancestors in the realm of the living? We never spoke about it in this language, but it was a logic that seemed to govern our existence.

Everyone dies. But Black death in America is too often premature, violent, spectacular. The particular nature of Black death haunts Black writing, as it haunts the nation. It haunts *this book*, born as it is from my own mourning of my father's premature death.

In much literature by Black American writers, death does not constitute an ending, but a change. Langston Hughes writes:

Dear lovely Death
That taketh all things under wing—
Never to kill—
Only to change
Into some other thing
This suffering flesh,
To make it either more or less,
But not again the same—
Dear lovely Death,
Change is thy other name.

Does not this understanding of death provide comfort? Not the comfort offered by the promise of heaven and everlasting life, but more akin to the law of conservation of energy, "Energy cannot be created or destroyed, it can only be changed from one form to another." A people who have suffered death at the hands of their oppressors may have developed an understanding and conception of it that rescues us from the temptation of despair.

Hughes's first line takes you aback. "Dear lovely Death"? If you have lost a loved one, you probably feel less tenderly toward death; it is neither "dear" nor "lovely." If they suffered badly, indeed it may have been ugly. Arnold Rampersad, Hughes's principal biographer, has noted that Hughes here might be echoing his admired Walt Whitman's "Come lovely and soothing death," from his 1865 elegy for Abraham Lincoln, "When Lilacs Last in the Dooryard Bloom'd." Hughes's second line, "That taketh all things under wing," is a more eloquent stating of the cliché "Death is the great equalizer." All living things die: bugs and butterflies, fish and fowl, flowers and trees. Death takes us outside of our raced and gendered bodies, takes us out of our human bodies even, reduces us or enlarges us into something other. "Only to change."

My father, his friends, and other members of our family—their lives were attenuated, not fully realized, except in the realm of love that they received and gave. Perhaps it was because of the absence of religious training in my youth, or the agnostic training of my father, that I never had a concept of Heaven, or an explanation of death such as Christianity provides. Maybe this is why I turned to literature and song. As an adult, I have often turned to Hughes's poem and its promise of transformation after the loss of loved ones. However, I think the death here is not only that of a living being, but also the death of an idea or a place: capitalism or the United States, for instance. The end is not the end, but a change. Personally, the poem confirmed for me what I have intuited about this thing with which I have so much experience but which continues to elude my understanding. Hughes closes the poem, "Change is thy other name." I have always known death to be change, to be the foreclosure of one set of possibilities and the opening of another.

In *The Art of Death: Writing the Final Story*, Haitian-American writer Edwidge Danticat turns to literature following the death of her mother. She writes: "I was so afraid of death that I wanted to desensitize myself to it. Now that my father and mother and many other people I love have died, I want to both better understand death and offload my fear of it, and I believe reading and writing can help." Like the persona of "Dear Lovely Death," Danticat writes: "I know now, having watched my mother die . . . I believe death is not the end." In this knowing, Danticat and I are sisters.

To write about death offers the possibility of stepping outside of race, not to avoid it or to transcend it, but to turn to a reality that predates it. In our society, death is both raced and without race. We all die; how we do so and how we respond to the loss of loved ones might very well be determined by race. And we all have something to teach each other about it, about tending to the dead, about our own dying. There are lessons to be learned and values to be shared. I have come to greatly admire Jewish mourning rituals, especially the weeklong Shiva, the year devoted to daily recitations of the Mourner's Kaddish, and the Unveiling of the headstone on the first anniversary of a loved one's death.

Langston Hughes offers a way of thinking about the inevitable. What it shares with Black Christianity is a notion that one leaves this suffering flesh, and in that way, there is a shared sense of transcendence. Where he departs from it is that there is nothing about going to heaven, "meeting Jesus," nothing about what one has to do in this life to get to heaven in the next. The death that is change here can be embraced by those who are religious or secular, by those who believe death transforms us into ancestors or into environmental energies, into stardust even.

Toni Morrison's *Sula* speaks of death as a subjective experience. After dying, the protagonist, Sula, thinks:

While in this state of weary anticipation, she noticed that she was not breathing, that her heart had stopped completely. A crease of fear touched her breast, for any second there was sure to be a violent explosion in her brain, a gasping for breath. Then she realized, or rather she sensed, that there was not going to be any pain. She was not breathing because she didn't have to. Her body did not need oxygen. She was dead.

Sula felt her face smiling. "Well, I'll be damned, "she thought, "it didn't even hurt. Wait till I tell Nel."

Sula's consciousness survives her death, as does her relationship with her childhood friend, Nel. She notices, fears, realizes, senses, smiles, and thinks, and she is dead. Sula is amused in death. Nel, the living friend, is devastated, encased in her own sorrow, and fully unaware that her estranged friend's spirit responds to her call. Walking back from the burial, she calls Sula's name: "'Sula?' she whispered, gazing at the tops of trees. 'Sula?'" In response, "Leaves stirred; mud shifted; there was the smell of overripe green things. A soft ball of fur broke and scattered like dandelion spores in the breeze." The language here echoes another moment of Nel's sorrow: when she mourns the demise of her marriage.

> "Why me?" She waited. The mud shifted, the leaves stirred, the smell of overripe green things enveloped her and announced the beginnings of her very own howl.
> But it did not come.
> The odor evaporated; the leaves were still, the mud settled. And finally there was nothing, just a flake of something dry and nasty in her throat. . . . There was something just to the right of her. . . . A gray ball hovering just there. Just there. To the right.

At Sula's death, Nel's sorrow is freed, the howl comes, and the ball of fur breaks. Sula's spirit, in the tops of trees, frees Nel to experience her sorrow, and thus to experience her life. Because one sure way of knowing you are alive is to fully experience the deep and explosive pain of grief.

Morrison's writing of Sula's death joins Hughes in that it

posits death as transcendent and transformative. It is in her later and most well-known work, *Beloved*, that Morrison offers her most wrenching portrayals of Black death. There is no transcendence here, nor is there the comforting presence of the dead as benevolent energy. No, *Beloved* gives us a haunting by what one character, Stamp Paid, calls "the Black and angry dead," those "people of the broken necks, of fire-cooked blood and Black girls who had lost their mothers." *Beloved* may mark a shift, a transition in literary representations of Black death. Stamp Paid says of Black people, "Very few had died in bed . . . and none that he knew . . . had lived a livable life." *Beloved*, though published later than *Sula*, is set in an earlier period. It calls into question the possibility of a transcendent death and insists we are always living in that perpetual state of grief from the "disremembered and unaccounted for" dead.

Following the path opened by Morrison, many contemporary Black writers posit death as the central marker, the major experience of Blackness. There has been renewed writerly attention to the tenacity of premature and violent Black death in the first two decades of the twenty-first century. The most widely read and influential theorists, especially the ever-eloquent Christina Sharpe, call our attention to the persistence of early death as foundational to an unrelenting climate of white supremacy. Some of this may have been prompted by the aftermath of Hurricane Katrina in 2005, George Zimmerman's murder of the teenager Trayvon Martin in 2012, and the litany of Black people killed by police and white vigilantes that followed:

Jordan Davis,
Rekia Boyd,
Lacquan McDonald,

Michael Brown,
Eric Garner,
Akai Gurley,
Tamir Rice,
Sandra Bland,
Freddie Gray,
Walter Scott,
The Charleston Nine,
Philando Castile,
Alton Sterling,
Korryn Gaines
Ahmaud Arbery,
Breonna Taylor
George Floyd . . .

The last two were murdered during the COVID-19 pandemic, which had already disproportionately killed Black and brown people. It was said that the virus killed us because of pre-existing health conditions like hypertension, obesity, diabetes, coronary disease. In fact, the preponderant pre-existent (public) health condition from which Black people suffer is racism. Here we had the convergence of a plague and slaughter.

This season of Black death (from Trayvon's murder in 2012 to the murder of George Floyd and Breonna Taylor in 2020) also has given us a burst of remarkable writing that bears witness, yet again, to Black lives under siege. The period has given birth to a new iteration of the long Black freedom struggle: Black Lives Matter. Some writing by Black writers in the contemporary moment seeks to bear witness: Black lives do in fact matter. Two of the most critically acclaimed writers of the time, Ta-Nehisi Coates and Jesmyn Ward, make the fear of dying and the actual deaths of peers the predominant experience of Blackness for their generation.

In *Between the World and Me* (2015), Ta-Nehisi Coates recounts his Baltimore childhood and his young adulthood at Howard University in a letter to his fifteen-year-old son. Because the epistolary form resembles that of James Baldwin's classic letter to his nephew, "Down at the Cross," published in *The Fire Next Time*, critics, following the lead of Toni Morrison's blurb for the book, hailed Coates as Baldwin's heir apparent. But the title is taken from Richard Wright's poem of the same name, and in its pessimism, Coates's view is much closer to that of Wright's. The persona of the Wright poem stumbles upon "a thing," a charred and lynched Black body and all the remnants that the mob has left behind, "buttons, dead matches, butt-ends of cigars and cigarettes, peanut shells, a drained gin-flask, and a whore's lipstick." As he stands there at the scene of the crime, "The ground gripped my feet and my heart was circled by icy walls of fear." It is this same fear that grips Coates, from his days as a bookish boy navigating the gang-worn streets of Baltimore, and later as the young man who, buoyed by the exuberance of attending college at Howard University—The Mecca—nonetheless still feels the threat of police who stand ready, in a split second, to kill young men with Black skin. Coates is raised by intellectual parents who believe neither in the American Dream nor in God. He writes that they "never tried to console me with ideas of an afterlife and were skeptical of preordained American glory." This rearing he believes "freed" him. It also left him skeptical of that thing that Baldwin never lost, hope. Coates recounts, "violence rose from the fear like smoke from a fire" in the form of a random and unprovoked teenager who points a gun at him, and a father who is quick to whip him with a belt as a form of disciplining

and "protecting" him from the death that surely will await a willful and disobedient Black child. Public schools further discipline
him: "The schools were not concerned with curiosity. They were
concerned with compliance." Coates at first finds explanation
and a role model in Malcolm X's autodidacticism and racial militancy. His interpretation of Malcolm leads him to a kind of crude
Black nationalism that celebrates Black kings, queens, rulers and
civilizations that mirror myths of Western Civilization but in
blackface. It is at the tutelage of Black poets whom he meets in
and around D.C. that he acquires a more nuanced understanding
of race and racism, and a critical understanding of Black identity.
As is the case with so many of us turned out and turned on by
the tradition of Black writing, he

> did not find a coherent tradition marching lockstep but
> instead factions, and factions within factions. Hurston
> battled Hughes, Du Bois warred with Garvey, Harold
> Cruse fought everyone. . . . I came looking for a parade,
> for a military review of champions marching in ranks.
> Instead I was left with a brawl of ancestors, a herd of dis-
> senters, sometimes marching together but just as often
> marching away from each other.

These same poets warn him of the police of Prince George's
County. The county sits just outside of D.C., "a great enclave of
Black people who seemed, as much as anyone, to have seized
control of their bodies . . . it was, to my eyes, very rich. Its residents . . . were Black people who elected their own politicians,
but these politicians, I learned, superintended a police force as
vicious as any in America." Although he will encounter the police
of Prince George's County, although he will be disrespected by

and afraid of them, they do not take his life. However, much of the second half of Coates's book is devoted to a young man named Prince Jones, whose life will be taken by a Prince George's County policeman. A Black policeman. Prince Jones is the literary son of Ralph Ellison's fictional Todd Clifton. Separated by more than half a century, both are beautiful, charismatic, and promising. Both are shot down by police. Todd Clifton prompts *Invisible Man*'s most eloquent speech, a eulogy in the tradition of that delivered by Mark Antony for Julius Caesar in Shakespeare's play. Similarly, some of Coates's best writing emerges from Jones's murder. "There are people whom we do not fully know, and yet they live in a warm place within us, and when they are plundered, when they lose their bodies and the dark energy disperses, that place becomes a wound." Here Coates is both describing his own experience of Jones's death, and also giving words to the collective loss Black people felt when we lost Trayvon, Tamir, Sandra, and George. Significantly, unlike the energy that lingered by my childhood bedside or just out of Nel's reach, here that "dark energy disperses," and the empty space it leaves becomes an open wound.

Of the memorial service for Prince Jones, which was held at Howard University's Rankin Chapel, Coates writes, "I know that I have always felt a great distance from the grieving rituals of my people, and I must have felt it powerfully then. The need to forgive the officer would not have moved me, because even then, in some inchoate form, I knew that Prince was not killed by a single officer so much as he was murdered by his country and all the fears that have marked it from birth." Whenever I have attended or viewed a Black funeral, especially those held in churches, I am buoyed and overwhelmed by the beauty of the rituals we've created around death—the music, the language, the majesty, the celebration of life, the acknowledgment of loss, even the lovingly prepared and delicious food that follows. I've never heard a call for forgiveness for the perpetrators of our deaths unless they were other young, Black people, but I do know that this is a part of our tradition that is now being called into question in ways that Coates describes. He continues

> And raised . . . in rejection of a Christian God, I could see no higher purpose in Prince's death. I believed, and still do, that our bodies are ourselves, that my soul is the voltage conducted through neurons and nerves, and that my spirit is my flesh. . . . I sat there feeling myself a heretic, believing only in this one-shot life and the body. For the crime of destroying the body of Prince Jones, I did not believe in forgiveness. When the assembled mourners bowed their heads in prayer, I was divided from them because I believed that the void would not answer back.

Here is where I depart from Coates. While in many instances I share his refusal of forgiveness, I do not believe that our bodies are ourselves or our only selves. I do not believe our spirit is only our flesh. And when my fellow mourners bow their heads, though I may not pray to Jesus, or only to Jesus, I, too, bow mine and join them in prayer.

In not believing the void would answer him back, Coates seems truly the son of Wright, not of Baldwin. Once, in a conversation, I told a beloved and wise elder that a friend said he wasn't sure he believed in an afterlife, to which she responded, "Tell him I said he doesn't have to, because the afterlife believes in him." This elder communed often with the dead, and I had no reason to question her.

Coates is a talented writer who has given voice to Black

fear, rage, and mourning, and who is perhaps one of the most celebrated Black authors of our time. He is one among many gifted writers who have emerged in the first two decades of the twenty-first century. Without question, Mississippi-born Jesmyn Ward is among the most compelling of writers of her generation. In three novels and one memoir, Ward writes of the Black, Southern poor who live in coastal Mississippi, near New Orleans. They are victimized by poverty, racism, and ecological disaster, especially in the form of hurricanes. She writes of people trying to stem the tide of premature death and losing. *Men We Reaped: A Memoir* (2013) focuses on five young Black men she knew, childhood friends and family members, who, between 2000 and 2004, "died, all violently, in seemingly unrelated deaths": Roger Eric Daniels, Desmond Cook, Charlie Joseph Martin, Ronald Wayne Lizana, and Ward's brother, Joshua Aidan Dedeaux, were between twenty and thirty-two years old when they died. One is murdered, one commits suicide, another dies of a heart attack after using cocaine, and two die in car accidents. Being Black, male, Southern, and poor is a common condition that contributes to their demise. It is the "seemingly unrelated" which holds the clue. For, as Ward shows, these individual deaths are anything but unrelated. She will term them an "epidemic": "the history of racism and economic inequality and lapsed public and personal responsibility festered and turned sour and spread."

Men We Reaped is a painfully beautiful work that alternates between autobiographical chapters and those devoted to each of the five young men. The autobiographical chapters have titles beginning with the word "We," while the other chapters are titled by each man's name, followed by his birth and death date: literary gravestones,

Roger Eric Daniels III
Born: March 5, 1981
Died: June 3, 2004

the pages that follow putting flesh onto the bones buried beneath. Alternating between memoir and memorial, this form shines a spotlight both on individual deaths (for their entire lives lead directly to their deaths; as readers, we are indeed anticipating death from the very beginning), and on the community, the "we" of which they are a part, also dying.

In the memorial chapter "Roger Eric Daniels III," Ward tries to comfort the deceased's sister, Rhea. Ward is at a loss for words, so she hugs her and whispers in her ear: "He will always be your brother, and you will always be his sister." She does not say fully what she wants Rhea to know, but she writes it:

What I meant to say was this: *You will always love him. He will always love you. Even though he is not here, he was here, and no one can change that. No one can take that away from you. If energy is neither created nor destroyed, and if your brother was here with his humor, his kindness, his hopes, doesn't this mean that what he was still exists somewhere, even if it's not here? Doesn't it? Because in order to get out of bed this morning, this is what I had to believe about my brother, Rhea.* But I didn't know how to say that.

This is what we believe: that our dead beloveds are always with us, an energy that holds all they were and surrounds us. We want to believe this because we must. We believe in order to "get out of bed in the morning," in order to keep living and not kill ourselves or someone else.

As with so much of Black literature, Ward portrays the specific funeral traditions of her community. Like the funerals of Morrison's *The Bluest Eye* or Gaines's *A Lesson before Dying,* in *Men We Reaped* "there is a gathering or a repast. Older women brought large pans containing casseroles and meat to [his mother's] house. We all found our way there. . . . We ate with plates balanced on our laps." But Ward's generation and location add a new element to these rituals of mourning. They sit on or partly in cars as they had done on numerous nights when he was alive, when they drank, smoked weed, played loud hip-hop, and reveled in each other's company. But now they wear memorial tee shirts emblazoned with pictures of the dead. "In this way, the young memorialize the young. . . . All of us crying and looking away from each other."

The final chapter, "We Are Here," tells of the lives of those left behind. "Grief scabs over like my scars and pulls into new, painful configurations as it knits. . . . We are never free from grief." That sense of profound loss is always with us, exacerbated by each new death. It is my mother and I calling each other when we hear of Baltimore's Freddie Gray in the ambulance and are both immediately snatched back to that Philadelphia night when the three of us—she, my father, and I—were in the back of the paddy wagon. It is every time we witness yet another police killing, or hear of yet another overdose. And in between, we live with the knowledge that the grief is just below the surface; there is no closure, just a scab that can be ripped off easily. "I carry the weight of grief even as I struggle to live. I understand what it feels like to be under siege."

In the closing pages Ward tells about writing a "history of loss," a narrative of remembrance, a memorial as much as a memoir. Such work is tiring, as is our living, which constitutes its own kind of remembrance.

And, when I am weary, I imagine this: After the moment
I die, I will find myself standing on the side of a long,
pitted asphalt road flanked on both sides by murmuring
pine trees, under a hot, high sun in a blue sky. In the
distance, I will hear a rumbling thumping, a bass beat. A
dull blue '85 Cutlass will cut the horizon, come growling
down the road before stopping in front of me. It will stop
so quickly the gravel will crunch, and then my brother
will swing the passenger door wide with one long tattooed arm, the other on the wheel. He will look at me
with his large dark liquid eyes, his face soft. He will know
that I have been waiting. He will say: Come. Come take a
ride with me. I will, brother. I'm here.

Ward insists that our Black lives are lived waiting to die. *Sula*
ends with the title character's consciousness extending past her
last breath. The afterlife is a given. Here, in *Men We Reaped*,
Jesmyn Ward ends with an imagining of her own life after death.
It is not a given, but it is a necessary imagining. "When I am
weary," as we all are—weary from the harshness of life, weary
from the persistence of death—when I am weary, "I imagine this."
Perhaps this is what the earlier writers of the tradition, from the
anonymous poets of the spirituals and the blues, to Hughes and
Morrison, have done for us: given language to our weariness, and
imagined for us that this harsh life is not the end.

7

The Transformative Potential of Love

In my family and community, my parents' love story was legendary. Recounting elements of it, tellers of the tale—aunts and uncles, cousins and neighbors, friends and casual observers—all seemed to find warmth and contentment. At first, my parents were buoyed by their youth—his brilliance and ambition, her fresh-faced beauty, creativity, and resourcefulness. Later, his addiction and ongoing attempts to rid himself of it halted their momentum, but not their devotion to each other.

Having met as children, Em and Mena were portrayed as a Black Romeo and Juliet, without the family feud. By some accounts she was twelve, too young for boy company, and he was thirteen, when they first met over games of jacks and double-dutch. She was the baby girl of a big brood that included two protective older sisters and a bevy of cousins, uncles, aunts, and grandparents, all of whom at one point or another shared living space. He was the young prince, the only child, of a striving young couple: the joy of his mother's life and the object of his contractor stepfather's resentment. He never knew his birth father, and did not know Alonzo Griffin was not his biological father until the day of his mother's funeral, when he was forty years old.

Mena and Em were new teen parents, aged fifteen and sixteen, when they ran away to marry, but a judge refused to render the service without Mena's parent's signature. Their baby daughter, Myra, continued to live with his parents even after the young couple successfully eloped. Finding their names in a *Philadelphia Inquirer* list of Applications for Marriage Licenses is an invitation to imagine them on the cusp of the life they would build together. She is listed by her maiden name, Wilhelmena Carson, living in the Ellsworth Street home I most identify with my grandmother, and he still resides in his parents' home, just around the corner from hers on Federal Street.

Following a brief stint in the Navy just after the end of World War II, and with the assistance of the GI Bill, Em purchased a house for his young bride from an Italian numbers runner, and earned an Associate's Degree in Architectural Engineering from Temple University. Blueprints and T squares found their way into the South Philadelphia row house he renovated over and over, while dreaming of furthering his education and making his way as an architect. Mena recalls standing on the sidewalk with him, looking up into the windows of architectural firms that didn't employ Blacks. The streets of Philadelphia were littered with many such places that practiced this unobtrusive form of discrimination. Yet, the couple's dreams were refreshed by going to jazz clubs like Pep's at Broad and South, or the basement of the Douglass Hotel, which housed the Showboat, near Broad and Lombard, where they heard the latest cutting-edge musical innovations of their peers. He befriended many of the musicians and she recalls him introducing her to a young Miles

Davis ("shy") and to Charlie Parker. They sat near the edge of the stage to watch and listen as Billie Holiday serenaded and mesmerized them.

Early mornings, before heading off to their jobs, they could be found swimming in the Wissahickon Creek, where they also filled jugs with fresh spring water. Mena found steady work in Philadelphia's many garment factories; in the evenings and on weekends she made clothing and did alterations for local women. Like many other degreed Black men, Em worked for the Post Office. He drove a "Dynaflow" Buick; she acquired a taste for D'Orsay pumps. Occasionally they drove to New York to visit friends on Sugar Hill in Harlem or to attend boxing matches at Madison Square Garden. Rare photos of them from this period show them dressed up amid friends, laughing and enjoying what must have been a rich social life. As a curious girl I found old paper coasters and cocktail napkins embossed with "Mena & Em," further evidence that they hosted parties I'd never witnessed, evidence of a mysterious and distanced life that preceded my entrance into their world.

Later, when my father became addicted, the plans for bigger homes and better jobs became ever more elusive. They settled into a life haunted by the anxiety of discovery by police, and worked as skilled laborers—she in factories and he in a shipyard—and gave birth to a second baby girl, whom they named Farah Jasmine.

My mother stayed on, through disappointment and setbacks. My father became a high-functioning addict, working every day and making various efforts to rid himself of his habit: methadone, group therapy, cold turkey. There were encounters with the police, and a year before my birth, he served a four-monthlong stint in prison for possession of the "residue of heroin." Throughout it all they leaned on the myth and reality of their romance. They were supported and sustained by loved ones, and they painstakingly mapped out a future for their youngest child. Guided by his vision and her ingenuity, I followed a path that generations of Civil Rights activists opened.

I first heard the love story from him. On the way to the library, as we passed familiar small businesses—corner stores, Italian bakeries, hardware stores—through the thoroughfare of Point Breeze Avenue, he relayed a fairy tale complete with a beautiful princess and her two sisters—One Eye and Three Eye—and a Prince Charming. Once we reached our destination, he scooped me in his arms and revealed that the sisters were "your aunts, Eartha and Eunice," the Princess, my mother, and, of course, he was the rescuing, heroic Prince. (Many years later when I heard Mary Lou Williams's "The Land of Oo-Bla-Dee," I realized my father's fairy tale was suspiciously similar.) Walking to my grandmother's home, in whose care my mother left me while she worked, she told me stories of eloping, describing in detail the dress she made and wore: "It was black with red rose print; in the back at the bottom of the V, I sewed a big red bow." Because of them, I never fantasized about being a princess bride, the center of attention at a big wedding. Eloping seemed so much more romantic. My aunts' and neighbors' versions of the story were recounted with soft, pleasant smiles. "Your daddy loved himself some Mena," said Aunt Eunice. Aunt Eartha recalled, "He bought her a house and filled it with furniture." And one of our neighbors, an older lady, told me, "I loved watching them holding hands when they came home in the evening."

Everyone seemed invested in the couple, who at one point or another represented possibility, love, marriage, education, home-ownership, and upward mobility. Later, they were an example of commitment and resilience in the face of life's challenges. My childhood friends watched in a kind of admiring disbelief at my parents' displays of affection. Their relationship was as passionate as it was affectionate, as playful as it was deadly serious. At his funeral, his life was framed by a version of their story, his final words reported as "Take me home to Muzzy." (Even then, I knew these were not his final words, because I had heard them in the ambulance. When the police van sharply turned the corner and the stretcher slid back, he hit his head and said, "Oh Muzzy, my head!" But that was too painful to recall and relay. The fairy tale needed a better ending.)

That story, their story, so often told, so celebrated and mourned, was nonetheless full of its own silence. No one mentioned the addiction that slowed their ambitious trajectory. Though known within our small, tight family circle, it was a secret, our family secret. These were the days before naloxone and sympathetic portrayals of opioid addicts on television and in print. These were the days when the possession of the smallest amount of narcotics guaranteed prison, and neither mercy nor sympathy. These were days when the public face of the heroin addict was a Black man, often a musician, not a young white person. (Although I vaguely remember discovering an issue of *Life* magazine that my father had saved along with the *Ebony*s, *Sepia*s, and other Black magazines, featuring a photo essay about a young white couple, both addicts.) There was no space in the public imagination for an intelligent, high-functioning addict, especially not a Black working-class one. So, we kept it a secret because so much was at stake: our beloved head of household, our well-being, our home. I was an inquisitive child who asked many questions, which my mother always answered, those answers followed by "Shush, you can ask me anything, but remember, we don't talk about these things to other people. Don't tell our family's business. Your daddy loves you."

As a child, I had no doubt of his love; I was fully aware that he cherished me. I knew that though he didn't celebrate Christmas, the season would bring shopping sprees, new dolls, shoes, and musical instruments, all bought by my father and not "some fat, white man in a red suit." I knew he worked hard to provide for us, going to work even on days when he didn't feel well. I knew that he dealt with small racist encounters on an almost daily basis; he recounted them at night when he returned home.

And yet, even as a small girl, I instinctively felt more secure in the presence of my mother than my father. My child's understanding of it was that though he would want to save me from an oncoming car or bus, my father's reflexes might be too slow to jump into action. My mother, on the other hand, would snatch me from harm's way in the blink of an eye, and if necessary, she would throw herself in front of the lethal vehicle. I trusted her judgment and her ability to handle anything that came our way.

Following my father's death, their story took on greater meaning. It was told to me to remind me that I was the product of Love. That no matter what the world, white people, and later bourgeois Black people, might think or say, my parents loved and respected each other and I was a result of that. My well-being, my gifts, my successes were a result of their investment in and of love.

For years I sought their story in books. Less Zora Neale Hurston's Teacake and Janie of *Their Eyes Were Watching God*, whom I would later discover, they were to my mind more like the young, beautifully doomed urban couples of James Baldwin's novels: Elizabeth and Richard of *Go Tell It on the Mountain*, Tish and Fonny of *If Beale Street Could Talk*. Both bear witness to the miracle of Black love in this hateful and unjust place we call home. Both have artistic, intellectual male leads, too sensitive for the raw and brutal injustices they encounter on an almost daily basis. And, the women are young, fiercely devoted, finding a deep inner strength they didn't know they possessed. (In "Sonny's Blues," Baldwin also writes about an addict with incredible sensitivity, and I love him for it.)

I read Baldwin as a teenager, about the same age that Mena and Em were when they had my sister. *Go Tell It on the Mountain* was my first James Baldwin. I read it the summer before I began attending The Baldwin School on scholarship. That summer of 1978 was my summer of James Baldwin. I recall reading *Giovanni's Room*, *If Beale Street Could Talk*, and *The Fire Next Time* in quick succession. I read in the kitchen as my mother straightened my hair, I read in my bedroom, and on the bus, and when not reading I thought about the characters like they were friends or family. I eventually made my way to Giovanni's Room Bookstore, on the corner of Twelfth and Pine, which I later found out was a gay bookstore. There, I was always greeted by kind and friendly white men, who welcomed me into their sunlit, book-filled space.

Fonny and Tish's romance is a boy-girl love story that sits at the center of a larger family and community love story. It is about the ways Black people nurture and nourish each other in the midst of a society that shows them no love. There is hope in young love, particularly young love that will result in new life. There is the desire to make a way for them, a sense of possibility invested in them. This is the kind of investment I think my family and community made in my parents' story. There was a softness that overcame them as they talked about how much

Emerson loved Mena. The older women even laughed when they learned of their quarrels because they knew these were love spats, neither destructive nor mean-spirited. Their peers were both protective of and sustained by them. Their relationship had outlasted other teen romances. I sometimes wondered how a young couple came to bear so much.

In his fiction, Baldwin, unlike Richard Wright or Ralph Ellison, is attentive to Black women. And, because he is attentive to Black women, he is attentive to Black love, to the love Black people have for each other, to their capacity to love in spite of the hatreds directed toward them. Baldwin, a gay Black man, sees the beauty of Black women and Black people; he attends to their tenderness and their desire for each other. Wright seems unable to imagine this tenderness. Ellison, though clearly a lover of Black culture, does not display the same affection for Black women. Unlike Baldwin's, Ellison's women characters lack substance and depth. In contrast, Baldwin's stories are often told from a woman's perspective. *Beale Street* is narrated by Tish, in the first person. She is the voice of authority; her interpretation of events shapes the way the reader receives the story.

To claim love as a theme of Baldwin's writing is almost cliché. Much has been written about his deep Christian sense of love as a requirement for and source of redemption for America. It is certainly an obsession of his, but religion isn't where it starts for me. What initially struck me upon my first readings of Baldwin, what strikes me still, is the way he writes about romantic love between Black people, and the way that romantic love radiates out, or does not, into families and communities. At the core, romantic love in Baldwin's writings can be the source of an ethics of community, of a radical spiritual survival, in a place set on destroying our souls. He does not romanticize Black life or the conditions under which Black people love each other. In fact, he explains them in harsh and unrelenting detail. These circumstances are what make love all the more profound, as miraculous as it is quotidian.

Though separated by twenty-one years, *Go Tell It on the Mountain* (1953) and *If Beale Street Could Talk* (1974) both provide meditations on young love blossoming while challenged by racism and poverty. The young couple Richard and Elizabeth, of *Go Tell It*, are not the novel's main characters. Their son, unaware of the circumstances of his birth or even of Richard's existence, is the novel's protagonist. Fonny and Tish are the central characters of the novel, and their story is the kernel around which Baldwin structures the story of a family and a people. Both Richard and Fonny, to differing degrees, reminded me of my father. An intellectual and an artist respectively, each is keenly aware of the societal forces seeking their destruction. Richard is defeated by them, while Fonny is sustained by the love of Tish, her family, his art, and the promise of his unborn child. My father was both sustained and defeated. Reading Baldwin and others, I began to understand his personal tragedy as a tragedy of our people.

Richard and Elizabeth are isolated and alone. Fonny and Tish are a source of inspiration and joy to family and sympathetic strangers; they are embraced, held, and cared for by a circle of kin and allies. Because those who make up this circle are angered by the injustice of white society, which incarcerates Fonny for a crime he didn't commit, Tish's family, the Riverses, recognize him as one of thousands of Black men who populate America's jails. The Riverses become a political force, a source of deep resistance. They are steeped in the history of the nation, enraged by injustice, and filled with love for the young couple and their unborn child. In *Go Tell It*, Richard commits suicide after his release from prison. At the end of *Beale Street*, Fonny—fully aware that the powers that be intend to keep him imprisoned, full of love for Tish, and of love from her, having claimed himself as an "artisan" whose work will create and sustain community—has eyes "like the eyes of a prophet." He is on fire.

Fonny and Tish exist in a world where the decks are stacked against them. When the novel opens, Fonny is already incarcerated on trumped-up charges of rape. The police are evil and the prosecutors are corrupt, the family that loves him is poor and the one that doesn't—his mother and sisters—are religious hypocrites with bourgeois aspirations and disdain for ordinary Black people. But Fonny, Tish, the Rivers family, and Fonny's father Frank are absolutely clear about what they are up against and willing to fight for his life and freedom by any means necessary. Each of the characters must discover ways to hold on to their sense of their own humanity. They must engage in acts of love and care toward one another, acts that serve as a bulwark against a society asserting that Black people are unworthy of either.

Tish's family does not judge her because she is pregnant and unmarried. They do not judge Fonny because he is incarcerated. They know Black unions were not given the sanctity and legal protection of marriage. They know Black men are subjected to wrongful arrest. Such incidents don't make people less worthy of love and support, but more so. They make use of the law, of pleading with the victim of a crime to tell the truth about her assailant, and of illegal means of hustling to raise money for bail. They are active, not passively accepting things as they are.

An orthodox Jewish landlord rents Fonny and Tish a loft when other white landlords refuse to do so; a group of Spanish restaurant owners and workers feed the young couple; an Italian store-owner defends them against a racist police officer; a young white lawyer takes Fonny's case, jeopardizing his own standing with the white establishment. All of these people, though not all Christians, enact biblical instructions to provide for the "least of these"—give food and shelter, bear witness to the oppressed's plight, and labor to free the captive. Together, these characters make up a multiethnic net that surrounds the young couple, a net of kinship embodying the possibility of a truly egalitarian America.

In *If Beale Street Could Talk*, family is not only the family you are born into, but the family you create. Tish is born into the Rivers clan. Fonny is not. But because they've known him since childhood, because Tish loves him and he loves Tish, and because he is the father of her baby, he is family. In form, Tish and Fonny become a family of sorts for Fonny's friend Daniel. Recently released from prison, having served a sentence for a crime he didn't commit, Daniel is deeply damaged and traumatized. He visits Fonny and Tish often. They feed him, listen to him, and take turns holding him when he cries. As a family, they care for him, and he too is nourished physically and spiritually by them. Tish recalls:

> We are happy, even, that we have food enough for Daniel, who eats peacefully, not knowing that we are laughing, but sensing that something wonderful has happened to us, which means that wonderful things happen, and that maybe something wonderful will happen to him. It's wonderful, anyway, to be able to help a person have that feeling.

Here is the answer that I had been seeking when I went in search of my parents' love story and why everyone who knew them seemed so invested in and lifted by it. They represented the possibility of something wonderful. Something that crooked cops, a racist workplace, and a country that will blame its victims for their failures, cannot break. They guarantee something as beautiful and wonderful as love can happen. Their love is to be cherished, and celebrated, and shared. Seeing themselves in the eyes of their friends and neighbors gave Mena and Em a sense of the importance of their own existence. They were as steady as a rock, a thing to be counted on, the stuff of movies, if only Hollywood weren't committed to stereotypes of Black life.

In an interview published in *The Black Scholar* (1973), Baldwin notes:

> The importance of the black family at this hour in the world's history is to be an example to all those other dispersed all over the world because in a sense, the American Negro has become a model . . . the vanguard of revolution which is now global, and it does begin with what you call the black family, my brother in jail, my sister in the street and my uncle the junkie, but it's my brother, and my sister and my uncle. So it's not a question of denying them, it's a question of saving them.

Context matters here. Baldwin said this in the aftermath of *The Negro Family: The Case for National Action*, better known as the Moynihan Report, published in 1965. Written by Daniel Patrick Moynihan, then Assistant Secretary of Labor under President Lyndon Johnson, it explored the causes of Black poverty in the United States. Moynihan's report concluded that one of the major causes of poverty was the high rate of Black single motherhood and a pathological Black culture. The report sparked decades of debate and controversy as a generation of Black scholars, art-

ists, and activists sought to counter its claims and policy recom-
mendations. In *The Black Scholar* interview, Baldwin provides
an alternative interpretation of the Black family, not pathological, but sitting at a vanguard of social change. The Black family
wasn't the cause of Black poverty and racial inequity, but a bulwark against it.

When I first encountered Baldwin, I had family members
and family friends who were junkies, family members who had
been incarcerated, family members who were unwed mothers,
family members who were "winos," family members who were
law-abiding citizens, and family members who were devout
Christians. And I loved and was loved by every one of them. I
knew and loved neighbors and family friends who had turned
tricks and boosted. And though my family aggressively protected
me from such a fate, they nonetheless insisted that I belonged to
this complex community and it belonged to me, and we were
fierce about the work of saving each other.

At the core of the Rivers family's—and thus ordinary Black
folks'—resistance is a refusal to take on white interpretations of
our lives as pathological. Racism and injustice abound. But we
love. We Resist. We save the souls, even if we cannot always free
the bodies, of those we love. And sometimes, because we love,
we are also enraged. In 1962, during a roundtable conversation
with Lorraine Hansberry, Langston Hughes, Alfred Kazin, and
Nat Hentoff on WBAI Radio, Baldwin asserted: "To be a Negro
in this country and to be relatively conscious is to be in a rage
almost all of the time. So that the first problem is how to control
that rage so that it won't destroy you." One way of controlling the
rage is to channel it into a love-fueled resistance.

I realize now that Baldwin saw this kind of unwavering, uncon-
ditional devotion to the "least of these" (who are us) as founda-

tional to a love ethic, to a politics informed by love for the Black poor and full of belief in love's transformative power. Earlier in his career, when he first emerged as an American prophet, he had faith in the power of love to transform white America and therefore the nation. But by the time of *Beale Street* he had to confront the seeming intransigence and violence of white supremacy and America's continued destruction of its Black sons and daughters. *Beale Street* turns inward, but never ceases looking for moments of genuine human connection across barriers of race and language and culture. (This fails miserably in one instance, when Tish's mother seeks to connect with the frightened Puerto Rican woman who has accused Fonny of rape, yet the desire to connect is meaningful.) In the novel, a precious few join forces to stand up for what is right and just. They model the possibility of what connection guided and inspired by love looks like. It is a set of concentric circles: the unborn baby encircled by Fonny and Tish, who are in turn encircled by the Rivers family, later joined by the Spanish restaurant workers, the Italian immigrant shopkeeper, the Orthodox Jewish building owner, the slowly awakening, ethical WASP lawyer. This is a glimpse of what America, guided and inspired by love, has the potential of becoming.

Because of my own experience of having been so deeply loved, I have no difficulty believing in its transformative power. But even I find it challenging to extend that love to those who cause long and lasting harm to the vulnerable. There are those I cannot imagine loving: a small and powerful group who are so deeply damaged that they enact evil; in some instances, they embody it. Dylann Roof, who was welcomed in a loving, prayerful embrace by Black parishioners, killed them in cold blood and has yet to display any remorse even in the face of their kin's forgiveness. Can love transform him? George Zimmerman? The 45th president of the United States? Perhaps these are just lost souls, driven primarily by fear. While I am uncertain that love can always transform those who embody evil, those sociopaths who lack a conscience, I do believe that the force of love can defeat and destroy such evil. To love the least of these is to be enraged by the conditions, if not the individuals, that enslave them. That love wins out over fear. That love inspires courage in the face of near-certain defeat. That love ought to be extended to babies in cages, to those in the throes of addiction, and to all those whom others would deny dignity and respect.

In truth, the people I loved and who loved me were flawed individuals. One of them disciplined her children too harshly. Others hit wives and girlfriends. (Too often, neighbors and kin loved and protected males more than females.) Some were homophobic even though family members they claimed to love were gay and lesbian. Some were damaged and in turn caused harm. Yet, none of this places them beyond the bounds of love. Love requires you hold folk accountable. At times, though not often enough, the abusers were called out, challenged. There were intense debates and arguments about right and wrong. Love meant you wanted people to acknowledge responsibility for the damage they'd done. On rare occasions, it was necessary to place distance. But in most instances, I have been fortunate to witness deep humanity and people's capacity for growth and change. And I am convinced that those who live on the margins, those who sit at the bottom, have a sense of compassion with a wider reach and a more bone-deep sense of love and loyalty than do many who have far better resources and are far more privileged.

In those years and months immediately following my father's death, my mother and I were enveloped in a communal embrace, wrapped in a love so thick that I feel it even now. Our family held us through tears and anger and confusion. My aunts clasped their baby sister close as she wept, all the while looking over her shoulder to reassure me that she would be alright, and they stepped in to help care for and nurture me. My male cousins and uncles and godfathers provided a ring of protection from all who would prey upon us. Our neighbors offered gifts of food, trips to the shore, and invitations to their families' gatherings. Folk stepped in and stepped up. They acted in love.

For Black people, America is a loveless place. The freedom fighters and justice seekers who have fought to make it less so have been motivated by a radical love modeling a new way of existing even as they try to bring it into being. The writer and theorist bell hooks writes extensively about all forms of love in a trilogy of books devoted to the topic. In *All About Love*, she writes that "all great movements for social justice in our society have strongly emphasized a love ethic." She asserts, "a love ethic presupposes that everyone has the right to be free, to live fully and well." A love ethic differs from a sentimental, overly romanticized understanding of love. It is "an action, rather than a feeling." Love is a choice. Love requires us to see each other and to commit to each other's humanity.

In *The Fire Next Time*, James Baldwin writes: "I use the word love here not merely in the personal sense but as a state of being, a state of grace—not in the infantile American sense of being made happy but in the tough and universal sense of quest and daring and growth." Malcolm X offered Black people the tools to resist self-hatred, to see their beauty, to recognize themselves as worthy of love. Martin Luther King Jr. called on Black people and their white allies to extend that love to their enemies, to the whites who violently opposed them and embraced policies that caused great harm. We are in desperate need of both loves—the Black self-love that builds moral and spiritual strength and conviction, and the love ethic embodied by King, that allows us to see our enemies as children of God.

The philosopher David Kyuman Kim posits the need for a conception of radical love in our public life. For Kim, a politics of love requires us to "render solidarity with the distant sufferer." Philosopher Michael Hardt warns that a political concept of "love of those like yourself has destroyed the possibility of love as a more generous and positive political concept." Had Hardt considered African American intellectuals and writers like King and Baldwin, he might have found a way out of this conundrum. Baldwin's, King's, and other thinkers' sense of Black love does not lead to a narrow ethnocentrism or nationalism. For Baldwin, love of those like yourself, if they are the powerless, allows for an extension of compassion to the unloved, to the different, to the stranger.

A literary heir to Baldwin, Toni Morrison took up the mantle of exploring the possibility of love and the existence of lovelessness. While her entire oeuvre grapples with the meaning of love, it is in the sermons her characters preach that we find the most powerful invocations. In *Beloved*, Baby Suggs famously tells the former slaves gathered before her in the clearing: "Here, . . . in this place, we flesh, flesh that weeps, laughs; flesh that dances on bare feet in grass. Love it. Love it hard. Yonder they do not love your flesh. They despise it." Baby Suggs calls upon them to enact self-love, Black love, community love, as an act of affirming themselves in the face of racist brutality.

Morrison also writes two wedding sermons on love in her novel *Paradise*. Weddings represent a community's investment in the future. They are rituals of renewal. Bearing witness to a young couple's public commitment is an act of committing to them and to the perpetuation of the group. The wedding of a young couple, K.D. and Arnette, allows the community to recommit to shared values. It also provides the opportunity for conflicting sides, especially the feuding families of the bride and groom, to come together. It offers an occasion for the officiants to provide a vision for the future. Morrison also uses the wedding as a literary device, to present the inner thoughts and concerns of the gathered wedding guests, families, and members of the bridal party. But most important for our purposes, the wedding is a space for readers to contemplate two conflicting theological perspectives on Love.

One of the wedding sermons, offered by the guest minister, the Senior Reverend Pulliam, an older traditionalist preacher, proffers a distant and indifferent God, one who humans can never deserve or even truly approach. He tells the young couple:

> You do not deserve love regardless of the suffering you have endured. You do not deserve love because somebody did you wrong. You do not deserve love just because you want it. You can only earn—by practice and careful contemplation—the right to express it and you have to learn how to accept it. Which is to say you have to earn God. . . . Love is not a gift. It is a diploma. A diploma conferring certain privileges. . . . How do you know you have graduated? You don't. . . . God is not interested in you. He is interested in love and the bliss it brings to those who understand and share that interest.

Rev. Pulliam's version of love and God are almost inaccessible. One can work to earn them—indeed one should work to do so; but such work provides no guarantee of God's favor or grace. The reason is most circular. This abstract thing for which you must work is the only thing that God is interested in, and yet Rev. Pulliam provides no instruction, offers little comfort, provides no reason to have faith that one will ever experience love and therefore ever experience or know God.

Reverend Misner, the young progressive pastor, thinks to himself: "God loves the way humans loved one another; loved the way humans loved themselves." He is so enraged by Pulliam's interpretation of God, he cannot articulate his opposition. He holds the cross before the congregation as evidence of God's care, concern, indeed love for human beings. While holding the cross he thinks a silent sermon.

Though the sermon is silent, Morrison nonetheless devotes pages of language to Misner's thoughts, his theology, and to the meaning of the cross. As he walks away from the pulpit to the back of the church, as he unhooks the cross from its place on the wall, as he carries it "past the empty choir stall, past the organ" for the gathered guests to witness, he thinks:

See what was certainly the first sign any human any-
where had made: the vertical line; the horizontal one.
Even as children, they drew it with their fingers in snow,
sand or mud; they laid it down as sticks in dirt; arranged
it from bones on frozen tundra and broad savannas; as
pebbles on riverbanks; scratched it on cave walls and
outcroppings from Nome to South Africa. Algonquin
and Laplanders, Zulu and Druids—all had a finger memory of this original mark. The circle was not first, nor
was the parallel or the triangle. It was this mark, this,
that lay underneath every other. This mark, rendered in

the placement of facial features. This mark of a standing human figure poised to embrace.

Here Morrison makes the cross a symbol more ancient than the religion that has claimed it. In her rendering it is a universal symbol across time, space, populations and beliefs; it is a symbol that unites us as human beings. So much so, in fact, that we draw it as naturally and with as much ease as children worldwide say some version of "dada" or "mama" as their first word. As he holds the cross before the congregation, Morrison has Misner think:

> See? The execution of this one solitary black man propped up on these two intersecting lines to which he was attached in a parody of human embrace, fastened to two big sticks that were so convenient, so recognizable, so embedded in consciousness *as consciousness*, being both ordinary and sublime. . . . See how this official murder out of hundreds marked the difference; moved the relationship between God and man from CEO and supplicant to one on one? The cross he held was abstract; the absent body was real, but both combined to pull humans from backstage to the spotlight, from muttering in the wings to the principal role in the story of their lives. This execution made it possible to respect—freely, not in fear—one's self and one another. Which was what love was: unmotivated respect.

Misner makes the crucified body of Christ into the lynched body that scars Black American history, and in so doing makes both the sacrifice that guarantees the love of God. In his view, God's love is the given. This is the promise of the New Testament and of the crucifixion. In Misner's theology, Love is not abstract. Love is unmotivated respect. There is no mystery. The instruction is clear: "Love one another. As I have loved you, so you must love one another." All of this, Misner concludes, "testified not to a peevish Lord who was His own love but to one who enabled human love. Not for His own glory—never. God loved the way humans loved one another, loved the way humans loved themselves; loved the genius on the cross who managed to do both and die knowing it." Through the refrain of the word "See" throughout the silent sermon, the visual sense takes primacy over the aural. If in fact the cross is a primal symbol, if because of Christianity, the absented body is always signified, then looking at and meditating upon the cross and its meaning ought to bring an understanding of the primacy of God's love for humankind.

At the level of narration, Morrison elevates Misner's unspoken sermon above that of Pulliam's. Pulliam's words, contained within quotation marks, open the chapter. Five paragraphs in his voice. There is no language devoted to describing the scene or to describing him, or the tone or register of his voice: it is unadorned and unremarked upon. But because Misner's sermon is silent, there is almost a merging of his inner voice with that of the omniscient narrator. In this way it is what literary scholars know as "free indirect speech," a form of narration that blends first and third person, whereby the voices of the character and narrator almost become one. As such, Misner's words, while not spoken to the other characters in the novel, are presented with authorial authority to the reader. They appear to be the thoughts, the perspective of the all-knowing narrator as well as the young minister. Morrison devotes elevated language to Misner's thoughts, thereby making them even more powerful and meaningful. Misner cannot speak calmly, so he holds the cross before the gathered and wills them to know "that not only is God interested in you; He is you."

There are important implications in Misner's silent sermon for all people of faith and for those of us who are secular as well. Suppose what we call God is nothing more than a conception of human beings loving each other, treating each other with mutual respect? Suppose we create and live in something divine each time we act lovingly and respectfully toward each other? Suppose humans are the only vehicles and vessels of Grace and Love? This kind of love is the basis of justice. This love is the conduit of freedom. This love is power beyond wealth, greed, and physical might.

8

Joy and Something Like Self-Determination

But I cannot leave it at that; there is more to it than that. In spite of everything, there was in the life I fled a zest and a joy and a capacity for facing and surviving disaster that are very moving and very rare. Perhaps we were, all of us—pimps, whores, racketeers, church members and children—bound together by the nature of our oppression, the specific and peculiar complex of risks we had to run; if so, within these limits we sometimes achieved with each other a freedom that was close to love. I remember, anyway, church suppers and outings, and later, after I left the church, rent and waistline parties where rage and sorrow sat in the darkness and did not stir, and we ate and drank and talked and laughed and danced and forgot all about "the man." We had the liquor, the chicken, the music, and each other, and had no need to pretend to be what we were not.

James Baldwin, *The Fire Next Time*

In walked—Us.

Amiri Baraka, "In Walked Bud"

Here is a departure, a brief detour, from the world of books to the landscape of sound. For it was not only the written word that shaped and formed my understanding of the world around me. In fact, it was not even primarily books. Music, more than anything, helped to define us in ways that were life-giving. It, along with food, accompanied those daily rituals that made of us a people.

I grew up in a working-class and working-poor Black family, similar to others in my neighborhood, and the larger Black community in Philadelphia. Although known for its rich history and importance in the founding of the nation, Philadelphia is also a city of Black migrants who arrived from the South in large numbers, the first wave occurring between World War I and the Great Depression, followed by a larger one during World War II and 1970. Upon their arrival they encountered an older Black population, many of whom were the descendants of free Negroes, those who founded the Mother Bethel AME Church and harbored fugitive slaves. Many of the migrants, like the ones about whom W. E. B. Du Bois wrote in his book *The Philadelphia Negro*, lived in streets so small they were barely more than alleys. They became a Black working class, and they created their own extraordinary music culture—jazz, gospel, and R & B—in the midst of what became an oppressive police state for Black Americans. I came of age in this Philadelphia, when Frank Rizzo, despised by large numbers of Black Philadelphians, was mayor, when the Black Panthers held conventions and served free breakfasts, and when musicians and entrepreneurs were creating the Sound of Philadelphia.

Although I recall the power of the books I encountered, it was music that was ubiquitous in the Philadelphia of my youth. So all-encompassing was it that I took it for granted. It accompanied everything we did: household chores, family gatherings, sitting outside in the summertime, cookouts in the park. There were small radios tuned either to the jazz station, WRTI (which we just called Temple Station because it was owned by the University), or the Black radio station, WDAS. We didn't turn the music on, because it was always on. It was beloved and necessary; it shaped our sense of ourselves as individuals and as a people. Telling someone about the music you listened to identified you in certain ways. My Aunt Eartha liked blues, organ trios, and R & B. I first heard Wes Montgomery's breezy guitar at the home she shared with Mr. Sweets (a man I never came to call uncle). Aunt Eunice was the hippest of the three sisters. She always listened to the newest thing first. She listened to Monk, and went to Labelle's Afrofuturistic concerts decked out in silver-sequined minidresses. At her house everyone debated the shift in Miles's music with the album *Bitches Brew*, and analyzed the cover of his *On the Corner*, or discussed the conspiracy theories about the model on Ohio Players album covers. Daddy was the jazz head, a bebopper, former hoofer, the intellectual who'd given up dance during his brief stint with the Nation of Islam. He stopped dancing, but never gave up jazz. My mother liked whatever he liked, but after his early death she turned to the Gladys Knight of "Neither One of Us Wants to Be the First to Say Goodbye," because Gladys articulated her mournful yearning for her husband. My big sister Myra and my cousins Irvin and Leon (all three of whom were nineteen to twenty-one years older than me) listened to Motown, which everyone loved and was sure to get multiple generations on the dance floor. Another cousin, Wilber, between their generation and mine, turned us on to Earth, Wind & Fire. And we, all of us—aunts and uncles, sister and cousins, mother and father—were stunned when an elderly Cab Calloway, in white tuxedo, came on television, shook that straight hair, and Mama, our beautiful, soft-spoken, Georgia-born matriarch, said "Oh my, it's the Hi-De-Ho Man!" in a desire-filled voice that none of us had heard before.

Saturday mornings were for household chores; Aretha helped us through them. On Sunday mornings Louise Williams played old-time and contemporary gospel on WHAT, another Black-themed radio station. Mahalia Jackson, Clara Ward, and the Philadelphia-based Dixie Hummingbirds were favorites. It was church "getting ready" music for some; for others it took the place of going to church. Our music was our life, our world. And while each person had a preference, nothing was off limits. We listened to it all.

We loved the musicians and the singers and talked about them like they were family or neighbors, preachers or prophets. We loved them because they were ours and we were theirs and their music shaped us and we shaped it too. So, when my Motown-loving cousins started quoting Marvin Gaye's "What's Going On" or "Mercy, Mercy Me" like scripture, they seemed to grow a little more serious too.

Sometime in the early '70s, my family owned a restaurant. Well, we called it a restaurant; as a matter of fact, we called it The Restaurant, but it was really a luncheonette. Most of my family lived in South Philadelphia. My grandmother, my cousins, my sister Myra and her children all lived within walking distance of my childhood home. My two aunts who lived in Germantown and West Oak Lane made frequent, sometimes daily trips to South Philadelphia. My maternal grandmother, who took care of me while my mother worked, lived two blocks away from my paternal grandparents. My mother, her siblings, and their children, as well as my father, attended elementary and junior high school in South Philadelphia. I say all of this to emphasize that we were of this place.

And yet, the part of South Philadelphia where our restaurant was located felt like a new and different world to me. It wasn't far, a two- or three-minute walk from my grandmother's, but it was "Cross the Road," Grays Ferry Avenue, and it seemed like another land all together. There were no trees that I can remember, but there was a vacant lot where huge sunflowers grew wild. I swear, one day I saw tumbleweeds rolling down Grays Ferry Avenue. I know now they couldn't have been tumbleweeds because I have since learned they don't grow in southeast Pennsylvania. But there was something dry, and big, and round, that rolled down the middle of the avenue on that wind-filled day, adding to the Wild West atmosphere of the area of South Philadelphia. Nearby, looming large, there were the gray, smoking tanks of an oil refinery, which gave the whole area an ominous feeling, not unlike the smoldering "valley of ashes" in Fitzgerald's *Great Gatsby*. There were small row houses in back of Grays Ferry, and the families who lived there had backyard vegetable gardens. On occasion, you might hear, but not see, a rooster. It was a Black community situated not far from a fairly hostile white one, and yet I can barely remember seeing a white person, except for two. The first was an older, seemingly wealthy woman who sometimes came to the bar next to the restaurant to visit her lover, the bar's owner. The second was a Jewish proprietor of a store that sold everything from cold cuts to inexpensive stockings in my mother's favorite shade, "Puff of Smoke." I remember him distinctly because he was a Holocaust survivor with a tattooed number on his forearm. I recall hearing him tell militant young Black men, "My people were slaves too." There had to have been police, but I have no memory of seeing them, though they were ever-present in other parts of South Philly.

Our restaurant had a Formica counter, red stools with spinning seats, an old-fashioned cash register, and a jukebox. The first time we went to clean it and prepare it for opening, there were already 45s in the jukebox. They were of another era. Chuck Jackson's "Any Day Now" (1962) and Bobbie Lewis's "Tossin' and Turnin'" (1961) stand out. Today I still remember the lyrics to many songs that were popular before my birth because I heard them in the restaurant. "That was on the jukebox," I often say when I hear them now, as I am taken back immediately to that space. My mother, aunts, and cousins gave me dimes so I could play those old songs when the restaurant wasn't full of customers who had their own favorites. It seems the other person who played the old songs was one of the men who lived in the boarding house upstairs from the restaurant. We also kept the jukebox stocked with the latest records—Jean Knight's "Mr. Big Stuff," Betty Wright's "The Clean Up Woman," The Impressions' "I'm So Proud," the O'Jays' "Love Train," Sly and the Family Stone's "Family Affair," and all of James Brown and Aretha Franklin. Even in that small, tight space, sometimes folks danced. Irvin, charismatic and working as a bartender next door, managed the restaurant and employed my mother, my grandmother, and one aunt. He would come in the door of the restaurant already dancing, flashing a million-dollar smile, and brightening our days. The music, like the space, was distinctly Black. It was mostly funky. It was often beautiful. The Dramatics' "I Wanna Go Outside in the Rain" was a favorite of one of the men who'd fallen in love with my unavailable mother. He'd play it when he came in, and sometimes, for effect, when it was raining, he'd stand outside and serenade her. A family friend, he at one time or another fell in love with each of my grandmother's daughters, in the order of their birth.

The music was as much a part of the ethos as the smell of burgers, fries, cheesesteaks, and fried chicken wings, which we served in wax paper–lined red-and-white paper baskets with white bread and hot sauce. My grandmother insisted we begin to serve breakfast sandwiches (egg and cheese on a buttered, toasted kaiser roll) because too many of the young schoolchildren came in before school, to purchase Now & Laters and other artificially colored sugar-filled products. Mama asserted, "Those babies are hungry." She behaved as if the marketing of neon sugar was a form of genocide. She probably gave away more food than we sold, much to my cousin's chagrin. But when word got out that we were serving breakfast, the hard-working men who were employed in nearby factories started to come for a cup of coffee, two eggs over easy, home fries, and conversation with one of the pretty ladies who served them.

Music sparked conversation and debate. On Tammi Terrell and Marvin Gaye: "Well you know Marvin ain't been right since Tammi died," they knowingly said. Though she died of a brain tumor, you couldn't convince them that her early death had not been initiated by David Ruffin's alleged abuse of her.

After Stevie Wonder's near-fatal car accident, his music took on a more spiritual turn, which prompted conversations about spirituality and religion, death and near death. The jukebox had his hits like "Signed, Sealed, Delivered," "For Once in My Life," "Superstition," and "You Are the Sunshine of My Life." But after the 1973 car accident, he, as a figure and an artist, took on an even deeper meaning. Many of the discussions suggested he wouldn't survive because he had already given us the deeply evocative *Innervisions*, which yielded: "Higher Ground," "Living for the

City," and "Golden Lady." Folk thought that may have been the last statement and the highest achievement of his genius. "Think about Trane," they said.

Our people came face to face with death on a regular basis, and among everyone who came into the restaurant it was a given that this life wasn't all there was. There was something after it. And if you faced Death and looked it down, you had to do something with the gift of time that was given to you. Stevie survived and came back to us to bear witness: "The only thing I know," he said, "is that I was unconscious, and that for a few days, I was definitely in a much better spiritual place that made me aware of a lot of things that concern my life and my future, and what I have to do to reach another higher ground." He later said, "What happened to me was a very, very critical thing, and I was really supposed to die." My father had said something similar following his first stroke in 1969. He recalled asking for two more years so he could "teach my baby." He got them and he did. So hearing this from Stevie and having the adults around me take it seriously as a cherished spiritual gift, I never saw cause to doubt it. The first album following the accident was *Fulfillingness' First Finale* (1974).

If Stevie's music took on a more spiritual bent, it also became more political. He was not the only one. When I think of music of that period, I also think of some of the most beautiful and political statements made by Black culture, music that both challenged and protested the condition of the world, but that also affirmed Black people. While there are those who debate the relationship between art and politics, between art for art's sake and propaganda, the most brilliant Black artists have shown that the dichotomy is a false one. As Toni Morrison said of her own art: "It has to be both beautiful and political."

Marvin Gaye's *What's Going On* proves it. When that album came out and we put selections from it on the jukebox, folks stopped, listened, and analyzed the lyrics. They talked about our involvement in Vietnam and the logic of young Black men fighting for a country that refused to recognize the value of their lives. Recall that the album opens with a moment of Black sociality. Even before launching into the lyrics, there are Black voices talking, almost like a group of brothers greeting each other on the street, happy to see each other, to be in each other's company. Following this exchange, Marvin's beautiful tenor enters with "Mother, Mother." "Mercy, Mercy Me" was also on our jukebox. I think this song stood out to me then as it does now for the capaciousness of its concerns with the environment, a song that suggested that it was not only Black people who were in peril, but the very planet upon which we lived. And it seemed to me that it issued a call that required our response. I remember begging my mother to get rid of aerosol cans. If only we got rid of ours, we would preserve a bit of the ozone layer!

The music marked this time of transition, not only in the nature of the lyrics or in the innovations in style, but also in the format. Although I often think of jazz in terms of albums and not singles, that had not been the case with Black popular music. The jukebox carried singles, but during this period, I heard more talk of albums than singles. People listened to the entire work, and discussed it as a whole. And while an album might yield a hit single, albums took on a feeling of importance and profundity. Stevie and Marvin gave us long-form works to discuss and debate. Listening to the albums together was an intimate, mind-expanding experience. The political nature of the songs and albums, especially those by Curtis Mayfield and Marvin Gaye, also echoed the sense of Black self-determination that informed the times. When I hear this music, I remember our history, laughter and love, food and dancing. My cousin Little Irvin (son of the restaurant's owner) and I knew even then that the adults around us were trying to build something for our futures: something that was ours, that belonged to us. When I think of this place, I think (and feel) *joy*: a joy made possible by unbreakable family ties, by a sense of community, a grounding in the music and food, all products of love. And these were made possible by and helped to make possible a sense of self-definition, a sense of autonomy, and perhaps, a quest for self-determination.

We knew our restaurant was a part of Black economic self-determination: a family-owned establishment, employing family, who in turn made possible its ownership. It was a business but it was also the center of our family and social life. It was a source of pride and self-definition. Later when I encountered Zora Neale Hurston's Eatonville in her autobiography *Dust Tracks on the Road*, or Morrison's fictional Ruby in *Paradise*, I recognized the impulse toward autonomy. One need not romanticize these places to recognize their value and significance. In fact, they are the sites where we gained a full understanding of our deeply flawed humanity. When whites are no longer the primary focus, one can see the contours of conflict, debate, and difference from within the Black community. The music gives voice to it all.

Around this time, folk began to talk about a new sound and set of artists in which they took special pride because they were based in Philly. Kenneth Gamble and Leon Huff founded Philadelphia International Records in 1971. Their studios were located on South Broad Street. Interestingly, though there was a roster of highly talented artists, I don't think any of them ever rose to the status that Stevie, Marvin, Aretha, or Curtis Mayfield had for the restaurant's customers. But that sound, those lush arrangements and soulful vocals, poured forth from car radios, home stereos, barbershops, beauty parlors, and for a while, our jukebox: The Delfonics, the O'Jays, Phyllis Hyman, Jean Carne, McFadden and Whitehead, Billy Paul, and of course, Harold Melvin & the Blue Notes and their breakout lead singer, the sexy and soulful Teddy Pendergrass. Oh, how the women loved Teddy. And because of him, the men, especially the dark-skinned ones, like my cousin Irvin, discovered just how good they looked in all white. The founding of this Black-owned record label and the music that came out of those studios was another symbol of Black economic independence and self-determination.

In Philadelphia during the early seventies there were also Black folk (including some from the neighborhood) running for state representative and city council. Hell, even the underground economy took on an air of Black self-determination. Young men sorely lacking employment opportunities engaged in illegal activities overseen by the newly constituted "Black Mafia." Restaurant folk spoke about the "Black Mafia" in hushed tones filled with fear and trepidation, but also a little admiration, because it had taken over enterprises formerly run by the Italian Mafia. In the restaurant it was spoken of in terms that gestured toward self-determination even as the intimidation, violence, and influx of drugs were a source of despair. I would be lying if I said some members of the Black Mafia didn't frequent the restaurant. They did, and they were respectful because they'd grown up with my cousins, and some of them even called my grandmother "Mama." Yes, drugs were rampant and some of my family members fell victim to them. But we all—gangsters and factory workers, politicians and entrepreneurs, Christians and Muslims—we all listened to and danced to and argued about and discussed the same music, while eating chicken and cheesesteaks—and, if my aunt felt like cooking on the weekend, ribs and chitlins too, although a bunch of folk didn't touch that "swine."

We were a people.

Through the door of that restaurant, in walked us.

I don't recall when or why our restaurant closed. It was after my father's death, after I left my neighborhood school for the magnet school. Perhaps it was around 1974. My cousin removed the records from the jukebox, put them in crates, and brought them to his home. Music continued to be central to our lives, but we never had the same sense of place or purpose that the restaurant had given us. We still gathered as a family; we convened in moments of crisis and celebration and everything in between. But that collective sense of building something for the future, as a family, disappeared. The way I experienced music changed as well. Instead of the jukebox, the radio became my primary way of listening, often alone and later, as a teen, with my peers. The Quiet Storm radio format mirrored the sense of interiority I rediscovered late at night, quietly listening to the radio. At that time, in addition to my ongoing love for Billie Holiday, I also became especially drawn to vocalists like Syreeta Wright, Minnie Riperton, and Deniece Williams. Significantly, all three, at different times, had been members of Stevie Wonder's backup group, Wonderlove. Riperton and Williams were coloratura sopranos. To me all three singers represented a kind of quiet, bohemian Black femininity to which I aspired. Feminine and flirtatious, their voices were also sensual and spiritual, distinctively grounded in Black musical traditions. Diana Ross's solo recordings, especially "Touch Me in the Morning" and "Do You Know Where You're Going To?," fall within this category of female vocals, though those tunes are more pop-oriented than the music of Wright, Riperton, and Williams. (Later, I purchased a secondhand copy of Betty Carter's debut album, *Out There with Betty Carter* [1958], at a thrift store, and I played it every day after school, memorizing the lyrics to each tune, as I transitioned to homework time.) These voices are the voices that I most associate with that period in my life.

Wright, Williams, and Riperton cleared a pathway for neo-soul artists like Erykah Badu, Philly's own Jill Scott, and later, singers like Solange and Chloe and Halle Bailey (Chloe x Halle). It seems Wright, Riperton, and Williams emerged at a time after the demise of the militant Black politics of the late sixties and early seventies and before the rise of disco and later, rap. It was an interstitial space, a space of protection and respite before the emergence of a new way of being.

Interestingly, during the COVID-19 pandemic, but before the global uprising for Black Lives, when the nation's leaders belatedly issued stay-at-home orders, and Americans joined people around the world sheltering in, the power of music to gather and heal us became evident once again. Ways of experiencing the music as both community and solitary individuals seemed to merge. In March 2020, DJ D-Nice (Derrick Jones) began spinning records on Instagram Live while quarantined in Los Angeles. On Saturday, March 21, over 100,000 people from around the world logged on to his nine-hour virtual dance party. Many were well-known celebrities, but most were just ordinary people drawn by the music and the need to connect with others. He played fifty years of Black music. Viewer-listeners sang and danced alone in their homes, together with thousands of others. Even this early in the pandemic, there had already been tremendous loss of life. The music helped to lessen the grief, providing a space of mourning that was also a celebration of resilience and community that reached out to others. The medium was no longer the jukebox or FM radio, but the result was much the same—a balm in difficult times, a space of joy and exuberance in the face of loss and uncertainty.

The virtual dance party was but one offering in the time of mass death. Grammy-winning producers Swizz Beatz and Timbaland began hosting a series of competitions, the Verzuz Battles, where music stars, producers, songwriters, and artists met in pairs to play from their repertoire of hits. Among the quarantined artists to stream from their homes on Instagram Live were Kenneth "Babyface" Edmonds and Teddy Riley, and Ludacris and Nelly. The Saturday evening in May that vocalist-songwriters Erykah Badu and Jill Scott shared their music transcended any notion of battle and redefined what was possible. Over 700,000 people joined. Audience members commented in real time on Instagram and Twitter. Scott and Badu came together not in a spirit of competition but instead of mutual admiration and appreciation. They shared stories of how they met, moments when one of them had enabled the career or performance of the other, and when Badu dropped out due to technical difficulties, Scott played one of her hits, "Tyrone." Because of the nature of neo-soul as a genre, the music was steeped in a sense of Black cultural history and an intention of celebrating and healing Black lives. It brought both a sense of nostalgia for the time in which it was produced, and evidence of its timelessness. It showcased the virtuosic vocal and songwriting genius of these two women. Jill Scott noted:

> People thought Erykah and I were enemies, which was never the case. . . . That's why I was initially dead-set against doing a Verzuz: "A battle? No." I like when women sing together for the sake of harmony, a fusion of sound. Two birds going at each other never sounds good. I don't want to try to tear anybody apart or have anybody

try to tear me apart. Erykah called me, and I said, "If we celebrate each other, honor each other, it will work." And we did it.

By evening's end, everyone who tuned in had to agree that the winner was "the culture," and those of us who participate in and are nurtured, healed, and transformed by it.

= 9 =

Cultivating Beauty

But through all of that and more, my mother tried to make
a small path through the wake. She brought beauty into that
house in every way that she could; she worked at joy, and she
made livable moments, spaces, and places in the midst of all that
was unlivable there, in the town we lived in; in the schools we
attended; in the violence we saw and felt inside the home while
my father was living and outside it in the larger white world
before, during, and after his death. In other words, even as we
experienced, recognized, and lived subjection, we did not *simply*
or *only* live *in* subjection and *as* the subjected.

                                        Christina Sharpe, *In the Wake*

And learn all the beautiful things around you, trees and birds.
And if there ain't no beauty, you got to make some beauty.

                                Earth, Wind & Fire, "All about Love"

S ometime in the summer of 2012 I encountered, for the first
time, Romare Bearden's collage *The Dressmaker (Mecklen-
burg Autumn, China Lamp)* (1983), at the Newark Museum,

where it was part of the exhibition "Romare Bearden: Southern Recollections." While my response to works of art is often emotional, I don't recall ever being as overwhelmed by the rush of feeling and memory that I experienced that day. I stood before it, drawn in by the shapes, the colors, and most importantly, by the subject matter. I made two more trips to the museum, just to be in its presence. As I sought information about it, I discovered another Bearden work, *Autumn of the Red Hat*, which also features a dressmaker and model or client.

These two works have much in common with many of Bearden's other collages that portray women: a nude younger woman stands, bathes, or dresses in the presence of a protective older one. In other works of this period, Bearden features Black women gardeners, conjurers, and quilters. In *The Dressmaker*, the color, the fabric, the curl of the tape measure echo the highlight that curls, vine-like, down the nude woman's back, behind, and legs. The seamstress, like the gardener and quilter, is an artist, a maker of beauty, a creator. They are all like the conjure woman in that they make something from nothing, they make magic, they make worlds. In *The Dressmaker*, the seamstress is an otherworldly figure. She is much larger than the nude woman. She is blue, not just her dress but the color of her arms, hand, and head. She is painted in profile, flattened, like the figures on Egyptian tombs. Is she a spirit, a priestess, a goddess? She is engaged in the act of transformation. The cloudlike circular shapes on her dress may seem to move like the wind. Perhaps they are energies, transferred to the smaller Black model, who reaches up and gestures toward the lamp, reaching for the light. She is about to put the garment on; the garment may constitute her transformation. And the dressmaker's gesture seems to be a soft nudge to the other side, through the light.

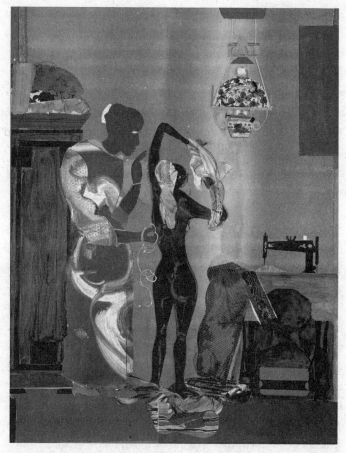

Romare Bearden, *The Dressmaker*. Private collection. Image courtesy of Michael Rosenfeld Gallery LLC, New York, NY. Art © 2021 Romare Bearden Foundation. Licensed by VAGA at Artists Rights Society (ARS), NY.

In *Autumn of the Red Hat*, the billowing tape measure gestures down to and echoes the broken guitar strap on the floor. By this means, Bearden brings the seamstress's tool together with the musical instrument, and the woman's work with that of the blues musician. Bearden admired and respected the artistry of musicians and portrayed them in a number of works. Critics have noted the importance of Black Southern women's quilts for Bearden's work as well. The seamstress and her craft belong with that of the musician, the gardener, and the quilter as subject and source of inspiration for him. Mary Schmidt Campbell notes that when Bearden married the elegant model, dancer, and choreographer Nanette Rohan, she "brought a new ethos into his life. . . . She often made her own clothes. Fabrics and patterns filled [their] Canal Street loft . . . and all became visual fodder for her husband."

In both *The Dressmaker* and *Autumn of the Red Hat*, I am drawn to the sewing machine. It is the first thing that catches my eye. Like the trains that are ubiquitous in Bearden's oeuvre, the sewing machine itself (not the cabinet) is Black and rectangular. As geometric form and color, Bearden's trains and sewing machines are functional objects of beauty, as significant for their design as their function. And both are almost placed in the background; they never take center stage, but they are central to the stories he seeks and invites us to create. I enter these images through the sewing machine and the other tools of the dressmaker's craft.

I am the daughter, granddaughter, and great-niece of seamstresses. Both my mother and grandmother had sewing machines, Singers, like the one depicted here. Among my earliest memories are sitting under or next to the machine as my mother sewed.

The quiet buzz of her sewing machine is barely audible over the sound of Miles, Marvin, or Earth, Wind & Fire. My mother prefers to sew after midnight: after the dishes have been washed and the kitchen straightened up, after I have bathed and gone to bed, after the noise of the day has quieted. By morning's light, she will have solved a puzzle, pushed past a momentary challenge, and she will have created something beautiful. She is meticulous: a finished seam, pressed flat with the iron, a collar stiffened just right, a yoke, a dart. She attends to every detail, even if it means ripping it all out and starting over. If I awaken, I come down the narrow, dark staircase to find her sitting at the shiny black Singer sewing machine with gold lettering. Our cat, a jet-black, green-eyed beauty named Velvet, is reclining at her feet. My mother is humming, and she seems—happy.

As a girl, I spent hours in bookstores with my father; hours more in fabric stores with my mother. Bolts of material were unwrapped and unfurled, measured by the yard, cherished for their color and texture. I early on learned the differences between designs and fabrics: tweed, houndstooth, gingham, paisley, and madras; wool, silk, cotton, crepe de chine, and chiffon. Notions, buttons, trimmings, spools of thread—these were the items that actually distinguished a sewer's garment. Buttons can change the whole story a piece tells. Buttons can be elegant or tacky. They can communicate military brass and strength, or delicate, ladylike refinement. Buttons are in and of themselves objects of beauty and delight. My hands grew especially adept at removing the cherished buttons from old garments, to be saved and used again. Some were treated as heirlooms: "That button I used on your coat comes from the camel hair wool jacket my Daddy bought for Mama in New York." The red wool swing coat closed with a single, large, statement-making black button just beneath the collar. It is one of many coats my mother made for me. It conjures images of a romantic past, of my grandmother—Mama (whose given name was Willie Lee, but called Billie by her oldest friends)—as she appears in sepia-tinted photos.

I grew up with the lore and language of dressmakers. When having a dress fitted, put your thumb in your mouth so you don't get stuck with a pin. A string or stray piece of thread on your clothing is a sign of money. My mother unknowingly introduced me to metaphor by describing natural phenomena in fashion terms. Trying to distract me from the cold as we walked to Mama's home, she would take me through a neighborhood park, point out the snow-covered trees, and say, "Look at how Mother Nature dresses her daughters in beautiful white fur coats. Some of them even have diamond jewelry." Together we'd count all the icicle "diamonds" we spotted until reaching my grandmother's, where warmth and good food awaited us. I was imbued with appreciation for the seamstress's art, though I had absolutely no desire to practice it. Reading and writing brought me the same delight sewing brought my mother.

My mother, through her sewing, engaged in the art of transformation. She transformed not only the fabric, but those of us who wore her clothing. She gave us confidence: "Mena made this for me" was a statement of pride. Translated, it meant, "Mena loves me."

My mother is self-taught. She often worked in garment factories. My grandmother sewed, but she was better known for her needlework: embroidery, needlepoint, and crochet. Some of my fondest memories are of my grandmother purchasing the equipment and teaching me how to embroider. And one of my favorite outfits was a slate-blue vest and skirt she crocheted for me when I started school. My great-aunt, my grandmother's baby sister Fannie, went to school for formal training. She drafted her own patterns and sewed for wealthy white women. In the home she shared with my great-grandmother, Lula, she had a pedestal where her clients stood before a three-way mirror and she clipped and pinned some loose fabric that would become a dress.

She had one of those headless dressmaker's mannequins, which thrilled and mystified me. The family proudly boasted that Aunt Fannie did alterations for Sophy Curson, an exclusive women's clothing store that still sits on Nineteenth Street, just a block away from ritzy Rittenhouse Square in Philadelphia.

In contrast, my mother worked in Philly's many garment factories. Philadelphia was a center of manufacturing, and she had no trouble finding work. "I used to quit a job on one floor, go downstairs and find another one in the same afternoon." She made everything from bras to men's ties. And in the eighties, just before the last of the good factory jobs went overseas, she made Adidas bathing suits as well as swimsuits for the United States Olympic Swimming team.

Though she found steady employment, she hated factory work. So, she often left it when other opportunities arose: She waitressed in our family's restaurant. She sought job training through a government program created by the Comprehensive Employment and Training Act (CETA). Unfortunately, Ronald Reagan cut funding for the program. She took in clothes at a dry cleaners owned by Italian mobsters who so loved my mother and grandmother, according to family lore, that they eventually gave each of them their own cleaners. In fact, these were storefronts where my mother and grandmother took in clothes and had them sent out to larger cleaning establishments. They also did small alterations for the cleaners' customers—fixing a fallen hem, replacing a button, adding cuffs to trousers—for which they were rewarded nicely with tips, boxes of candy, and Christmas cash that came in plain envelopes. I never met the gangsters, but they loomed large in the tales my mother told. I did know my mother's Italian clients, especially my favorite, Mrs. Rizzo.

Even when she worked in garment factories, in the evenings

my mother sewed for family, neighbors, and friends. Though she hated doing alterations, she did them because they were lucrative. She often did them for Mrs. Rizzo, or better yet, Mrs. Rizzo's teen daughters. Mrs. Rizzo owned a corner store with her husband, a friendly man with a round belly. They were a kind couple who served generous portions of ice cream and, unlike other white store owners in the neighborhood, didn't seem to hold their predominantly Black clientele in contempt. In the summer, my mother made dresses or altered garments for the Rizzo girls, outfits that they took with them to their summer vacations at the Jersey Shore. These were most often sundresses made of printed cotton. Some were more like caftans or muumuus and had larger floral designs. During the holiday season Mrs. Rizzo had my mother work on garments for various formal functions. When we delivered those, freshly pressed and neatly wrapped, Mrs. Rizzo would invite us upstairs to the family's living quarters on top of the store. There she had a Christmas display almost as dazzling as that of Wanamaker's Department Store.

Other women came to my mother to have dresses made, or taken in or out, and to talk. Those fittings passed on whispered gossip, laughter, stories of troubled children, men loved and left, stories of "going back home" told with soft Southern accents, or of sending children there for the summer. I loved hearing these stories, these conversations; the texture and tone of the voices, the grown woman troubles they discussed, the depth of their laughter all filled my ears and created a landscape of imagination.

These people brought in much needed extra income, but truthfully, my mother preferred sewing for her family. Her home was her sanctuary, and she didn't like to have "just anybody" in it. People brought all kinds of energy, some of which unnerved the quietude she tried so hard to cultivate. Not so with her family, her sisters, daughters, and mother. They brought joy. Sewing for them was the project that found her working from midnight to daybreak, the time flying by. She could make clothing for the women she loved without even fitting them. One of my aunts was feeling down because she put on a little weight; don't worry, Mena reassured her, and sewed something flattering that made her feel beautiful. Another lost the use of her right arm following a stroke; it just hung there, dangling and useless. My mother continued to make her dresses, and always crafted a beautiful sling of silk or chiffon that complemented the outfit. What had been a disability became a style statement. When my sister was overwhelmed by her four small children, my mother grew concerned over what she thought was Myra's descent into dowdiness. So, she made a few minidresses for her. "She's got the long legs for them." Later, she affectionately expressed dismay for having done so: "I put that girl in short dresses, and now I can't get her out of them!" My sister preferred the mini long after they'd disappeared from the pages of the pattern catalogues. They signified a kind of youth, vitality, and freedom that she longed for and that she came to embody.

Like the women in her life, our home was the beneficiary of my mother's skills and talents. She reupholstered chairs, refinished secondhand furniture, and applied new coats of paint and wallpapered rooms on a rotating basis, and she made curtains and draperies for our windows and changed them seasonally.

Creating beautiful things for the people and spaces she cherished was a process that brought my mother focus and concentration. Listening to Miles, she created a rhythm, a meditative state that set her flowing. This was even more the case after my father's death, when she turned to her sewing more and more, though she took in fewer clients. In those first days when, finally, she emerged from a period of formal mourning ("Baby, it's time to come out of that black," her sisters tenderly whispered to her), my mother entered into a new phase of her life. I witnessed her blossoming. I watched as she stepped more fully into the person she had always been. At forty-five she was a widow and the mother of one girl on the threshold of adolescence and the other a young mother. She embraced both of these roles. But she was also a homeowner, a still youthful-looking grandmother of four. She was resourceful and intelligent. The small resources provided by my father's life insurance, social security, and veteran's benefits provided a modicum of financial security. She didn't have to work for our survival, which meant she didn't have to put up with exploitative factory conditions, including foremen who sexually harassed workers, and mean-spirited floor ladies. She could work in our family's restaurant if she liked. She could set her own hours so as to be at home when I returned from school. She'd always painted and wallpapered our home, but to these skills she added basic household chores and repairs: replacing a washer, caulking a tub, changing a fuse, replacing a windowpane, and, before we switched to gas heat, banking a fire in the coal furnace. Finally, she was free from the stress, the secrecy and responsibility of managing my father's addiction. She had no desire or intention of ever getting married again. In this way, she was like Zora Neale Hurston's Janie, of *Their Eyes Were Watching God*, who after the death of her husband, Jody Starks, emphatically tells her friend Pheoby, "Tain't dat ah worries over Joe's death, Pheoby. Ah jus' loves dis freedom."

She made the occasional prom gown and bridesmaid's dress, but she took on those jobs because she welcomed the challenge, and enjoyed the opportunity to be creative, not because she needed to do it. Occasionally when times got a little rough, she'd find factory work again; she refused welfare, Medicaid, or food stamps. (In this way, she was both prideful and conservative. She felt these were good, temporary solutions, but not to be relied upon if work was available.)

When I think of these years, I think of the beautiful space she created for us: the sound of Miles, shades of blue (her favorite color), and the scent of lavender. We turned inward. We prioritized my education and the conditions necessary for me to be successful. "My job is to take care of you; your job is to do well in school." In fact, we took care of each other. Like many children who have lost one parent, I became especially attentive to my mother's every breath, and desirous of her happiness. Which is why I loved hearing the buzz of that sewing machine in the wee hours of the morning, which is why I worked hard to bring her the A's she so craved of me. Our connection grew even deeper, and we cultivated a sensibility of me and you against the world.

Watching her pin a pattern on fabric that she would then cut and sew, I learned that the care given to your work brought a blissful solitude and satisfaction. Notebooks, stationery, and writing pens brought me the same pleasure that fabric and notions brought her. Writing and reading brought me that quiet high that seemed to engulf her as she sewed. Eventually my grandmother came to live with us, and we became an intergenerational household of women, a household that was quiet, beautiful, and filled with maternal love.

At the beginning of the fall of 1972 following my father's death in March, I began attending a magnet school, the Julia Reynolds Masterman Laboratory and Demonstration School, on Seventeenth and Spring Garden Avenue. Masterman is still considered the city's best public school; it was housed in an elegant neoclassical building where students from neighborhoods throughout Philadelphia were taught by an interracial group of deeply devoted and brilliant teachers. I awoke each morning, ate breakfast, walked to the bus stop accompanied by my mother, said goodbye to her, and then boarded the first of two buses to school. Dressed in an outfit she made for me, I sat under the watchful eyes of women I thought of as the "bus mothers." I read, at first, my father's books—a paperback about the Panthers was my favorite—and eventually my own books. Looking up from the window, I watched as my familiar neighborhood disappeared and there emerged another, cleaner and greener one, then the business district of Center City, followed by another stretch of green and stately high-rises and brownstones I later learned were in federalist style.

At one bus stop, just past the statue of Rodin's *Thinker*, on Philadelphia's Benjamin Franklin Parkway, a light-skinned Black woman sometimes boarded the bus. We got off at the same stop and caught the same connecting bus. One day, we talked, and she asked what I was reading. I was wary of strangers, but told her. I learned that her name was Mrs. Aurelia Waters and she was a history teacher at Masterman. Made curious by my manner, my reading, and yes, my clothing, Mrs. Waters soon inquired about my mother, and she eventually visited our home, and quickly became my guide and my mentor. She was one of those activist Black teachers who always expressed concern over all children, whether they were her students or not. She joined my mother as one of my greatest advocates through the public-school system.

Sometime during my Masterman years, over summer break, I first read Toni Morrison's *Sula*. I think I was thirteen years old. The girls on my block spent summer afternoons braiding hair, jumping rope, and exchanging books. We read Richard Wright's *Black Boy*, Nathan Heard's *Howard Street*, Jacqueline

Susann's *Valley of the Dolls*, anything by Iceberg Slim, and *Sula*. We shared a paperback of the novel. I distinctly recall the cover with its painting of a pretty brown woman—her hair in a soft Afro—seated, bent knee, her chin resting on top of one hand,

Cover art for the 1975 paperback of Toni Morrison's *Sula*. *All Rights Reserved.*
Roger K. Kastel. Photograph by Nivea Castro.

the other hand placed across her thigh. On top of her image the book's designer has placed a single yellow rose, with a few loosened petals floating around her form. As girls, we knew *Black Boy* was IMPORTANT—some of the older kids had read it in school. Iceberg Slim and Jacqueline Susann we read for the sex. *Howard Street* was the entryway to *Manchild in the Promised Land*: both mirrored the worst of our reality. But *Sula* . . . *Sula* changed my life. Toni Morrison wasn't my first Black woman writer. Lorraine Hansberry and Nikki Giovanni preceded her. In fact, because of *The Black Woman*, I'd read Toni Cade (she was not yet Bambara), as well as Sherley Anne Williams, Alice Walker, and others before that first encounter with Morrison. But *Sula* felt like the beginning of a new knowing. Here was a world in some ways familiar and in other ways completely different from the one I knew. Here was a language that sounded like the language the women around me spoke, but presented in a way so that I heard its imagery, its beauty, its rhythm. This was the beginning of the written word entering into my consciousness in the way that others imbibed the words of the Bible. From here on, more than any scribe of the Old or New Testament, Morrison would inform my understanding of my family, my history, and the nation that I called home. She would also shape my voice, my juvenile attempts to use language to describe the world around me.

After learning that her grandmother, the woman who raised her, is dying, the beautiful but imperious Helene Wright prepares to travel from the fictional Medallion, Ohio, to New Orleans in the Jim Crow South, to say her final goodbye. As part of her preparation, she takes to her sewing machine:

> Helene thought about the trip South with heavy misgiving but decided that she had the best protection:

her manner and her bearing, to which she would add a
beautiful dress. She bought some deep-brown wool and
three-fourths of a yard of matching velvet. Out of this
she made herself a heavy but elegant dress with velvet
collar and pockets.

Helene creates a garment as armor. Along with her dignified
bearing, her dress is both an assertion and protection: "I am a
woman of dignity and purpose," it seeks to communicate. And
its refinement brings confidence. I felt a kinship with her daughter
Nel, who attentively watched her mother cut the pattern and
then sew far into the night.

Unfortunately, Nel also bears witness to her mother's humiliation.
The dignified bearing and beautiful dress, the respectability,
do not protect her from the indignities of racism. The train
conductor berates her, saying she ought to have gotten on the
Jim Crow Car instead of walking through the one reserved for
Whites. When she needs to relieve herself, she must do so in the
bushes because there are no bathrooms for Blacks on the train,
or at the rest stop. By the time the train reaches New Orleans,
neither her light skin, which elsewhere guarantees a modicum of
privilege, nor her dress, nor her sophistication have armored her
against such debasement.

Fortunately, I was spared ever having to see my mother
humiliated before whites. We encountered people of other races
and cultures often, living on the borderline between Black and
Italian South Philadelphia. Shop owners were Jewish, Italian,
and eventually Vietnamese. However physical proximity did not
bring familiarity. Except on very rare occasions, we did not visit
each other's homes, and for the most part, we engaged each other
with cordial distance. (This would change when I attended high

school, where for the first time I made lifelong friendships with classmates of all races.) I understood Helene's impulse to put the respectable version or image of herself forward. I was raised not to be a stereotype or an embarrassment to Black people. "Get to school early because white people say we are always late." "Speak proper English." "Get A's because they have low expectations of us." "Do not let them give you a nickname; they are to call you by your given name." And, most importantly, "Do not tell white people our business." "They" were not a dominant physical presence, but what "they" thought of us informed our encounters with "them." A certain way of acting and presenting oneself was indeed a kind of armor.

However, the beauty my mother cultivated was not for the white world. It was to nurture, sustain, and please us. Less armor, it was a respite, a kind of sanctuary, a source of identity, creativity, and pleasure. We lived in a complex, challenging world that did not center whites—they were a marginal, if ultimately powerful, presence.

This is the world of Morrison's novels as well—not the constant confrontation with brutal racism that one finds in *Black Boy*, nor the unrelenting life of *Howard Street*. The Bottom, the neighborhood where Sula and Nel reside, is full of fascinating characters, drama, humor, tragedy, and a multitude of beauty.

Helene Wright is conventionally beautiful, respectable, and Creole. She so cherishes the dominant standards of beauty that she forces Nel to sleep with a clothespin on her nose. Hannah Peace, Sula's mother, is gorgeous, generous, sensual, and sexually free. Where Helene is perfectly girdled and armed in heavy wool and velvet, Morrison tells us of Hannah, "without ever a pat of the hair, a rush to change clothes or a quick application of paint, with no gesture whatsoever, she rippled with sex. . . . [S]he made men aware of her behind, her slim ankles, the dew-smooth skin and the incredible length of neck." Morrison's description of Hannah's sensual allurement never mentions the color of her skin or the texture of her hair. She calls our attention instead to the grace of her movement, the proportion of her limbs, the smoothness of her skin. Morrison allows her readers to imagine Hannah's physicality, to fill it in with our own sense of what makes a woman beautiful. However, it is not only the women who are physically attractive. Ajax, Sula's lover, is jet-black and exquisite. Adding to his own splendor, Ajax practices the cultivation of beauty in his courtship and seduction of Sula: a blue glass bottle filled with milk and a jar of butterflies let loose in her bedroom.

Beyond the physical attractiveness of the characters or of the objects described, the novel in its language and structure is itself a thing of beauty. When I first encountered this book as a teenager, I took tremendous pleasure in reading the language aloud, in thinking about the characters when I was away from them; and upon finishing it, I wondered, why did I now see my world, my family, my neighbors differently? Why did it seem so overwhelmingly beautiful, and why did it seem to even stretch my own understanding of what "beauty" is or means? Even the protagonist's death holds a sense of wonder and possibility. And Nel, in the depth of her grief over Sula, is compelled to look for and sense her presence in the trees above her.

I now know that reading *Sula* at thirteen constituted my first real step toward separating myself from my mother. I was never a rebellious teen. My sister had been rebellious enough for both of us. I was obedient because I thought my mother's way paved a path I wanted to follow. I never wanted to embarrass her or to make her life difficult. The one and only time I skipped school, I went to the shoe department of the luxury department store, Bonwit Teller, where I ran into the singer Patti LaBelle. While graciously granting my request for an autograph, she asked, "Why aren't you in school, young lady?" I was rendered speechless, but fearing my mother might hear of my transgression, I went home and I confessed.

Morrison's novel, and then works by other Black women, provided other female voices of authority, in addition to my mother's and my aunts', about what my life could become. My mother may have carved the path, laden with beauty and strict codes of behavior, but those works by Black women writers established the destination. Their content, indeed their very existence, gave meaning and purpose to the art of living.

In *Sula* Toni Morrison attends to the lives of ordinary people with great care. Although the main characters of the novel are the most compelling, it is Morrison's description of the anonymous community, where she embeds a sense of the ethics driving her characters, that holds meaning. This is a constant throughout her oeuvre. It is an anonymous but omnipresent "they," who are Black, observant, and judging. *Sula* reveals it as one of the greatest sources of beauty:

What was taken by outsiders to be slackness, slovenliness or even generosity was in fact a full recognition of the legitimacy of forces other than good ones. They did not believe doctors could heal—for them none ever had done so. They did not believe death was accidental—life might be, but death was deliberate. They did not believe Nature was ever askew—only inconvenient. . . . The purpose of evil was to survive it and they determined (without ever knowing they had made up their minds to do it) to survive floods, white people, tuberculosis, famine and

ignorance. They knew anger well but not despair, and
they didn't stone sinners for the same reason they didn't
commit suicide—it was beneath them.

In moments like these, Morrison takes a people deemed sim-
plistic by whites, and reveals the worldview they've created, the
theories, philosophies, analyses, and ethics they've invented and
lived by. As with the chorus in Greek tragedy, these moments of
communal revelation comment on the action but also contain
the community's values. She honors the meaning these people
have given to their lives. Her texts reveal the depth and dignity
of ordinary people whose values are often quite distinct from
those of the dominant society. The repetition of "they did not
believe" elevates the language here, signifies that this moment
in the text is special, separate from dialogue and description.
There is a rhythm and symmetry that makes the language and
the meaning it seeks to relay beautiful.

Morrison does not romanticize the community in passages
like these; nor does she provide sentimental nostalgia. She never
turns away from the harsh realities of Black life. In a piece of
eyelet lace, a hole is surrounded and reinforced with a closely
stitched thread. The holes allow air and light to come through.
They are the space of vulnerability, but woven together in a pattern, they create a thing of beauty. The fabric is sturdy. It is light
and airy but not as delicate as other forms of lace. In those sum-
mers of my reading, eyelet also became a favored fabric of mine.
(I later requested a dress made of the fabric for my ninth-grade
graduation from Masterman.) The novel Sula reveals Black life to
be like eyelet: so beautiful, such strength and vulnerability, both
ordinary and extraordinary.

The Black women writers I discovered as a teenager asserted

that the concept and consideration of beauty need not be oppressive. Both my mother and these writers acknowledged how aesthetic ideals, particularly those informed by white supremacy, were unfair, indeed even violent to Black women. Colorism was and is real. And although "Black Is Beautiful" was a slogan of the Black Power movement, that news hadn't reached the streets of South Philadelphia, where some young playmates (all Black) greeted me with "ugly Black thing" with such frequency it felt like torture. Beautiful custom-made clothing was no armor for that, and only my family's love and reassurance provided a balm against the hatefulness with which that phrase was hurled. Even as a young teen, when "ugly Black thing" was replaced with "pretty to be so Black," the language associated with dark skin was biting. It still triggers. Early in my life, when I first encountered colorism, my father tried to counter it by telling me that my playmates had been brainwashed by white supremacy. He tried to explain that the white dolls they played with only reinforced it. He said things about "self-hatred" and promised that after the revolution my true dark-skinned beauty would be recognized and revered. I knew *he* believed this, but I had serious doubts about the veracity of his predictions. My mother and Black women writers I later encountered succeeded where my father's efforts to explain and reassure me had not.

One day, in ninth grade, I came home distraught because a classmate told me about an exchange she had with an English teacher. Let's call them Luvenia and Mrs. Ready. Mrs. Ready was a well-dressed Black woman. As I recall, she claimed to be friends with Diahann Carroll, an association which only underscored her glamour in our eyes. She wore lovely outfits, and she was always fully made up: thick, light-hued foundation and drawn-on eyebrows are what I remember most. Once a week, before the school day started, Mrs. Ready met with a group of girls for whom she'd organized a club—a kind of charm school. I did not participate, but Luvenia did. On this particular day, she reported, the girls were talking about other girls they found "cute." When my name was mentioned, Mrs. Ready allegedly proclaimed, "Farah is not cute. She just knows how to make the best of what she has." I was devastated. I hadn't thought much about being "cute." I knew the girls who were designated as such and I didn't believe myself to be one of them. Then as now, I was always surprised when someone complimented me on my looks. But I did not feel unattractive. I was popular enough, pretty enough. But knowing that an adult, a self-proclaimed expert on such things, had made this pronouncement about me to my peers, hurt.

When I arrived home from school, I told my mother. I remember she was sitting in one of the chairs she had recently reupholstered, and I sat on the other side of the room, in the middle of the couch. The blinds were open and the sun framed her face, as she sat there patiently listening to me. When I finished, she said, "Listen to me. I am only going to tell you this once. Mrs. Ready is right." I was crestfallen. She continued, "You are not cute. Babies and monkeys are cute. You are beautiful. I haven't wanted to tell you because I didn't want you to value your looks too much. You are beautiful and it means absolutely nothing. It says nothing about what kind of person you are. It says nothing about your heart or your intelligence or your kindness. Mrs. Ready probably said that because you are dark-skinned, and unfortunately a lot of people are still color struck. Mrs. Ready is one of those people. She's not the first you've encountered and she won't be the last. For God's sake, she covers her face in pancake makeup to make herself three shades lighter and she draws under her lip line to make her lips look thinner. She has no business talking about you. She's pitiful. Now go do your homework." What I remember most about that moment was thinking, "My mother thinks I'm beautiful. Wow."

In the pages of books by Morrison, Gwendolyn Brooks, and other Black writers, the destructive nature of intra-racial colorism has devastating consequences. It is the subject of Morrison's first novel, *The Bluest Eye*, and Brooks's main protagonist in *Maud Martha* is victimized by it as well. Maud Martha is saved by her tremendous sense of self and her capacity for seeing and creating beauty on her own terms. It is not surprising that Black women writers should address the oppressive beauty standards of white supremacy and Black people's internalization of them. The gifted musician Me'Shell Ndegeocello puts it most concisely, "Her beauty cannot be measured by the standards of a colonized mind."

Although the earliest Black women writers, from the antebellum authors through to those of the Harlem Renaissance, adhered to notions that celebrated fair skin and straight hair, the writers who emerged in the sixties and seventies, as well as the words of my own family members, asserted without qualification the physical beauty of all Black women, regardless of shade. For them, physical beauty is equally spread across skin tones. But more importantly, perhaps most importantly, beauty is not only the province of human beings.

Brooks has Maud Martha love dandelions. She

would have liked a lotus, or China asters or the Japanese Iris, or meadow lilies—yes, she would have liked meadow lilies, because the very word meadow made her breathe more deeply, and either fling her arms or want to fling her arms, depending on who was by, rapturously up to whatever was watching in the sky. But dandelions were what she chiefly saw. Yellow jewels for everyday studding the patched green dress of her back yard. She liked their demure prettiness second to their everydayness; for in that latter quality she thought she saw a picture of herself, and it was comforting to find that what was common could also be a flower. . . . [I]t was hard to believe that a thing of only ordinary allurements—if the allurements of any flower could be said to be ordinary—was as easy to love as a thing of heart-catching beauty.

This passage both captures and embodies the aesthetic. It describes Maud Martha's appreciation for the beauty of a wildflower commonly thought to be a weed. But who can deny the beauty of a field of green peppered with petite yellow blossoms? The language of this poet-turned-novelist relays the experience that it represents. Like my mother's metaphors, dandelions are yellow jewels for every day, studding, like exquisite buttons, the green "dress" of her backyard. They are the very notion that one adorns oneself every day. Nature daily provides experiences of beauty. Even the most ordinary flower is nonetheless a thing of loveliness, to be cherished.

In an essay titled "Beauty Is a Method," Christina Sharpe (whose mother also created objects of beauty, including clothing for her daughter) writes, "I've been revisiting what beauty as a method might mean or do: what it might break open, rupture, make possible and impossible. How we might carry beauty's knowledge with us and make new worlds." This, I believe, is what my mother and what that innovative group of Black women writers did. They cultivated beauty as a way of making possible new ways of understanding who we were, what we might become, and the worlds we might build.

The cultivation of beauty in life and literature is the cultivation of the aesthetic dimension of our lives. That kind of beauty is a necessary balm to be found or created. It is not something given to us, or judged by white people, or by Black men even. The cultivation of and appreciation for beauty enhances everyday life. It requires neither fortune nor status. It is our birthright. It is a state of being, a way of navigating the world that cannot be taken away or stolen. It is a source of solace and pleasure. Sometimes it emerges after we have been forced to confront pain. It is to be found in the most mundane and quotidian aspects of our lives: a garden or a single flower, a flourishing houseplant, an intricately woven textile, a cobalt blue bottle, a languorous cat, a Miles Davis solo, Aretha singing "Day Dreaming," the rare stillness and silence provided by a quick but weighty summer storm, or the luxury of reading a sentence that leaves us breathless.

⟆ 10 ⟆

Of Gardens and Grace

> What we suffer now are just less intense moments of being despised, but any reprieve from death is welcome, if only because it allows one to spend hours, days, years cultivating one's roses, at home, or in the imagination.
>
> Hilton Als

My Aunt Eartha, my mother's middle sister, loved yellow roses. When I moved back to Philadelphia as a young professor in 1993, and purchased my first home, a pair of adjacent townhouses in a gentrifying neighborhood, within walking distance of my childhood home, she gave me a rosebush that promised to yield bright yellow flowers: "So you will have something to remember me when I die," she told me. I believe because I did not want to think of a time when she was no longer in my life, I neglected the plant. When I relocated my mother from our South Philadelphia row house to one of my townhouses, she rescued the bush and replanted it in her own garden. Now, long after I moved from Philadelphia to New York, and over a decade since my aunt's passing, the bush still blooms.

Also, at the home Aunt Eartha occupied during the final years of her life, a home that has been in our family for over seventy years, the yard is seasonally awash in yellow roses—untamed, climbing up the fence, and spilling over into the alley. I consider this burst of roses a visitation from my Aunt's spirit, an eruption of beauty given to me (to all of us), in spite of my neglect, to be a gift of grace.

Mama migrated from Georgia to Philadelphia with her parents and siblings in 1923. There she married a South Carolinian named David Carson, and they gave birth to three girls, Eunice, Eartha, and the baby, my mother, Wilhelmena. The daughters had never tilled soil or picked cotton, and though the two oldest did domestic work, they quickly found employment outside of white women's homes. They worked in factories, hospitals, and office buildings, joined unions, and tried, with varying degrees of success, to pursue their dreams. They wore stylish clothing purchased with hard-earned money or sewn by my mother. They loved hard, and when the situation demanded it, my aunts left the men who they felt were no longer worthy of them. They laughed, danced, married, gave birth, and kept beautiful homes. Aunt Eunice's was filled with art, some of which she painted herself, as well as a nude painting for which she had been the model. Aunt Eartha found inspiration in the sunny glamour of one of her style icons, Doris Day. During the good times, one of her homes was furnished with round beds and chandeliers. As for my mother, the first homeowner of the three, her house was her canvas. Inside she papered and painted walls, uphol-stered chairs, and made draperies for windows she'd repaired or replaced, which she also washed regularly. Outside she joined the daily morning ritual of other housewives on our block as they, clad in crisp cotton housedresses, swept the small pavements in front of their homes, occasionally going so far as to scrub them with buckets of soapy water. If they had white marble steps, they regularly scrubbed those down as well. At various times, these women, including my mother, had some type of planter, large and round—a basket, a painted stoneware pot, or even an intricately cut car tire—which contained several flowering plants. These were placed close to the house, under a window, or next to a step if there was room.

The women in my family loved flowers and plants. My grandmother and each of her daughters had gardens. They exchanged clippings and gardening tips, but each had a distinctive aesthetic, a different way of tending to her small plot of earth. They were working-class women who cultivated beauty in every aspect of their lives: their clothing, their adorned bodies, their table settings, and their gardens. Occasionally they grew tomatoes, cucumbers, green beans, but mostly they grew flowers. Until this day I associate white trumpet vines and blue hydrangea bushes with Aunt Eunice and her Germantown cottage, and yes, yellow roses with my Aunt Eartha and her West Oak Lane semi-attached single-family home, and later the South Philadelphia family home to which she returned after a failed relationship. That house had been my grandmother's; there she'd raised or helped to raise three generations. She'd rented it for decades until my cousin Leon, Aunt Eartha's oldest son, purchased it upon his return from Vietnam. Mama had a flowerbed in back, which Aunt Eartha took over and cultivated until her death. My mother preferred marigolds, morning glories, and an abundance of tiger lilies.

After my father's death, my mother used some of his life insurance money for a variety of home repairs, including replacing the fence around our tiny yard, which she re-cemented as well. My cousin Irvin did most of this work, and he also created a space for a garden bed. My mother preferred growing her flowers from seed; she loved watching the entire process of their growth. Occasionally she planted gifts of bulbs given her by her sisters. I think this was the case with the tiger lilies. But for the most part she planted seeds without identifying them, often forgetting what she'd sown: Would it be a sweet pea or snapdragon, zinnia or pansy? She delighted in the surprise. It was entirely unplanned, except in the fact that her planting would yield something colorful and pretty.

Two memories of my mother's garden stand out to me. The first isn't really about the garden, but about the wild honeysuckle vine that grew, attaching itself to the row of fences, in the alley behind our yard. After a summer rain, the scent was thick and intoxicating. I remember the contrast: that the alley, a place of danger that my playmates and I were warned to avoid, could also yield such perfumed pleasure. The second memory is of my mother in her garden, and it stands out to me in its quiet power and significance. I was at the kitchen sink, looking out the window at her as she watered her garden with a green hose. Afterward, as she stood there looking at the flowers, I saw her gently point her index finger. As if it had been summoned, a large, graceful butterfly flew from the clothesline to land on her finger, where it seemed to rest for an eternity. Two inexplicable gifts: the serenity and beauty of the butterfly a gift to my mother; the entire scene, framed by the wooden window like a painting, a gift to me.

I think of my grandmother less with her garden and more with her abundant houseplants, cared for and nurtured as we all were under her care. I especially recall an ancient rubber tree, reaching over and across the ceiling, shaking, as did the whole house, as freight trains passed atop that ominous elevated bridge. My grandmother had a green thumb, and her houseplants fared much better than the "little old plant" that Mama Lena Younger is always tending. Younger is the matriarch of Lorraine Hansberry's pioneering play *A Raisin in the Sun*, and her plant is one of the work's most consistent images. We are told that it is "a feeble little plant growing doggedly in a small pot on the windowsill." Throughout, it is a reminder of the resilience, of the will to life, in spite of its stifled circumstances. It survives because Mama never ceases to tend to it. She seems to place much of her hope and aspirations into her care of it, as she does with the family who shares her small, cramped living space. Mama Lena aspires to live in a house and to tend to a garden: "Well, I always wanted me a garden like I used to see sometimes at the back of the houses down home. This plant is as close as I ever got to having one." In the play's final scene, as the family prepares to move into their new home, they give Mama a gift of gardening tools. Yet in the play's final moment, she "comes back in, grabs her plant, and goes out for the last time."

One summer, when I was seven or eight years old, my grandmother enrolled me in her neighborhood 4-H Club. A few days a week, after I arrived at her home, I would join my cousin Irvin Jr., leave the house, cross the street, say hello to Mrs. Mary or her husband Mr. Ernest, and walk through a vacant lot we called Cowboy Hill, to the small desolate alley-like street that sat just behind Mrs. Mary's. Alter Street had few remaining row houses, one of which was occupied by Mrs. Wilson, who oversaw a variety of programs, including a Cub Scout troop to which Little Irvin belonged, as had his father before him. (Little Irvin so loved Mrs. Wilson that he flew into a fitful rage when my aunts commented that she was unattractive.) I longed for a Brownie troop, primarily because I envied Irvin's uniform, but alas, that wasn't to be. So, I joined the 4-H Club, about which I remember absolutely nothing, except gardening and a long bus trip to visit the Pennsylvania Amish 4-H Club near Lancaster. They were the friendliest white children I'd ever encountered. In fact, at that time in my life, they may have been the only white children with whom I had any extended interaction. They had farms and raised cows and pigs!

We had neither farm nor livestock on Alter Street, but we did have little plots of a community garden for which we were responsible. I grew tomatoes and coleus, marigolds, and four o'clocks. I loved the four o'clocks for the magical way they opened and closed, twilight cousins to poet Rita Dove's "Evening Primrose":

> They'll wait until the world's
> tucked in and the sky's
> one ceaseless shimmer—then
> lift their saturated eyelids
> and blaze, blaze
> all night long
> for no one.

Gardening gave me something in common with the women in my family. I felt so proud bringing Mama tomatoes, which she'd use on our sandwiches and in our salads (with iceberg lettuce and Catalina Salad Dressing). I could join my mother and aunts as they appraised each other's gardens, or offer my mother advice on which packets of seeds to purchase from the hardware store or supermarket. I loved the cool shade and quiet of the Alter Street garden, which stood in stark contrast to the scalding heat that arose from the asphalt left bare to the brutal sun because of the prevalence of vacant lots. That garden was a such a good place to daydream.

In African American literature and visual art, Black women's gardens are usually located in the South. Romare Bearden's *Maudell Sleet's Magic Garden* and most famously, Alice Walker's Black feminist aesthetic manifesto, "In Search of Our Mothers' Gardens," are two works that portray the beauty and complexity of Black women's gardening practice. These artists surely came to inform my understanding and interpretation of my beloved gardeners, but there is something significantly different. I think of my family's urban gardens as expressions not only of their artistry but also their desire for a breathing space, a space that mirrored their own lovely softness amid the harsh concrete world they inhabited.

Flowers are objects of gratuitous beauty. While I know there are scientific reasons for their variety of shape, shade, color, and scent, nonetheless they seem to exist just to give us a glimpse of their glory. And noticing them, attending to them, admiring them is an expression of gratitude. Our attentiveness to and expressions of gratitude for them is a prayer of sorts. They, like the songbirds overhead, are a reminder that though the world is full of ugliness, meanness, hatefulness, there is always, also, this: Grace, unmerited reward given to humans by the Divine. There is nothing we can do to earn it. It just is.

The enslaved often tended their own garden plots; they planted vegetables that supplemented their meager diets. Occasionally, with their master's permission, they also sold some of their produce at market. Historians Eugene Genovese and Dianne D. Glave have documented these gardens and the ways the enslaved worked their plots late at night and on Sunday. They are said to have grown cabbages, collards, turnips, corn. The gardens provided a modicum of independence and allowed them to use their labor for the sustenance of their own families. In addition to foodstuffs, sometimes the enslaved also grew flowers, for their scent, for their oils, and "In the grim framework of slavery these gardens [were] a tiny patch of painful light." The freed people continued to cultivate gardens, and their descendants who migrated to Northern cities brought these practices with them.

Toni Morrison, whose family migrated to Lorain, Ohio, loved flowers. She kept a beautiful multilayered garden and took great joy in the geometry and color of seasonal cut-flower arrangements. It is no wonder that flowers and gardens grace her entire oeuvre. Flowers signal meaning in her text. In *The Bluest Eye*, the earth is unyielding of marigolds as punishment, and in *Sula*, a blackberry bush torn from its roots signals the dispossession of the Black community that is destroyed to make way for a golf course. But it is in *Beloved* that the flower is a revelation and gift of grace. Sethe has to bring the yellow flower of the salsify root to help her escape the drudgery of working in her mistress's kitchen: "A few yellow flowers on the table, some myrtle tied around the handle of the flatiron holding the door open for the breeze." Myrtle is an herb that grows a small white flower, a small firework-like burst of a blossom. In that same novel, when Paul D escapes the chain gang, he goes to the Cherokee, who saw off his chains and point him toward freedom: "'Follow the tree flowers,'" they tell him. "So, he raced from dogwood to blossoming peach," to the cherry blossom, and when, finally, he reached the apple tree whose blossoms were turning to fruit, he had reached freedom. Even under slavery and the conditions of captivity that follow its formal end, the human soul longs for beauty and seeks grace. For Black people, grace most often manifests in momentary bits of freedom, a hint of the broader freedom for which we still struggle.

Even in the midst of crisis, the flowers bloom. Especially in moments of crisis, their blooming is a reminder of something that transcends the moment, a reminder of a deep, deep sense of time, reaching back and stretching forward.

In the spring of 2020, when the pandemic hit and New York emerged as an early hotspot, Mom and I decided it best that she stay in her Philadelphia townhouse. At 92, she is healthy and independent. Her petite stature belies her physical strength.

We are blessed with a beautiful network made up of family and a multiracial group of friends. Mia, Laura, and Laura's daughter Madison drop off delicious meals and fresh produce and visit Mom from a safe distance on the sidewalk. Neighbors Judy and Lorene check in frequently and offer to make grocery runs. Mom's great-granddaughter Karen (named for her mother, one of my mother's deceased granddaughters) sends care packages and calls frequently. Irvin regularly parks across the street, sits in his car or pickup, and keeps an eye on the house. I visit from New York every two weeks.

At first Mom kept busy sewing masks, but when threading the needles becomes a challenge, my friend Barbara (who is like a second daughter to her) and I encourage her to spend more time in her garden. The yellow roses are first to bloom, and Barbara and I discover two sources for them, the rescued bush that had been given me by my Aunt Eartha, and a vine, which Barbara had given Mom. It now climbs deep in the crepe myrtle tree (also a gift from Barbara). The hydrangeas have been especially abundant and glorious, in shades of blue, purple, and magenta.

Barbara rakes and cleans the tiny yard. She buys a trellis around which she wraps the rose vine. I buy a four-tiered planter in which we grow petunias, geraniums, and, on the bottom tier, some impatiens, since they don't need a lot of light. Barbara adds a potted lavender plant, and Mom surrounds it with white begonias. Michelle sends a pot of mint from her home in the Berkshires, and Julia drives in from Germantown to drop off lettuce plants.

The death count continues to grow. We lose a family member and cannot be there to comfort his loved ones. Philadelphia becomes a major site of the uprising for Black Lives Matter. Mom expresses love and gratitude for the protestors, but she is also concerned for their safety. The Frank Rizzo statue comes down.

When the news becomes unbearable, she puts on a CD, something pretty like *Roy Hargrove with Strings: Moment to Moment*. She goes out to her garden and communes with the spirits of her sisters. "Eartha," she recalls, "loved a yellow rose."

ACKNOWLEDGMENTS

This book is an offering to the people and place, Philadelphia, that made me, and to the writers, music makers, and visual artists who helped me have a better understanding of and appreciation for both. As I brought this project to a close in the fall of 2020, Philly, true to its history, emerged, once again, as an important site in our nation's struggle for democracy.

My life and writing have been visited both by deep love and profound loss. My family members who are no longer living continue to exist vividly in my memory and my dreams: my father, Emerson Maxwell Griffin, my maternal grandmother, Willie Lee Carson, my aunts Eartha Mordecai and Eunice Cogdell, my sister Myra Griffin-Lindsay, and my nephew and nieces, Kenneth, Phyllis, and Karen Lindsay. That life—my life—continues to be graced with the presence of those who still bless my days, especially my cherished mother, Wilhelmena Griffin, who gave me permission to tell some of our story here, and my cousin Irvin Carson Sr., who doesn't always share my opinions about our family, but who nonetheless has loved, supported, and protected me so that I could write my version of their story and who clarifies the vagaries of my memory. His son, my cousin Irvin Carson Jr., my nephew Warren Lindsay, and my first friend, Cassandra Singleton (Sandra), were all just a call or text away when I needed to check a fact, recall a name, place, or event, or just laugh. Constant companions during my childhood, we "knew each other when," and they still brighten my days. Sandra joins Vanessa Garrett Harley and Crystal Jones Lucky as my three oldest friends; like Sula and Nel, "we was girls together."

Similarly, I am fortunate to have a cherished group of wonderful friends of my mind: Daphne Brooks, Jamal Calloway, the late James H. Cone, Angela Davis, Thadious Davis, Gina Dent, Michael Eric Dyson, Brent Edwards, Maxine Gordon, Diedra Harris-Kelley, Saidiya Hartman, Régine Jean-Charles, Serene Jones, Deborah Paradez, Robert O'Meally, Michelle Ores, Imani Perry, Kevin Quashie, Christina Sharpe, Salamishah Tillet, and Richard Yarborough. My colleagues in the African American and African Diaspora Studies Department at Columbia University are a constant source of support and inspiration. Thank you to Kevin Fellezs, Robert Gooding-Williams, Steven Gregory, Frank Guridy, Kellie Jones, Natasha Lightfoot, Mignon Moore, Sam Roberts, Josef Sorett, and Mabel Wilson. During the time I wrote this book and several of you were writing your own, we founded and built a department. May both the books and the department be a contribution to the collective intellectual and political project to which we are committed. Shawn Mendoza and Sharon Harris make all we do possible. I treasure all of you.

I have also benefited from the insights of those with whom I've shared portions of the book in talks and lectures at Columbia, Dartmouth, Morgan State, Wayne State, and Yale universities as well as the University of Massachusetts Amherst and the University of Pennsylvania. Graduate and undergraduate students in my seminar, African American Novelists and the Question of Justice, and in my lecture survey course, Introduction to

African American Literature, have greatly shaped how I think about this body of literature.

Much of this book was written during visits to Easton's Nook in Newark, New Jersey. Founded by Jacquie and Nadine Mattis, Easton's Nook provides a beautiful space for scholars, artists, and activists to work, to build, and to dream. At important stages in my writing, the Nook, especially Nadine's warmth, love, and delicious food, helped me forge ahead on the journey to completion. When the pandemic hit and we could no longer be in residence, Jacquie and Nadine created a weekly virtual writing space and community that continued to sustain and nurture. Makers of magic are they.

I have been fortunate to have an extraordinary group of research assistants: Elleza Kelley, Alexis Johnson, and Bérénice Sylverain. Each of them is a beautiful writer and promising scholar in her own right. Brianna Barrett provided assistance helping me prepare the manuscript for publication. I am thankful for her efforts.

Rene Boatman, Valerie Boyd, Carol Taylor, and Brandee Younger each helped to save the day on more than one occasion. This is a much better book for their generous assistance.

Many people nurtured my writer self; without their support this book, in this form, would not have been possible. Tanya McKinnon is more than an agent. She is a visionary who sees the writer you can be, want to be, even when you cannot see it yourself. Of the many gifts Michael Eric Dyson has given me, bringing me to Tanya is one of the greatest. I am deeply appreciative of both of them. Amy Cherry is a dream editor. Her intelligence, her sensitivity, and her thoughtfulness have helped to make this book much better. The time and care she devoted to it are more than I could have ever asked for. Jan Clausen, Beverly

Gologorsky, and Jane Lazarre invited me into their community of writing women, attended to my drafts with care, coaxed my writing and welcomed it into the world. Our writing group has been an incredible personal, political, and creative space for me.

Jan and Jane join my dearest friends Barbara Savage, Elizabeth Alexander, and Cornel West, all of whom read the entire manuscript, offered suggestions and encouragement, and shored up my confidence that I'd produced the book I hoped to write.

At Norton a talented group of professionals has seen the manuscript through to book form: Jodi Beder, Bee Holekamp, Huneeya Siddiqui, Amy Medeiros, Bob Byrne, Rose Sheehan, and Sarahmay Wilkinson. Thank you for your patience and for lending your talents and attention to this project.

Finally, I owe a debt of gratitude to the woman to whom this book is dedicated, Toni Morrison, for her friendship, words, work, and freedoms granted. And to Obery, whose love sustains me and whose courage and brilliance inspire me every day.

NOTES

1. Legacy, Love, Learning

7 **"both lighthouse and anchor"**: Ayana Mathis, *The Twelve Tribes of Hattie* (New York: Vintage, 2013), 302.

8 **"Outdoors, we knew, was the real terror of life"**: Toni Morrison, *The Bluest Eye* (New York: Vintage, 2007), 17.

8 **It goes against Christ's dictum**: Matthew 25:35–40 KJV.

> 35 For I was an hungred, and ye gave me meat: I was thirsty, and ye gave me drink: I was a stranger, and ye took me in:
>
> 36 Naked, and ye clothed me: I was sick, and ye visited me: I was in prison, and ye came unto me.
>
> 37 Then shall the righteous answer him, saying, Lord, when saw we thee an hungred, and fed thee? or thirsty, and gave thee drink?
>
> 38 When saw we thee a stranger, and took thee in? or naked, and clothed thee?
>
> 39 Or when saw we thee sick, or in prison, and came unto thee?
>
> 40 And the King shall answer and say unto them, Verily I say unto you, Inasmuch as ye have done it unto one of the least of these my brethren, ye have done it unto me.

9 **"There was a difference between being put *out* and being put out*doors*"**: Morrison, *The Bluest Eye*, 17–18.

10 **ethic of care:** I borrow the term "ethic of care" from feminist theorists such as Carol Gilligan and others who have called our attention to the ways people within communities depend upon one another and who have insisted that the most vulnerable members of a community deserve special consideration and attention. According to this mode

of thinking, care is an ethical issue that can and should govern how we behave in community. While Gilligan has been criticized for the essentialist implications of her theory, which claims women act or behave in ways that emphasize empathy or compassion, I nonetheless find the notion of an ethic of care is useful when divorced from notions of inherent gender differences. For instance, most recently, it has been taken up by the field of disability studies. Eva Feder Kittay notes: "Care is an indispensable, and even a central good—one without which a life of dignity is impossible and which is itself an expression of a person's dignity. The ability of a being to give and receive care is a source of dignity for humans no less than the capacity for reason." Eva Feder Kittay, "The Ethics of Care, Dependence, and Disability," *Ratio Juris* 24, no. 1 (March 2011): 52. More recently, social scientists Jacqueline S. Mattis, Nyasha A. Grayman, Sheri-Ann Cowie, Cynthia Winston, Carolyn Watson, and Daisy Jackson discuss altruism and care among African Americans in a New York housing project. See Mattis et al., "Intersectional Identities and the Politics of Altruistic Care in a Low-Income, Urban Community," *Sex Roles* 59 (2008): 418–28.

11 **"Love, thick and dark . . . does not want me to die":** Morrison, *The Bluest Eye*, 12.

11 **"She came with nothing":** Ibid., 18.

2. *The Question of Mercy*

18 **The Baldwin School:** Interestingly, The Baldwin School has inspired at least two fictional representations by Black women writers. See Andrea Lee, *Sarah Phillips* (New York: Random House, 1984), and Asali Solomon, *Disgruntled* (New York: Farrar, Straus and Giroux, 2015).

20 **"On Being Brought from Africa to America":** Phillis Wheatley, *Phillis Wheatley: Complete Writings*, ed. Vincent Carretta (New York: Penguin, 2001), 13.

20 **Celebrated, reviled, and eventually revisited:** Henry Louis Gates Jr., *The Trials of Phillis Wheatley* (New York: Basic/Civitas, 2013).

21 **"a dirty carpet":** Margaretta Matilda Odell, *Memoir and Poems of Phillis Wheatley: A Native African and a Slave* (n.p.: Franklin Classics, 2018; originally Geo W. Light, 1834), 85.

22 **"a young negress":** Ibid., 72.

22 **"Until then Phillis had been somebody's child":** June Jordan, "The Difficult Miracle of Black Poetry in America: Something Like a Sonnet for Phillis Wheatley," in *Some of Us Did Not Die: New and Selected Essays* (New York: Civitas, 2003), 175.

22 **Senegambia:** Term used by the British to refer to settlements in Senegal and The Gambia. (The Confederation of Senegal and The Gambia was created on February 1, 1982.)

23 **"uncommon intelligence":** Odell, *Memoir and Poems of Phillis Wheatley*, 85.

23 **"The problem of internalizing the master's tongue":** Toni Morrison, *Race-ing Justice, En-gendering Power: Essays on Anita Hill, Clarence Thomas, and the Construction of Social Reality* (New York: Pantheon, 1992), xxv.

24 **Wheatley's most astute biographer:** Vincent Caretta, *Phillis Wheatley: Biography of a Genius in Bondage* (Athens: University of Georgia Press, 2011), 29.

26 **"To wrest dominion over another is a wrong thing":** Toni Morrison, *A Mercy* (New York: Alfred A. Knopf, 2008), 196.

26 **In an extraordinary book of poems inspired:** Honorée Fanonne Jeffers imagines Wheatley's life in Gambia and explores Mercy as it relates to her relationships with other Black people. Jeffers, *The Age of Phillis* (Middletown, CT: Wesleyan University Press, 2019), 13–16.

27 **"There is no reason for you to try to become like white people":** In *The Fire Next Time* (New York: Vintage, 1993), 8.

28 **"There is no protection":** Morrison, *A Mercy*, 195.

28 **The theologian Reinhold Niebuhr tells us:** I am grateful to James Cone for directing me to Niebuhr. Reinhold Niebuhr, "The Assurance of Grace," in *Reflections on the End of an Era* (New York: Charles Scribner's Sons, 1934), 286.

28 **"Justice is getting what you deserve":** Natashia Deón, *Grace: A Novel* (Berkeley: Counterpoint, 2016), 34.

30 **"Should you, my lord, while you peruse my song":** Wheatley, *Complete Writings*, 39.

31 **"from the state of [her] teeth":** Morrison, *A Mercy*, 6.

3. Black Freedom and the Idea(l) of America

43 **"What Have I, or those I represent"**: Frederick Douglass, "What to the Slave Is the Fourth of July?" in *The Portable Frederick Douglass*, ed. John Stauffer and Henry Louis Gates Jr. (New York: Penguin, 2016), 203.

44 **"We hold these truths"**: The Black Panther Party's original Ten Point Program as it appeared in Black Panther, May 15, 1967, reprinted in Joshua Bloom and Waldo Martin, *Black Against Empire: The History and Politics of The Black Panther Party* (Oakland: University of California Press, 2016), vii.

45 **"What, to the American slave, is your 4th of July?"**: Frederick Douglass, "What to the Slave Is the Fourth of July?," in *The Portable Frederick Douglass*, ed. John Stauffer and Henry Louis Gates Jr. (New York: Penguin, 2016), 207.

46 **"In that instrument I hold"**: Ibid., 219.

47 **"Notwithstanding the dark picture"**: Ibid., 220.

49 **"If speech alone"**: Frederick Douglass, "The Ballot and the Bullet," in *The Life and Writings of Frederick Douglass*, ed. Philip S. Foner, vol. 2 (International Publishers, 1975), 458.

51 **"That's why, in 1964"**: Malcolm X, "The Ballot or the Bullet," in *Malcolm X: Selected Speeches and Statements*, ed. George Breitman (New York: Grove Press, 1994), 25.

52 **"In the North"**: Ibid., 30.

52 **"When you expand the civil-rights struggle"**: Ibid., 34.

52 **"Uncle Sam's hands"**: Ibid., 35.

53 **"We didn't land on Plymouth Rock"**: All subsequent Malcolm X quotes are from an earlier version of "The Ballot or the Bullet" delivered in Washington Heights on March 29, 1964. AMDOCS: Documents for the Study of American History, http://www.vlib.us/amdocs/texts/malcolmx0364.html.

54 **"party of money rather than a party of morals"**: Frederick Douglass, "Lessons of the Hour," January 9, 1894, in *The Portable Frederick Douglass*.

56 **"Malcolm X's . . . repeated acts"**: Barack Obama, *Dreams from My Father* (New York: Broadway Books, 2004), 86.

58 **"danger, in the minds of most white Americans"**: James Baldwin, "My Dungeon Shook: Letter to My Nephew on the One

Hundredth Anniversary of the Emancipation," in *The Fire Next Time*, 9.

59 **"I can no more disown him"**: This and the following quotations are from the transcription of his speech "A More Perfect Union," at the National Constitution Center, Philadelphia, PA, March 18, 2008, in *We Are the Change We Seek: The Speeches of Barack Obama*, ed. E. J. Dionne and Joy-Ann Reid (New York: Bloomsbury, 2017).

65 **"It is not permissible that the authors of devastation"**: Baldwin, "My Dungeon Shook," 5–6.

66 **"all those Americans"**: Richard Rorty, *Achieving Our Country: Leftist Thought in Twentieth-Century America* (Cambridge, MA: Harvard University, 1998), 9.

66 **"We hold these truths to be self-evident"**: Obama, *Dreams from My Father*, 437.

67 **"I felt very powerfully patriotic"**: "Toni Morrison: 'I want to feel what I feel. Even if it's not happiness,'" with Emma Brockes, *The Guardian*, April 13, 2012, https://www.theguardian.com/books/2012/apr/13/toni-morrison-home-son-love.

4. The Quest for Justice

72 **My uncle was one of hundreds**: Allen M. Hornblum, *Acres of Skin* (New York: Routledge, 1998).

73 **There was the story of a young woman**: "Detective Judged Innocent of Assault on Girl, 14," *Philadelphia Tribune*, March 9, 1974.

76 **"I can't take upon myself the blame"**: Richard Wright, *Native Son* (New York: Perennial Classics, 2005), 287–88.

76 **"Mr. Max!"**: Ibid., 429.

77 **"What I killed for, I am!"**: Ibid., 428.

78 **"lord have merce sweet jesus"**: Gaines, *A Lesson before Dying*, 233.

79 **"day breakin"**: Ibid., 237.

81 **"a young Negro boy"**: Toni Morrison, *Song of Solomon* (New York: Vintage, 2004), 80

85 **In *Song of Solomon***: In *God Help the Child* (New York: Vintage, 2016), Morrison portrays two self-absorbed young adults who don't fully develop their sense of humanity until they come together to

care for an infirm elder. The act of bathing her becomes their spiritual practice, what Morrison calls "an act of devotion." She tells us "They worked together like a true couple, thinking not of themselves, but of helping somebody else" (167).

87 **"Have mercy"**: Toni Morrison, *Home* (New York: Vintage, 2013), 124.

87 **"Cee was different"**: Ibid., 121.

88 **In the posthumously published "Goodness"**: Toni Morrison, "Goodness: Altruism and the Literary Imagination," *New York Times*, August 7, 2019; originally presented as a lecture at Harvard Divinity School in 2012.

89 **"This Cee was not the girl who trembled at the slightest touch"**: Morrison, *Home*, 128.

89 **"What, in this instance, does justice require?"**: Shatema Threadcraft, *Intimate Justice: The Black Female Body and the Body Politic* (New York: Oxford University Press, 2016), viii.

90 **"Justice is love correcting"**: Sarah van Gelder, "The Radical Work of Healing: Fania and Angela Davis on a New Kind of Civil Rights Activism," *Yes Magazine*, February 19, 2016, https://www.yesmagazine.org/issue/life-after-oil/2016/02/19/the-radical-work-of-healing-fania-and-angela-davis-on-a-new-kind-of-civil-rights-activism/.

91 **"If things are restored"**: Zaheer Ali, text exchange on Messenger, February 8, 2020; conversation with author.

91 **"I think that restorative justice"**: Van Gelder, "The Radical Work of Healing."

92 **"a satisfactory or good ending"**: Morrison, "Goodness."

93 **"Mercy grants freedom from the bondage of harms"**: Serene Jones, *Call It Grace: Finding Meaning in a Fractured World* (New York: Viking, 2019), 267.

5. *Rage and Resistance*

97 **"If we must die"**: Claude McKay, *Complete Poems*, ed. William J. Maxwell (Urbana: University of Illinois Press, 2008), 177.

100 **"The Whites have always been"**: All references to David Walker, *Appeal to the Coloured Citizens of the World*, are taken from David Walker, *Appeal in Four Articles*, docsouth.unc.edu/nc/walker/walker.html.

101 **"believe this, there is no more harm":** Ibid., 29–30.

101 **"Brethren and Fellow Citizens":** Henry Highland Garnet, "An Address to the Slaves of the United States of America," August 16, 1848, in *The Norton Anthology of African American Literature*, 3rd ed. (New York: W. W. Norton, 2014), and https://digitalcommons .unl.edu/etas/8/.

102 **"Let your motto be *resistance*!":** Ibid.

105 **"Philadelphia, the eastern Underground Railroad headquarters":** Margaret Washington, "Frances Ellen Watkins: Family Legacy and Antebellum Activism," *Journal of African American History* 100, no. 1 (Winter 2015): 59.

106 **Jane Johnson and her two children:** The incident provides the inspiration for Lorene Cary's *The Price of a Child* (New York: Alfred A. Knopf, 1995).

107 **Born in Baltimore:** One scholar notes her death certificate lists 1824 as her birth year. I have reconstructed Harper's life from the following sources: Margaret Hope Bacon, "'One Great Bundle of Humanity': Frances Ellen Watkins Harper (1825–1911)," *Pennsylvania Magazine of History and Biography* 113, no. 1 (1989): 21–43; Melba Joyce Boyd, *Discarded Legacy: Politics and Poetics in the Life of Frances E. W. Harper, 1825–1911* (Detroit: Wayne State University Press, 1994); Hazel V. Carby, "'Of Lasting Service for the Race': The Work of Frances Ellen Watkins Harper," in *Reconstructing Womanhood: The Emergence of the Afro-American Woman Novelist*, ed. Hazel V. Carby (New York: Oxford University Press, 1987), 62–94; Frances Ellen Watkins Harper, *A Brighter Coming Day: A Frances Ellen Watkins Harper Reader*, ed. Frances Smith Foster (New York: Feminist Press, 1990); Harper, *The Complete Poems of Frances E. W. Harper*, ed. Maryemma Graham (New York: Oxford University Press, 1988); Washington, "Frances Ellen Watkins."

109 **"What would you do if you were in my place?":** Quoted in Daniel Yacovone, "Sacred Land Regained: Frances Ellen Watkins Harper and 'The Massachusetts Fifty-Fourth,' A Lost Poem," *Pennsylvania History* 62, no. 1 (Winter 1995): 90–110. Originally published in William Still, *The Underground Rail Road*, https://www .gutenberg.org/files/15263/15263-h/15263-h.htm#fharper.

109 **Ned Davis case:** Marcia Robinson, "The Tragedy of Edward 'Ned' Davis: Entrepreneurial Fraud in Maryland in the Wake of the 1850

Fugitive Slave Law," *Pennsylvania Magazine of History and Biography*, April 2016, 179.

110 **"Upon that grave I pledged myself"**: Still, *The Underground Rail Road*, 95.

110 **"Anger . . . births change, not destruction"**: Audre Lorde, "The Uses of Anger: Women Responding to Racism," in *Sister Outsider: Essays and Speeches* (New York: Crossing Press, 2007), 131.

110 **"a blow has been struck"**: Still, *The Underground Rail Road*.

113 **In the clarity of language:** Boyd, *Discarded Legacy*, 49–51.

114 **Harper affiliated herself:** Still, *The Underground Rail Road*.

115 **One man, Aaron A. Stevens:** Boyd, *Discarded Legacy*, 67.

117 **Her essays, short stories, and novels:** The pioneering edited volume, *The Black Woman* (1970), two collections of short stories, *Gorilla, My Love* (1972) and *The Sea Birds Are Still Alive* (1977), and two novels, *The Salt Eaters* (1980) and the posthumously published *Those Bones Are Not My Child* (1999).

118 **"neighbors, lovers, and family members"**: Linda Holmes, *Joyous Revolt: Toni Cade Bambara, Writer and Activist* (Santa Barbara, CA: Praeger, 2014), 78.

118 **"Resistance is the secret of Joy!"**: Alice Walker, *Possessing the Secret of Joy* (New York: Harcourt Brace Jovanovich, 1992), 279.

119 **"built schools and hospitals for themselves"**: Toni Cade Bambara, *The Seabirds Are Still Alive* (New York: Vintage Books, 1982), 33–38.

120 **It became one of the largest protest movements:** Larry Buchanan, "Black Lives Matter May Be the Largest Movement in U.S. History," *New York Times*, July 3, 2020.

120 **Black feminist Brittney Cooper:** See Brittney Cooper, *Eloquent Rage: A Black Feminist Discovers Her Superpower* (New York: St. Martin's Press, 2018), 4, and Salamishah Tillet, "The Art that Confronts Racism," *New York Times*, June 4, 2020. Tillet explores Black rage as a necessary political tool in her forthcoming *All the Rage: "Mississippi Goddam" and the World That Nina Simone Made.*

121 **"Do what you say this country is supposed to be about"**: My own transcription of Mallory's speech, https://www.youtube.com/watch?v=8Jzku_jx5DQ.

122 **"You broke the social contract"**: My transcription of Kimberly Jones, "How Can We Win," https://www.youtube.com/watch?v=llci8MVh8J4.

6. Death

130   **"deaths of despair"**: In 2020, journalists like Nicholas Kristof and economists like Angus Deaton and Anne Case wrote of "deaths of despair" among the white working class: "the surge of mortality from alcohol, drugs and suicide." "Who Killed the Knapp Family?," *New York Times*, January 12, 2020, Sunday Review.

130   **All of their days were cut short:** Linda Villarosa, "The Refinery Next Door," *New York Times Magazine*, August 2, 2020, 28–35.

132   **"Dear Lovely Death":** Langston Hughes, "Dear Lovely Death," in *The Collected Poems of Langston Hughes*, ed. Arnold Rampersad (New York: Vintage Books, 1995), 127.

133   **"I was so afraid of death":** Edwidge Danticat, *The Art of Death: Writing the Final Story* (New York: Graywolf Press, 2017), 37.

136   **"the Black and angry dead":** Toni Morrison, *Beloved* (New York: Vintage, 2004), 234.

136   **"Very few had died in bed":** Ibid., 234.

139   **"did not find a coherent tradition":** Ta-Nehisi Coates, *Between the World and Me* (New York, Spiegel & Grau, 2015), 49.

140   **"There are people whom we do not fully know":** Ibid., 64.

141   **"And raised . . . in rejection of a Christian God":** Ibid., 79.

142   **"the history of racism and economic inequality":** Jesmyn Ward, *Men We Reaped* (New York: Bloomsbury, 2013), 8.

143   **"What I meant to say was this":** Ibid., 38.

144   **"there is a gathering or a repast":** Ibid., 40–41.

144   **"All of us crying and looking away from each other":** Ibid., 239.

144   **"I carry the weight of grief":** Ibid., 240.

145   **"And, when I am weary":** Ibid., 251.

7. The Transformative Potential of Love

148   **Finding their names:** *Philadelphia Inquirer*, Sept. 2, 1948, 11.

150   **Many years later:** In 1949, Mary Lou Williams co-wrote the "Land of Oo-Bla-Dee" with Milton Orent, which she arranged for Dizzy Gillespie's band. Gillespie later recorded it with vocalist Joe Carroll.

151   **Although I vaguely remember:** The story, featuring the photography of Bill Eppridge and writing by James Mills, followed addicts

Johnny and Karen, who lived in "Needle Park," on the Upper West Side of Manhattan. *Life*, February 26, 1965.

157 **"We are happy"**: James Baldwin, *If Beale Street Could Talk* (New York: Dial Press, 1974), 105.

158 **"The importance of the black family"**: "The Black Scholar Interviews James Baldwin," *Black Scholar* 5, no. 4: 140.

159 **"To be a Negro"**: The Roundtable, "The Negro's Role in American Culture," in *Cross-Currents* and *Negro Digest*, March 1962.

162 **"all great movements"**: bell hooks, *All About Love: New Visions* (New York: William Morrow, 2000), xix.

162 **"a love ethic presupposes"**: Ibid., 87.

162 **"an action, rather than a feeling"**: Ibid., 13.

162 **"I use the word love here"**: James Baldwin, *The Fire Next Time*, 95.

163 **"render solidarity"**: David Kyuman Kim, "Love's Labor's Found" (unpublished paper), 17.

163 **"love of those like yourself"**: Leonard Schwartz, "A Conversation with Michael Hardt on the Politics of Love," *Interval(le)s* 2, no. 2–3, no. 1 (Fall 2998/Winter 2009), 810–21, http://labos.ulg.ac.be/cipa/wp-content/uploads/sites/22/2015/07/73_shwartz.pdf.

163 **"Here, . . . in this place"**: Morrison, *Beloved*, 103.

163 **Morrison also writes:** Toni Morrison, *Paradise* (New York: Vintage, 2014), 141–47.

164 **"You do not deserve"**: Ibid., 141–42.

165 **"God loves the way humans loved one another"**: Ibid., 146.

165 **"See what was certainly the first sign"**: Ibid., 145.

166 **"See? The execution of this one solitary black man"**: Ibid., 146.

167 **"Love one another"**: John 13:34, New International Version.

168 **"that not only is God interested in you"**: Morrison, *Paradise*, 147.

8. Joy and Something Like Self-Determination

182 **"People thought Erykah and I were enemies"**: A. D. Amorosi, "How Verzuz DJ Battles Became a Lockdown Phenomenon: Swizz Beatz, Timbaland, Jill Scott Explain," *Variety*, May 22, 2020, https://variety.com/2020/digital/news/verzuz-dj-battles-swizz-beatz-timbaland-jill-scott-1234614586/.

9. Cultivating Beauty

186 **Perhaps they are energies:** I came to this reading of the painting following a generative conversation with an especially engaged audience after my lecture on the painting. "Ride the Air: Romare Bearden, Mobility, Movement, and Migration," High Museum of Art, Atlanta, January 25, 2020.

188 **"brought a new ethos into his life":** Mary Schmidt Campbell, *An American Odyssey: The Life and Work of Romare Bearden* (Oxford University Press, 2018), 177.

188 **Like the trains:** Bearden talks about the centrality of trains in his collages in the short film *Trains, Snakes, and Guitars: The Collages of Romare Bearden.* He notes, "When I first began to do collages I had no idea that I was going to develop such symbols that run through my work, like the train, the serpent, the guitar. . . . I use the train because so many of the lives of Black people had to do with the train" (https://www.sfmoma.org/watch/trains-snakes -and-guitars-the-collages-of-romare-bearden/). Some collages that depict trains are *The Train* (1975), *Daybreak Express* (1978), *The Afternoon Northbound* (1978), *Sunset Limited* (1978), *Moonlight Express* (1978), *Prelude to Farewell* (1981), *Sunset Express* (1984).

194 **"Tain't dat ah worries over Joe's death":** Zora Neale Hurston, *Their Eyes Were Watching God* (New York: Amistad, 2006), 93.

200 **"without ever a pat of the hair":** Morrison, *Sula* (New York: Vintage, 2004), 42.

202 **"What was taken by outsiders":** Ibid., 90.

207 **"I've been revisiting what beauty as a method":** Christina Sharpe, "Beauty Is a Method," *e-flux* 105 (December 2019), https:// www.e-flux.com/journal/105/303916/beauty-is-a-method/ (originally published in the Winter 2020 issue of *Brick: A Literary Journal*).

10. Of Gardens and Grace

213 **"a feeble little plant":** Lorraine Hansberry, *A Raisin in the Sun* (New York: Vintage, 2004), 39; 52.

213 **"Well, I always wanted me a garden":** Ibid., 52.

213 **"comes back in":** Ibid., 152.

214 **"They'll wait until the world's":** Rita Dove, "Evening Primrose," *Collected Poems: 1974–2004* (New York: W. W. Norton, 2017), 407.

215 **The enslaved often tended:** Eugene Genovese, *Roll Jordan Roll: The World the Slaves Made* (New York: Random House, 1974), 535; Dianne D. Glave, *Rooted in the Earth: Reclaiming the African American Environmental Heritage* (Chicago: Chicago Review Press, 2010). In a wonderful chapter on "Women and Gardens," Glave beautifully documents the history and practices of Southern Black women gardeners during and after slavery.

216 **"In the grim framework of slavery":** Robin Lane Fox, "Reflections on Slave Gardens," *Financial Times*, September 21, 2018.

216 **"a few yellow flowers":** Morrison, *Beloved*, 27.

216 **"Follow the tree flowers":** Ibid., 133.

BIBLIOGRAPHY

Amorosi, A. D. "How Verzuz DJ Battles Became a Lockdown Phenom-
    enon: Swizz Beatz, Timbaland, Jill Scott Explain." *Variety*, May 22,
    2020. https://variety.com/2020/digital/news/verzuz-dj-battles-swizz
    -beatz-timbaland-jill-scott-1234614586/.
Angelou, Maya. *I Know Why the Caged Bird Sings*. New York: Ballantine
    Books, 2009.
Baldwin, James. *If Beale Street Could Talk*. New York: Dial Press, 1974.
———. "The Black Scholar Interviews James Baldwin." *The Black Scholar*
    5, no. 4 (Dec. 1973–January 1974): 33–42.
———. *The Fire Next Time*. New York: Vintage, 1993.
———. *Go Tell It on the Mountain*. New York: Vintage, 2013.
———. "Sonny's Blues." In *Going to Meet the Man*. New York: Dial Press,
    1965 (originally published in *Partisan Review*, 1957).
———, Lorraine Hansberry, Nat Hentoff, and Langston Hughes
    (The Roundtable). "The Negro's Role in American Culture."
    Cross-Currents, and *Negro Digest*, March 1962.
Bambara, Toni Cade, *The Salt Eaters*. New York: Vintage, 1992.
———. *The Seabirds Are Still Alive*. New York: Vintage Books, 1982.
———, ed. *The Black Woman*. New York: Washington Square Press,
    2005 (originally 1970).
Blight, David. *Frederick Douglass: Prophet of Freedom*. New York: Simon
    & Schuster, 2018.
Boyd, Melba Joyce. *Discarded Legacy: Politics and Poetics in the Life of
    Frances E. W. Harper 1825–1911*. Detroit: Wayne State University
    Press, 1994.

Brooks, Gwendolyn. *Maud Martha*. Detroit: Third World Press, 1992.

———. "We Real Cool." In *Selected Poems*. New York: Harper Perennial, 2006.

Buchanan, Larry. "Black Lives Matter May Be the Largest Movement in U.S. History." *New York Times*, July 3, 2020.

Campbell, Mary Schmidt. *An American Odyssey: The Life and Work of Romare Bearden*. New York: Oxford University Press, 2018.

Carby, Hazel. "'On the Threshold of Woman's Era': Lynching, Empire, and Sexuality in Black Feminist Theory." In *"Race," Writing, and Difference*, ed. Henry Louis Gates Jr. and Kwame Anthony Appiah (Chicago: University of Chicago Press, 1992), pp. 301–16.

———, ed. *Reconstructing Womanhood: The Emergence of the Afro-American Woman Novelist*. New York: Oxford University Press, 1987.

Caretta, Vincent. *Phillis Wheatley: Biography of a Genius in Bondage*. Athens: University of Georgia Press, 2011.

Cleaver, Eldridge. *Soul on Ice*. New York: Delta, 1969.

Coates, Ta-Nehisi. *Between the World and Me*. New York: Spiegel & Grau, 2015.

Cooper, Brittney. *Eloquent Rage: A Black Feminist Discovers Her Superpower*. New York: St. Martin's Press, 2018.

Danticat, Edwidge. *The Art of Death: Writing the Final Story*. New York: Graywolf, 2017.

Davis, Angela. *Angela Davis: An Autobiography*. New York: International Publishers, 2013.

———, ed. *If They Come in the Morning*. New York: Verso, 2016.

Delany, Martin. *Blake; or, The Huts of America*. Cambridge, MA: Harvard University Press, 2017.

Deón, Natashia. *Grace: A Novel*. Berkeley: Counterpoint, 2016.

Douglass, Frederick. "The Ballot and the Bullet." In *The Life and Writings of Frederick Douglass*, edited by Philip S. Foner, volume 2, 457–58. New York: International Publishers New World Paperbacks, 1975.

———. *Frederick Douglass: Autobiographies*. New York: Library of America, 1994.

———. "What to the Slave Is the Fourth of July?" In *The Portable Frederick Douglass*, edited by John Stauffer and Henry Louis Gates Jr. New York: Penguin, 2016.

Dove, Rita. *Collected Poems: 1974–2004*. New York: W. W. Norton, 2017.

Du Bois, W. E. B. *The Philadelphia Negro: A Social Study*. Oxford University Press, 2007.

———. *The Souls of Black Folk*. New York: Penguin, 2002.

Dyson, Michael Eric. "American Society and Christian Faith," in *Reflecting Black: African American Cultural Criticism*. Minneapolis: University of Minnesota Press, 1993.

Ellison, Ralph. *Invisible Man*. New York: Vintage, 1995.

Fox, Robin Lane. "Reflections on Slave Gardens." *Financial Times*, September 21, 2018.

Fulks, Bryan. *Black Struggle: A History of the Negro in America*. New York: Delacorte Press, 1969.

Gaines, Ernest. *A Lesson before Dying*. New York: Vintage, 1994.

Garnet, Henry Highland. "An Address to the Slaves of the United States of America." In *The Norton Anthology of African American Literature*, 3rd ed. New York: W. W. Norton, 2014.

Gates, Henry Louis, Jr. *The Trials of Phillis Wheatley*. New York: Basic/Civitas, 2013.

Genovese, Eugene. *Roll, Jordan, Roll: The World the Slaves Made*. New York: Random House, 1974.

Gilligan, Carol. *In a Different Voice: Psychological Theory and Women's Development*. Cambridge, MA: Harvard University Press, 1982.

Glaude, Eddie S., Jr. *Begin Again: James Baldwin's America and Its Urgent Lessons for Our Own*. New York: Crown, 2020.

Glave, Dianne D. *Rooted in the Earth: Reclaiming the African American Environmental Heritage*. Chicago: Chicago Review Press, 2010.

Greenidge, Kaitlyn. "My Mother's Garden." *New York Times*, Opinion, March 26, 2016.

Greenlee, Samuel. *The Spook Who Sat by the Door*. Detroit: Wayne State University, 1989.

Jordan, June. "The Difficult Miracle of Black Poetry in America: Something Like a Sonnet for Phillis Wheatley." In *Some of Us Did Not Die: New and Selected Essays*. New York: Civitas, 2003.

Hansberry, Lorraine. *A Raisin in the Sun*. New York: Vintage, 2004.

Hardt, Michael, with Leonard Schwartz. "A Conversation with Michael Hardt on the Politics of Love." *Interval(le)s* 2, no. 2–3, no. 1 (Fall 2998/Winter 2009): 810–21. http://labos.ulg.ac.be/cipa/wp-content/uploads/sites/22/2015/07/73_shwartz.pdf.

Holloway, Karla F. C. *Passed On: African American Mourning Stories: A Memorial*. Durham, NC: Duke University Press, 2002.

Holmes, Linda. *Joyous Revolt: Toni Cade Bambara, Writer and Activist*. Santa Barbara, CA: Praeger, 2014.

hooks, bell. *All About Love: New Visions*. New York: William Morrow, 2000.

Hornblum, Allen M. *Acres of Skin*. New York: Routledge, 1998.

Hughes, Langston. *The Collected Poems of Langston Hughes*. Edited by Arnold Rampersad. New York: Vintage Books, 1995.

Hunter, Marcus. *Black Citymakers: How the Philadelphia Negro Changed Urban America*. New York: Oxford University Press, 2013.

Hurston, Zora Neale. *Their Eyes Were Watching God*. New York: Amistad, 2006.

Jackson, George. *Soledad Brother: The Prison Letters of George Jackson*. Chicago: Lawrence Hill Books, 1994.

Jeffers, Honorée Fanonne. *The Age of Phillis*. Middletown, CT: Wesleyan University Press, 2019.

Jones, Kimberly. "How Can We Win." Video. https://www.youtube.com/watch?v=llci8MVh8J4, 2020.

Jones, Serene. *Call It Grace: Finding Meaning in a Fractured World*. New York: Viking, 2019.

Jones, Tayari. *An American Marriage*. Chapel Hill, NC: Algonquin Books, 2019.

Kim, David. "Love's Labor's Found." Unpublished paper.

Kittay, Eva Feder. "The Ethics of Care, Dependence, and Disability." *Ratio Juris* 24, no. 1 (March 2011): 52.

Kristof, Nicholas. "Who Killed the Knapp Family?" *New York Times*, Sunday Review, January 12, 2020.

Lee, Andrea. *Sarah Phillips*. New York: Random House, 1984.

Lorde, Audre. "The Uses of Anger: Women Responding to Racism." In *Sister Outsider: Essays and Speeches*. New York: Crossing Press, 2007.

Malcolm X. "The Ballot or the Bullet." In *Malcolm X: Selected Speeches and Statements*, edited by George Breitman. New York: Grove Press, 1994.

———, with Alex Haley. *The Autobiography of Malcolm X: As Told to Alex Haley*. New York: Ballantine Books, 1965.

Mallory, Tamika. "State of Emergency." May 29, 2020. https://www.youtube.com/watch?v=8Jzku_jx5DQ.

Marshall, Paule. *The Chosen Place, The Timeless People.* New York: Vintage, 1984.

Mathis, Ayanna. *The Twelve Tribes of Hattie.* New York: Vintage, 2013.

Mattis, Jacqueline S., Nyasha A. Grayman, Sheri-Ann Cowie, Cynthia Winston, Carolyn Watson, and Daisy Jackson. "Intersectional Identities and the Politics of Altruistic Care in a Low-Income, Urban Community." *Sex Roles* 59 (2008): 418–28.

McKay, Claude. *Complete Poems.* Edited by William Maxwell. Urbana: University of Illinois Press, 2008.

Morrison, Toni. *Beloved.* New York: Vintage, 2004.

———. *The Bluest Eye.* New York: Vintage, 2007.

———. *God Help the Child.* New York: Vintage, 2016.

———. "Goodness: Altruism and the Literary Imagination." *New York Times,* August 7, 2019.

———. *Home.* New York: Vintage, 2013.

———. *Jazz.* New York: Vintage, 2004.

———. *Love.* New York: Vintage, 2005.

———. *A Mercy.* New York: Vintage, 2009.

———. *Paradise.* New York: Vintage, 2014.

———. *Race-ing Justice, En-gendering Power: Essays on Anita Hill, Clarence Thomas, and the Construction of Social Reality.* New York: Pantheon, 1992.

———. *Song of Solomon.* New York: Vintage, 2004.

———. *Sula.* Vintage, 2004.

———, with Emma Brockes. "Toni Morrison: 'I want to feel what I feel. Even if it's not happiness.'" Interview, *The Guardian,* April 13, 2012. https://www.theguardian.com/books/2012/apr/13/toni-morrison-home-son-love.

Niebuhr, Reinhold. "The Assurance of Grace." In *Reflections on the End of an Era.* New York: Charles Scribner's Sons, 1934.

Obama, Barack. *Dreams from My Father: A Story of Race and Inheritance.* New York: Broadway Books, 2004.

———. *We Are the Change We Seek: The Speeches of Barack Obama.* Edited by E. J. Dionne and Joy-Ann Reid. New York: Bloomsbury, 2017.

Petry, Ann. *Ann Petry: The Street, The Narrows.* New York: Library of America, 2019.

Rorty, Richard. *Achieving Our Country: Leftist Thought in Twentieth-Century America.* Cambridge, MA: Harvard University, 1998.

Rossen, Johnny Appleseed. *The Little Red White and Blue Book: Revolutionary Quotations by Great Americans*. New York: Grove Press, 1969.

Sharpe, Christina. "Beauty Is a Method." *e-flux* 105 (December 2019). https://www.e-flux.com/journal/105/303916/beauty-is-a-method/. Originally published in *Brick: A Literary Journal* (Winter 2020).

——. *In the Wake: On Blackness and Being*. Durham, NC: Duke University Press, 2013.

Solomon, Asali. *Disgruntled*. New York: Farrar, Straus and Giroux, 2015.

Still, William. *The Underground Rail Road: A Record of Facts, Authentic Narratives, Letters, &c.* Philadelphia: Porter & Coates, 1872. https://www.gutenberg.org/files/15263/15263-h/15263-h.htm.

Threadcraft, Shatema. *Intimate Justice: The Black Female Body and the Body Politic*. New York: Oxford University Press, 2016.

Thurman, Howard. *Jesus and the Disinherited*. Boston: Beacon Press, 2012.

Tillet, Salamishah. *All the Rage: "Mississippi Goddam" and the World That Nina Simone Made*. Forthcoming.

——. "'Mississippi Goddam' (1964)." In "Art that Confronts and Challenges Racism: Start Here." *New York Times*, June 8, 2020.

van Gelder, Sarah. "The Radical Work of Healing: Fania and Angela Davis on a New Kind of Civil Rights Activism." *Yes Magazine*, February 19, 2016, https://www.yesmagazine.org/issue/life-after-oil/2016/02/19/the-radical-work-of-healing-fania-and-angela-davis-on-a-new-kind-of-civil-rights-activism/.

Villarosa, Linda. "The Refinery Next Door." *New York Times Magazine*, August 2, 2020, 28–35.

Walker, Alice. *Possessing the Secret of Joy*. New York: Harcourt Brace Jovanovich, 1992.

Walker, David. *Walker's Appeal in Four Articles: Together with a Preamble, to the Coloured Citizens of the World, but in Particular, and Very Expressly, to Those of the United States of America, Written in Boston, State of Massachusetts, September 28, 1829*. docsouth.unc.edu/nc/walker/walker.html.

Ward, Jesmyn. *Men We Reaped: A Memoir*. New York: Bloomsbury, 2013.

Washington, Margaret. "Frances Ellen Watkins: Family Legacy and Antebellum Activism." *Journal of African American History* 100, no. 1 (Winter 2015): 59–86.

West, Cornel. "Never forget that justice is what love looks like in public." Facebook post. https://www.facebook.com/drcornelwest/posts/never-forget-that-justice-is-what-love-looks-like-in-public/119696361424073/.

Wheatley, Phillis. *Complete Writings*, edited by Vincent Carretta. New York: Penguin, 2001.

———. *Memoir and Poems of Phillis Wheatley, a Native African and a Slave*. Memoir of Wheatley's life by Margaretta Matilda Odell. Boston: George W. Light, 1834.

Wideman, John Edgar. *The Lynchers*. New York: Harcourt Brace Jovanovich, 1973. Reprinted by the author, 2010.

Wright, Jeremiah. "Confusing God and Government, " Trinity United Church, Chicago, April 13, 2003. Transcript https://www.blackpast.org/african-american-history/2008-rev-jeremiah-wright-confusing-god-and-government/.

———. "The Day of Jerusalem's Fall." Trinity United Church, Chicago, September 16, 2001. https://www.youtube.com/watch?v=HV5B4uZCSt0.

Wright, Richard. "Between the World and Me." *Partisan Review* II, no. 8 (July–August 1935): 18–19. *Partisan Review* Online. Howard Gotlieb Archival Research Center, Boston University. http://archives.bu.edu/collections/partisan-review/search/detail?id=283895.

———. *Native Son*. New York: Perennial Classics, 2005 (originally published 1940).

Yacovone, Daniel. "Sacred Land Regained: Frances Ellen Watkins Harper and 'The Massachusetts Fifty-Fourth,' A Lost Poem," *Pennsylvania History* 62, no. 1 (Winter 1995): 90–110.

DISCOGRAPHY

Ammons, Gene. "Didn't We," by Jimmy Webb. *The Boss Is Back*, Fantasy, 1970.

Davis, Miles. *'Round About Midnight*. Columbia, 1957.

———. *Miles Ahead*. Columbia, 1957.

———. *Porgy and Bess*. Columbia, 1958.

———. *Kind of Blue*. Columbia, 1960.

———. *Bitches Brew*. Columbia, 1970.

Earth, Wind & Fire. *That's the Way of the World*. Columbia, 1975.

Franklin, Aretha. "Day Dreaming." Atlantic, 1972.

Gaye, Marvin. *What's Going On*. Tamala, 1971.

Hargrove, Roy. *Moment to Moment: With Strings*. Verve, 2000.

Heron, Gil Scott, and Brian Jackson. *Winter in America*. Strata East, 1971.

Jackson, Chuck. "Any Day Now," by Burt Bacharach and Bob Hilliard. RCA, 1962.

Knight, Jean. "Mr. Big Stuff." Stax Records, 1971.

Lewis, Bobbie. "Tossin' and Turnin'," by Ritchie Adams and Malou Rene. Beltone, 1960.

Mayfield, Curtis (The Impressions). "I'm So Proud." ABC-Paramount, 1964.

O'Jays. "Love Train," by Kenny Gamble and Leon Huff. Philadelphia International Records, 1972.

Ripperton, Minnie. *Perfect Angel*. Epic, 1974.

Ross, Diana. "Touch Me in the Morning," by Michael Masser. Motown, 1973.

———. "Theme from Mahogany (Do You Know Where You're Going To)," by Michael Masser and Gerry Goffin. Motown, 1975.

Sly and the Family Stone. "Family Affair." Epic, 1971.

Williams, Deniece. *This Is Niecy*. Columbia, 1976.

Wonder, Stevie. "For Once in My Life." Tamla, 1968.

———. "Signed, Sealed, Delivered I'm Yours." Motown, 1970.

———. *Talking Book*. Tamla, 1972.

———. *Innervisions*. Tamla, 1973.

———. *Fulfillingness' First Finale*. Motown, 1974.

Wright, Betty. "Clean Up Woman," by Clarence Reid and Willie Clarke. Alston, 1971.

Wright, Syreeta. *Stevie Wonder Presents: Syreeta*. Motown, 1974.

INDEX

Notes: Page numbers in *italics* refer to illustrations.
Page numbers after 222 refer to the Notes section.

ABOUT THE AUTHOR

Farah Jasmine Griffin, the inaugural chair of the African American and African Diaspora Studies Department at Columbia University, is the William B. Ransford Professor of English and Comparative Literature. She is the author of numerous books, including *If You Can't Be Free, Be a Mystery: In Search of Billie Holiday* and *Harlem Nocturne: Women Artists and Progressive Politics During World War II*. The recipient of a 2021 Guggenheim Fellowship and a Society of Columbia Graduates Great Teacher Award, she has also been a fellow at the Cullman Center for Writers and Scholars. Griffin lives in New York.

READ UNTIL YOU
UNDERSTAND

Farah Jasmine Griffin

READ UNTIL YOU UNDERSTAND

Farah Jasmine Griffin

DISCUSSION QUESTIONS

1. Like Farah Jasmine Griffin does in *Read Until You Understand*, if you were to undertake a survey of the works that have shaped you, what writers, artists, and musicians would feature prominently? How did these works influence your understanding of yourself and your place in the world?

2. Did you like the structure Griffin uses in the book, exploring universal themes and the Black experience in America through a blend of literary analysis, cultural history, and "autobiographical meditation" (p. xii)?

3. Griffin writes: "As a form, the novel can raise questions about the possibilities and goals of justice. It allows us to imagine what a society governed by an ethic of care, a society devoted to restoring and repairing those who have been harmed, giving them the space for transformation, might look like" (p. 91). Do you agree? Do you think an increased emphasis on the reading of literature could improve empathy and encourage greater participation in the collective work of creating a society that honors all human beings?

4. Have you read many of the books referenced here? Were there any excerpts or works that particularly moved you?

5. "Each year a multiracial group of students take my class, and each semester they encounter ideas that challenge their understanding of themselves, their relationships to each other, and what they thought they knew about the nation's history. They are forced to rethink their notion of what the United States is and their place within it and within the world" (p. xi). In your own education, were the works of Black Americans featured prominently? If so,

what lessons or perspectives most impacted you? If not, what does that absence, that silencing, reveal to you?

6. "Everyone dies. But Black death in America is too often premature, violent, spectacular. The particular nature of Black death haunts Black writing, as it haunts the nation. It haunts this book, born as it is from my own mourning of my father's premature death" (pp. 131–32). Reading Griffin's account of her father's death is harrowing and heart-wrenching. Did her family's experience resonate with your own or a loved one's experiences or did it challenge an assumption that authority figures will act for the well-being of all in times of crisis? Do you think your perspective of this moment was at all influenced by the recent Black Lives Matter movement?

7. "Black Americans' understanding of America is too realistic, too cautious, too conscious of the lessons of history to possess an unbridled patriotism. We know that at best, our country is a work in progress and that the battle to perfect it is an uphill climb" (p. 67). Do you feel a sense of patriotism? Have your feelings changed over time?

8. How do you see "the struggle over the idea(l) of America" (p. 68) at play in your own community? Did this book move you to take action? How?

Meghan Kenny	*The Driest Season*
Nicole Krauss	*The History of Love*
Don Lee	*The Collective*
Amy Liptrot	*The Outrun: A Memoir*
Donna M. Lucey	*Sargent's Women*
Bernard MacLaverty	*Midwinter Break*
Maaza Mengiste	*Beneath the Lion's Gaze*
Claire Messud	*The Burning Girl*
	When the World Was Steady
Liz Moore	*Heft*
	The Unseen World
Neel Mukherjee	*The Lives of Others*
	A State of Freedom
Janice P. Nimura	*Daughters of the Samurai*
Rachel Pearson	*No Apparent Distress*
Richard Powers	*Orfeo*
Kirstin Valdez Quade	*Night at the Fiestas*
Jean Rhys	*Wide Sargasso Sea*
Mary Roach	*Packing for Mars*
Somini Sengupta	*The End of Karma*
Akhil Sharma	*Family Life*
	A Life of Adventure and Delight
Joan Silber	*Fools*
Johanna Skibsrud	*Quartet for the End of Time*
Mark Slouka	*Brewster*
Kate Southwood	*Evensong*
Manil Suri	*The City of Devi*
	The Age of Shiva
Madeleine Thien	*Do Not Say We Have Nothing*
	Dogs at the Perimeter
Vu Tran	*Dragonfish*
Rose Tremain	*The American Lover*
	The Gustav Sonata
Brady Udall	*The Lonely Polygamist*
Brad Watson	*Miss Jane*
Constance Fenimore Woolson	*Miss Grief and Other Stories*